A Short History of
INDONESIA

A Short History of
INDONESIA

Ailsa Zainu'ddin

PRAEGER PUBLISHERS
New York • Washington

BOOKS THAT MATTER
Published in the United States of America in 1970
by Praeger Publishers, Inc.
111 Fourth Avenue, New York, N.Y. 10003

Library of Congress Catalog Card Number: 78–117479

Printed in the United States of America

Contents

List of Illustrations

MAPS

Foreword

China, Japan, India and Indonesia are, in their several ways, of tremendous importance to their neighbours and to the world at large. The progress of Communist revolution in China's vast agrarian society, the success story of Japan's industrial revolution, the efforts of India to combine the pursuit of economic development with the preservation of democratic institutions, and the problems of political stability and of population pressure in modern Indonesia, are issues of general and crucial significance. It is therefore surprising that the study of these countries in Australian schools should have been delayed until the 1960s. The present series of volumes is designed to aid that study. While directed specifically to a particular syllabus it hopes, at the same time, to offer a treatment which can interest the general reader.

The authors of the four individual studies which go to make up the series have been left considerable freedom in handling their subjects as they see them, but they have accepted one common principle. They share the view that the study of any Asian country cannot be seen solely in terms of its recent history and its present situation. They recognize the persistence of tradition into the present and the way in which contemporary behaviour may reflect the long established patterns of ancient societies. They share also the view that, quite apart from its importance in interpreting the present, the study of traditional societies is worthwhile for its own sake.

Each of these volumes therefore is concerned to place 'modern' history in the context of the longer history of the country concerned, whether it is the shape of early Asian trade and the rivalry of maritime and land-based kingdoms in the Indonesian archipelago, the artistic triumphs of the Gupta period in India, the character of Confucian thought in China or the contribution of a feudal order in Japan. If history must have a utilitarian purpose it is hoped that, in this way, not only will students be led to a more subtle understanding of the character of the modern countries of Asia, but that they will acquire a measure of respect and sympathy for systems of thought and ways of behaviour which are far removed from their own.

J. D. Legge
Monash University

(ix)

Acknowledgments

I acknowledge permission to quote from the following works: Brown, C. C. Sejarah Melayu or 'Malay Annals' in *Journal of the Royal Asiatic Society, Malay Branch*, Vol XXV, Parts 2 and 3, Oct. 1952; Furnivall, J. S. *Netherlands India: A Study of Plural Economy*, Cambridge University Press, 1967; Kartini, *Letters of a Javanese Princess*, The Norton Library, W. W. Norton & Co., New York, 1964; Multatuli (Douwes Dekker), *Max Havelaar* (tr. by Roy Edwards), A. W. Sijthoff/Heinemann, 1967; Skinner, C. 'Sja'ir Perang Mengkasar' in *Verhandelingen van Het Koninklijk Institut voor Taal-Land-en Volkenkunde*, Martinus Nijhoff, 1963; Pigeaud, Dr Th. *Java in the Fourteenth Century*, Vol. III, Martinus Nijhoff, The Hague, 1960; Sjahrir, Soetan. *Out of Exile*, Copyright © 1949 by the John Day Company, Inc., reprinted from *Out of Exile* by Soetan Sjahrir by permission of the John Day Company, Inc., publishers; Van Leur, J. C., *Indonesian Trade and Society*, 'Essays in Asian Social and Economic History' (*Selected Studies on Indonesia, Vol. I*), published for the Royal Tropical Institute, Amsterdam, by W. van Hoeve, The Hague, 1955.

I would like to thank Mr Bill Wight for permission to use the colour photograph which appears on the cover; the Victorian Education Department for the photo of girls in traditional dress; the Melbourne *Herald* for permission to use the portrait of Sukarno; C. P. J. Van Der Peet, Amsterdam, for permission to use a plate from Bernet Kempers, *Ancient Indonesian Art*, Harvard University Press, Massachusetts, 1959, the aerial view of Borobodur; Mr Ivan Southall, Mr Ken Wells, UNESCO and David Davies for permission to use their photographs. The maps were prepared by the technical staff of the Geography Department of Monash University and I am most grateful to them for their assistance.

For all the illustrations otherwise unacknowledged I am indebted to the Information Section, Embassy of Indonesia, Canberra, and through them to Deparlu, Deppen and Kempen. I am especially grateful to the Embassy for their generosity in allowing me to borrow so many illustrations for so long and for their co-operation in helping me to find the material I wanted.

Author's Note

When I was studying history at secondary school I had the great good fortune to be taught by Miss Ellen Christensen. We 'finished the syllabus' each year but we also explored many by-ways and learned not only about the past but about the present and about ourselves. 'Chris' communicated to us her own interest in history and presented us, not with ready-made answers, but with the big questions. As this stage of a person's development, no history book can possibly serve as substitute for such a teacher; the best that I can hope for is that this book may serve as a useful starting point for the same kind of vigorous discussion that we enjoyed. Indeed no teacher can really teach history effectively except by joining in this kind of joint enterprise with fellow students and seeking, not factual knowledge only, but some measure of understanding of the past and, through it, the present.

The history we learned at school, apart from a brief glance at Australia as an outpost of Empire, was firmly Europe-centric. So were my university studies of history. Not till my post-graduate years was I introduced to a meaningful study of Australian history by Professor Manning Clark, whose concern also is with the big questions. I would like to think that my debt to him is apparent. It is certainly very great. He was also indirectly responsible, because he appointed me as his research assistant, for my meeting with the Canberra Indonesian community, among whom was my future husband.

My introduction to Indonesia's past began with involvement in its present when, between 1954 and 1956, I spent two years as a Volunteer Graduate in the Ministry of Education, Djakarta. My husband and those of his generation were the *pemuda*, the young people who had lived through the Japanese occupation and who were not prepared to accept the return of their former colonizers, the Dutch. He was a participant in the struggle for independence. one of the many thousands who risked their lives for the cause of the Republic because he knew from his own experience what it was like to live under colonialism. Through him I met other Indonesians and found that their vision of the world, in differing from my own, both illuminated it and in time may even have modified it. He has taught me a good deal about how Indonesians see themselves, each other and the world around them.

Others have also read and commented on earlier drafts of this book and even when, on occasions, I have not taken their advice, I have valued it. My thanks are due to Mrs Lois Carrington, Professor Manning Clark, Mrs Betty Feith, Professor Herbert Feith, Mr Alan Gregory, Miss Melva Hutchison, Professor Anthony Johns, Miss Lindsey Reber, Rev. David Webster, Mr David Webster junr and Mr Ken McAdam.

Mrs Betty Bradly and Miss Melva Hutchison produced order out of the chaos of my draft typescript and I am very grateful to both of them. Mrs Lois Carrington and my mother helped us with the proof reading. My mother also helped in many ways far too numerous to mention, by acting as general backstop in moments of domestic crisis.

My thanks are also due to various members of the Indonesian Embassy, Canberra, in particular Mr Alex Marentek, for their willingness to be of help.

Finally I must acknowledge my considerable indebtedness to Professor John Legge as editor. Without his 'gentle pressure' this book would have taken longer to write and would have been longer when written. Apart from this he let me say what I liked— as long as I could justify it. I have enjoyed working with him tremendously in what I feel has been the true spirit of *musjawarah*, *mufakat* and *gotong royong*.

Ailsa Zainu'ddin
Monash University, 1968

PART I

Introductory

CHAPTER ONE

Country and People

There is a sense in which it is true to say that all history begins from the present and is related to it. The historical questions which we ask about the past usually arise from our own preoccupations in the present. Certainly this study of the past must begin from the present, because it is the present Republic of Indonesia, not much over twenty years old, whose history we are going to trace. We will find that this particular unitary state is in some ways a recent creation, while in others its past goes back long before recorded time.

Before looking more closely at the history of Indonesia let us look first at the stage setting, the country to which this history belongs and from which it has sprung. Geographical features are not the only ones determining historical events, but they do provide an important framework, which can sometimes set the limits to historical events.

The Republic of Indonesia, which proclaimed its independence on 17th August, 1945, stretches from Sabang to Merauke (and a little beyond), a distance of over 3,000 miles; it contains a total of 13,667 islands of which 6,044 are named and only 992 inhabited.[1] 'From Sabang to Merauke' was one of the slogans which sustained Indonesians in their struggle for Independence. Sabang is a small island just off the northern tip of Sumatra; Merauke is near the border between West Irian and Papua-New Guinea. From north to south, Indonesia stretches for only about 1,300 miles, 6° north to 11° south of the Equator, from the border with Sabah on the island of Kalimantan, to the small island of Roti, about 300 miles from the coast of northeast Australia.

The total land and sea area is about two and a half times the land area of Australia, but the total *land* area is only about 735,381 square miles, about one and a half times the area of New South Wales, or a little larger than Queensland. Indonesians refer to their homeland as *Tanah Air Kita* (literally 'Our Earth

[1] Nugroho, *Indonesia, Facts and Figures* (Terbitan Pertjobaan, 1967), p.11.

and Water'),[2] and the sea has played as important a part in Indonesia's history as has the land.

Look first at the Indonesian archipelago on a globe. It straddles the Equator between the Indian Ocean to the west, and the Pacific Ocean to the east. To the north are China and Japan, to the north-west India and Arabia. The Indonesian islands, particularly Sumatra and Java, are, from one direction, a doorway from India to China, and from the other a doorway from China to India. The ebb and flow of trade, for the centuries preceding the steamship and aeroplane, were determined by the monsoonal and trade winds. The Indonesian islands, and the Malay archipelago, provided a convenient midway point where the merchants of the civilized world met and exchanged goods. They also, with less awareness of what was happening, exchanged ideas.

If you look at Indonesia on several maps of the world you find a curious thing. In the atlases commonly used in Australian or Indonesian schools, Indonesia is in the centre of the world. A map of the world published in America places the Americas at the centre of the world, while a map published in England shows Greenwich (Long. 0) as the centre of the world and Indonesia is in the Far East. Maps are not objective. They embody a particular point of view. Our view of the world, both in time and space, is very much determined by the place at which we stand in it.[3]

Indonesia has been called a girdle of emeralds strung around the equator, and green predominates in the Indonesian landscape, the sombre green of tropical rain forests, the varied greens of coconut palm and banana plant, the brilliant green of young rice in the terraced ricefields. Unlike her large, dry, sunburnt neighbour in the south, Indonesia is a country with plentiful rainfall. Large areas of western Sumatra, north-western Kalimantan, western Java and West Irian average over 120 inches of rain annually. The city of Padang (western Sumatra) averages 173 inches a year. Bogor, a town in western Java, not very far from Djarkata, has about 322 thunderstorms a year and an average rainfall of 165.5 inches. This combination of very heavy rainstorms and mountainous country in Java, where much of the natural growth has been cleared, leads to considerable erosion. It

---

[2] Although it signifies not only the sustenance drawn from both land and sea but also the combination of earth and water on which the fertility of the region depends — irrigated ricefields.

[3] *Atlas of South East Asia* with an introduction by D. G. E. Hall (Macmillan, 1964), although expensive, should be in every school library not only for its maps but for its accompanying illustrations and text.

Girls in the traditional dress of Minangkabau (Central Sumatra). The headdress is said to symbolize buffalo horns.

Terraced ricefields stretch right up the mountainside . . .

. . . and down to the edge of the stream

has been estimated that Java loses, through erosion, about two hundred million tons of top-soil every year.

Most of the rest of the country averages between 60 and 120 inches. Only a few areas in Sulawesi, and some of the islands closest to Australia, have a rainfall below 60 inches a year. This combination of heavy rainfall and tropical heat makes the climate, particularly in coastal areas, very humid, and it is also a very even climate, with a temperature range, at the coastal level, from about 75°F to about 85°F. The humidity may be as high as 97% and is seldom, if ever, less than 75%.

Indonesia has no seasons comparable with the four with which we are familiar, although they distinguish between the hot season and the wet. The only differences between them, to a newcomer from more temperate regions, are that the hot season is slightly hotter and not quite so wet as the wet season, while the wet season is slightly wetter and not quite so hot as the hot season. The length of day and night remains constant throughout the year, with sunrise at about 6 a.m. and sunset at 6 p.m.

In some of the islands east of Java and Bali the seasonal differences are pronounced. Even within Java some districts have a sufficiently marked dry season to suffer drought at times, but in the rest of Java, and Bali, this regular and even climate means a rhythm of life for the Indonesian farmer based less on the annual fluctuation of the seasons than on the growth pattern of his crops, and in the areas with heavy rainfall and terraced rice-field cultivation there is no set planting season or set harvest, but a continuing flow of activity, where one hillside may demonstrate the whole cycle of rice cultivation—ploughing the muddy fields, planting seedbeds, planting out the young seeds, right through to the reaping of the harvest and to the scruffy-looking stubble on harvested and as yet unploughed plots. This gives a marvellous patchwork effect in greens, brown and gold, while in between the young, newly planted out seedlings, the water in which they stand reflects the blue sky.

This reminds us of the great antiquity of Indonesian civilization. Historians believe that rice cultivation on irrigated fields, intricately terraced to follow the slope of the land, has been known for over two thousand years. The Javanese peasant, wading behind his buffaloes, steering his wooden plough, or hoeing the muddy plot with a simple hoe, is like those countless Javanese peasants who have preceded him. The cars which travel along the macadamized highway between towns, seem to be the intruders as they overtake lumbering ox-carts drawn by matronly buffaloes in carpet-slippers or by hump-backed, dew-lapped zebu.

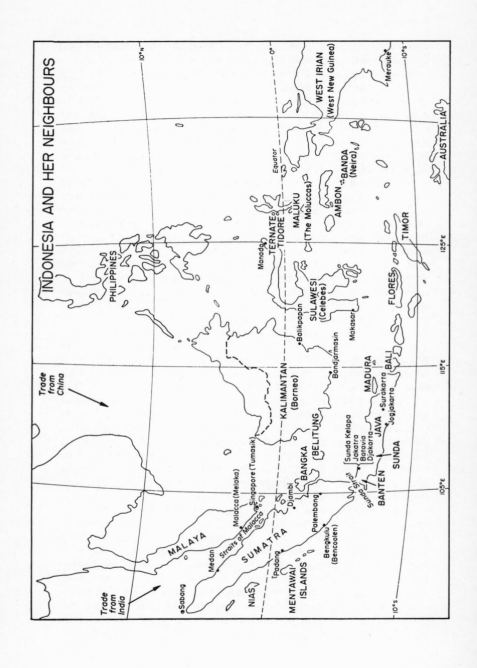

INDONESIA AND HER NEIGHBOURS

Trade from China

Trade from India

PHILIPPINES

MALAYA

Sabang

Medan

Straits of Malacca

Malacca (Melaka)

Singapore (Tumasik)

Padang

NIAS

MENTAWAI ISLANDS

SUMATRA

Bengkulu (Bencoolen)

Djambi

Palembang

BANGKA

BELITUNG

KALIMANTAN (Borneo)

Balikpapan

Bandjarmasin

Sunda Strait

BANTEN

Sunda Kelapa
Jakarta
Batavia
Djakarta

SUNDA

JAVA

MADURA

Surakarta

Jogjakarta

BALI

Makasar

SULAWESI (Celebes)

Manado

TERNATE
TIDORE

MALUKU (The Moluccas)

AMBON

BANDA (Neira)

FLORES

TIMOR

WEST IRIAN (West New Guinea)

Merauke

AUSTRALIA

Equator

10°N

0°

10°S

105°E

115°E

125°E

Harvesting, too, is done with hand tools, a rice knife wielded delicately and unobtrusively to avoid disturbing the spirit of the rice-goddess. In Bali, harvest offerings woven from rice straw into the shape of a goddess, are placed in the fields, dedicated to Dewi Sri, goddess of agriculture and fertility.

Running like a backbone down the western coast of Sumatra is a long range of mountains, which continues through Java, Bali and the Lesser Sundas. The backbone of bird-shaped New Guinea is another mountain range, some mountains of which are snow-capped, despite their closeness to the equator. North-central Kalimantan and the orchid-shaped island of Sulawesi are also mountainous.

Scattered along the mountain range from Sumatra to Flores, with a strong concentration on the island of Java, are many volcanoes. In 1883, one of these—the island of Krakatau in the Sunda Straits—blew its top right off; and the resulting tidal wave killed over thirty thousand people. The volcanic dust caused brilliant sunsets throughout the world for two years. In 1963 a large part of Bali was devastated by the eruption of the sacred mountain, Gunung Agung. This, many Balinese believe, was a sign of the wrath of the gods. It will be many years before the ricefields in that half of the island, devastated by lava flow and by volcanic ash, will again be fertile. In eastern Java the local people, the Tenggerese, still offer a propitiatory sacrifice to the Bromo mountain whose crater, with its faint plume of smoke, dominates the landscape.

If you look at a vegetation map of Indonesia[4] you will see that, apart from small areas along the coast and the rivers, and a rather larger cultivated area on the island of Java, most Indonesian islands are covered with tropical rain forests. Along the east coast of Sumatra, the south coast of Kalimantan and West Irian, and much of the north coast of Java, is swampy, low-lying land, covered, in many cases, with mangrove swamp. This land results from a continuing process of erosion, whereby topsoil has been washed down the rivers by the heavy rains. These torrential downpours also wreak havoc with Indonesian roads, which deteriorate into a series of potholes unless constantly repaired.

Indonesia's jungles contain a great variety of wild life: some, like the giant Komodo lizard,[5] are unknown elsewhere in the world. Tigers, elephants, orang utang, wild buffalo and rhinoceros inhabit Sumatra and Kalimantan, and even in the late

[4] D. G. E. Hall, *Atlas of South East Asia*, pp. 28-29. Compare this with the map on pp.18-19.
[5] Described vividly in *Zoo Quest for a Dragon* (see p. 16).

seventeenth century, could still be found near Batavia. Chinese
traders were prepared to pay dearly for rhinoceros horn, which
they believed to have medical-cum-magical qualities. Even in
present-day Java, where pressure of population has reduced the
amount of jungle, a troop of monkeys may swing across the main
road between Djakarta and Bandung. It has been estimated that
88% of the land area of Indonesia consists of forest, marsh or
bare highlands.

What has been said so far about the tropical vegetation and
the mountainous terrain, together with the fact that Indonesia
is composed of a series of islands, suggests that communication
between the different islands, or between different parts of one
island was more easily achieved by sea than by land. Not only
has Indonesia, for centuries, stood at the crossroads of world
trade and so attracted traders from far away, but also for communication between the different islands, and between the
different parts of the various mountainous, jungle-clad islands,
her own traders and seafarers have been very important.

Indonesia has attracted this world trade because many local
products were unique to this part of the world and were very
much sought after in other countries. Foremost were the spices
which gave the name 'Spice Islands' to the archipelago. In the
days before refrigeration, spices served the dual purpose of preserving food, meat in particular, and of disguising the flavour
of that which could not be adequately preserved. Sumatra was
famous for pepper, gold, and benzoin (an aromatic gum valued
especially by the Chinese); but the real spice islands, for whose
products merchants ventured more than halfway around the
world in small sailing vessels, and for whose control bitter and
cruel battles were fought, are mere specks in the seas beyond
Sulawesi. Ternate and Tidore, islands off the coast of Halmahera, and Ambon and Banda, islands further south in the
Maluku area, were the home of the nutmeg and clove. These
were used as spices and preservatives, in the manufacture of perfumes, and for medicinal purposes.

More recently, Indonesia's products have included oil, palm
oil, rubber, tin, copra, tea, coffee, quinine, sugar and kapok;
while as far back as records can be traced—perhaps even further
—Indonesia has been a rice-producing area. This generalization
is not true for the whole of present-day Indonesia. As we move
from west to east we move from islands where the staple diet is
rice to those where maize—or sago, in the extreme east—either
supplements or replaces it as the staple. Nowadays Indonesians

consume all the rice they produce, and it is distributed through her inter-island shipping. In earlier times, too, the rice produced in Java was exported, not only to the spice islands of the east but further afield.

The rhythm of international, including inter-insular trade, was determined in the days of sailing ships by monsoonal winds. From about April to September, the south-west monsoon, and from about October to March the north-east monsoon, controlled the sea routes.[6] By choosing the time carefully it was possible to travel to the Indies by one monsoon and back by the other. Where this was not possible the trader had to spend several months at one of the trading centres in the Malay peninsula or the Indonesian archipelago. Traders came from China, India and Arabia, while south-east Asian traders went as far afield as China, India, and even Madagascar. In the sixteenth century European traders also found their way to the fabled riches of the Indies.

From this way of life emerged a number of city-state harbour principalities located along the coasts of Sumatra, Malaya, Java and Kalimantan, adjacent to the trade routes, with others in the eastern islands, such as Makasar or South Sulawesi. Their rulers often participated actively in the sea trade which was the economic basis of their city, and derived additional income from customs and harbour dues, or from tribute, and piracy directed against rival ports. The urban population in these towns was usually poor, widely separated from the ruler and his aristocratic advisers. The population included both permanent inhabitants and many foreign traders, often with their own quarters in the city.

Not all Indonesians were traders. Some Indonesian communities turned their backs on the sea and lived a life centred on the raising of crops and livestock, the weaving of cloth and other activities related to their own subsistence and independent community life. The Balinese, for whom Bali is the centre of the universe, offer an example of this *sawah* or wet rice cultivation. The inland cities of Java were also less directly concerned with the outside world. At different periods Java has been the cradle of land-based civilizations, linked more closely to agriculture than to trade and the sea. Here the palaces (*kraton*) of princes developed, and became the centre of Javanese culture.

[6] See G. B. Cressey, *Asia's Lands and People* (McGraw-Hill, 3rd Edn., 1963), p. 500, for maps showing the wind conditions in South East Asia month by month.

A leisured class, an aristocracy, developed the arts of dancing and courtly literature, while drawing their wealth from their control of the surrounding villages. Such a civilization during the ninth century left behind it the great monument, Borobudur.

A third kind of civilization predominated in sparsely settled areas of Sumatra, Kalimantan and western Java. These people were peasants who moved from one place to another, following a form of shifting cultivation or *ladang*, sometimes known as swidden farming. They cleared an area of its jungle vegetation on the slash-and-burn principle: clearing and then burning off the jungle growth to speed up the normal process of decomposition enriching the soil sufficiently to plant a variety of crops for their own consumption, and others, such as pepper, mainly for trade. The pepper crop was delivered to the chief of the tribe and then exchanged by barter for the products needed from overseas. When, in a year or two, the soil ceased to be sufficiently fertile the community would move on, clear yet another area of land and cultivate it, while the jungle reclaimed its former territory. Eighty-nine per cent of the total area, and about one third of the population of Indonesia are still involved in shifting cultivation.

In some islands other than Java, dwellers in the interior have been cut off from contact with outsiders for centuries, and have retained a form of culture dating back, in some cases, to the Stone Age. In the interior of southern Sumatra, the Kubu tribe had no knowledge of the outside world, and was barely known to outsiders, until guerrilla fighters operating against the Dutch in the struggle for independence came into contact with them. Some authorities believe they were descendants of the original inhabitants of the islands, who came originally from Ceylon. Similar groups have been found in central Sulawesi and in the interior of Kalimantan and West Irian. Along with their Stone Age culture they have retained belief in animism, a religion based on worshipping and placating the spirits which they believe inhabit the natural world around them.

In West Java live the Badui, who quite deliberately withdrew to the mountains when Java became predominantly and officially Moslem in religion. Since then they have had only minimal contact with their non-Badui neighbours.[7] The Balinese have retained the Hindu religion and preserved a culture dating back to the period when much of Sumatra, Java and Bali were Hindu-Buddhist. In Java itself, modern Javanese practices reveal influences which are Hindu and Buddhist rather than Moslem, and

[7] See Nina Epton, *Palace and Jungle.*

behind these again influences dating back to the period when Animism was the religion of the people.[8]

According to census statisticians modern Indonesia is about 90 per cent Moslem, although some areas—for example, Minahassa in the north of Sulawesi—are almost 90 per cent Christian. The Batak Church in Sumatra is another Christian minority group; while in Flores, where Portuguese influence remained strong, there are many Roman Catholics. The Minahassans and Bataks are predominantly Protestant, the former linked with the missionary activity of the Dutch Reformed Church, the latter with Lutheran missionary activity in Sumatra. We shall have to ask how and why these different religious beliefs came to spread in this way, and what influence they have had on Indonesian life.

Indonesia's national motto is *Bhinneka Tunggal Ika*, an Old Javanese phrase meaning: 'They are many; they are one' or, as more usually translated, 'Unity in Diversity'. There are many underlying geographical similarities between the different islands, but partly because of their relative isolation from each other in the past, considerable diversities have developed among the different people of these islands. The history of Indonesia—the present unitary Republic of Indonesia—is the history of these diversities and of the continuing attempt to create a united nation without destroying the diversity.

A map of the language distribution throughout the archipelago[9] shows that all the languages spoken throughout Indonesia, except those of North Halmahera and Papua, belong to the same Malayo-Polynesian linguistic family; and that many different languages are found within this family.

There are five main language groups in Sumatra: Atjehnese, Batak, Minangkabau, Lampung and the language spoken along the east coast (opposite the Malay Peninsula) known originally as *Melayu* or Malay, now the official, unitary Indonesian language. To the east, the island of Sulawesi has at least six distinct language groups. Although the languages of the interior of Kalimantan form a distinct sub-family, in parts of the coastal areas and along the river systems Indonesian is spoken, while smaller coastal enclaves speak the language of south Sulawesi.

[8] Some of you may be interested to dip into a very fascinating book — C. Geertz, *The Religion of Java* (Free Press of Glencoe, 1960) — which is a study of religious beliefs and attitudes in a small town in east central Java. Read the introduction carefully; but then you may prefer to use a dip and skip technique, skipping the bits which seem too technical, and looking more particularly at the extracts from interviews which the writer had with various Javanese informants.
[9] D. G. E. Hall, *Atlas of South East Asia*, pp. 28-29 has such a map.

This provides linguistic evidence of trading contacts both between Kalimantan and Sumatra/Malaya and also between Kalimantan and the Buginese sailors of south Sulawesi. On the basis of similar linguistic evidence, historians believe that the early Malay and Indonesian sailors and traders had contacts with Madagascar.

Java has three main languages: Sundanese, spoken in west Java; Javanese, spoken in central and east Java; and Madurese, spoken on the island of Madura and in the adjacent district of Java. Sundanese and Javanese, like Balinese, each consist of different levels of language—one used when speaking to an inferior (mother to child, master to servant); one when speaking to an equal; and one when speaking to a superior (child to mother, servant to master). There are some nice social distinctions to be observed here, and there can be awkward moments even for the native speaker. Yet another courtly level exists for use when speaking to the Sultan. This is more than a difference between polite or formal usage and everyday speech. These levels of language have different vocabularies even for everyday things. This is one reason why the Javanese—the single largest ethnic group in Indonesia—realized that Javanese was too complicated to become the national language.

Instead, as far back as 1928, Indonesian was chosen as the national language. 'One country, one people, one language' was a national slogan before national independence was achieved. This national language, *bahasa Indonesia* (lit: the language of Indonesia) is now the language of instruction in all classes after third grade of primary school. Until third grade, children may be taught in their own local language—for example Javanese in a Javanese village, Batak in a Batak village; the language they would speak at home—but in those first three years at school the children learn Indonesian, and the national language is used for the rest of their primary and secondary education. (By university level they are expected also to have learnt sufficient English, now the first foreign language of Indonesia, to read English language books as well as Indonesian for their study.)

The Indonesian language has sprung from the form of Malay used as a lingua franca, the language of trade, for centuries. In the early eighteenth century one writer reported that: 'A person who can speak Malay can be understood from Persia to the Philippines.' As spoken, it is close enough to the language spoken in the Malay peninsula for Malay and Indonesian to be mutually intelligible. This development of a national language is an example of the attempt to achieve unity in diversity, one which has, to date, been very successful.

An ethnological map of south-east Asia[10] shows that, except for parts of West Irian, the islands of Indonesia are inhabited by the one ethnic group—the Malayan section of the Malayo-Polynesian group. Most of Java, apart from a few areas in the south, has quite a high concentration of overseas Chinese—also found on the tin island of Bangka; in various coastal areas of Sumatra, particularly the east coast and round about Medan; in some Kalimantan coastal areas; and near the northernmost and south-western corners of Sulawesi. The Chinese form an important minority group, especially since they are highly concentrated in several urban areas, where they often have near monopoly of retail trade. Many Chinese families have lived in Indonesia for four or five generations or longer, yet remain distinctively Chinese. How this has come about is one of the puzzles which we must examine later.

Although ethnologically—apart from some Papuans, the overseas Chinese groups and a few other foreign minority groups—all Indonesians are Malay; yet within this general group, as we have already seen, there is much diversity of culture. This is based partly on language differences, often linked with religious differences, but also related to differences in *adat*—the customary law governing the lives of the different communities. There are about nineteen different areas of *adat* law, again with basic similarities but with considerable variations as well. Different areas have different ceremonies and laws associated with birth, marriage and death; different traditional dances and festivals and even different dietary patterns. Some of these latter depend on the different products of each area, some are religiously based; for example the Moslem eats no pork and regards the dog as unclean also, while some Bataks regard dog as a prize delicacy: 'Especially black dog,' they say, when setting out to shock foreigners.

The basis of these differences can often be found in the past history of the different groups. For example the legend of how the Minangkabau people got their name goes back to a period when they were at war with people from Java. Instead of fighting with armies they agreed to abide by the outcome of a buffalo fight. The people of west Sumatra met the superior strength of the Javanese, represented by their great champion buffalo, by the use of superior cunning. The Minangkabau selected a little calf, starved him for a day or two and tipped his horns with steel. When the Javanese buffalo came into the arena and looked for an opponent worthy of his mettle, he saw only a little calf, which

[10] D. G. E. Hall, *Atlas of South East Asia,* p. 6.

he did not deign to attack. The calf, by now very hungry, ran to
the larger animal vainly searching for nourishment, but as he
ran beneath the bull, the steel-tipped horns struck the larger
animal a fatal blow. *"Menang kerbau"* (or Minangkabau), 'the
victorious buffalo', became the name of the people of this area.
Such a legend is not historical evidence of the events it records,
but does provide evidence of the attitude of the Minangkabau
people both to themselves and to the Javanese.

The past history of Indonesia as far back as the available
evidence will take us, shows an emerging pattern from about the
seventh century onwards. First there is evidence of an empire
(Srividjaya) based on trade, and tribute from traders, centred in
South Sumatra. It controlled the Straits of Malacca, and sought
also to control the Sunda Straits and to dominate the area. By
the tenth and eleventh centuries it was being challenged by a
kingdom in east Java, with a relatively large, mainly agricultural
population and a stratified bureaucratic social organization.
Initially these two states had been complementary rather than
competitive; but gradually the two became competitors for
sovereignty over other small principalities, and rivals for control
of the spice trade.

From this rather confused situation there arose by the second
half of the fourteenth century another Java-based kingdom, the
Empire of Madjapahit, while Srividjaya disintegrated into a
number of independent principalities and poor states. The move
had been from complementary systems through a period of direct
rivalry and struggle to one in which the Javanese empire had
established its superiority. The balance of power was restored
with the rise of the Empire of Malacca, centred on the peninsula
side of the Straits, but exercising control over both sides, and
basing its power on trade rather than any products of its own.
The ports along the north coast of Java came within its commercial orbit, and it was also in contact with the rest of the
archipelago, in particular the spice islands.

With the capture of Malacca by the Portuguese in 1511 the
decline of the empire had begun; but this same shifting balance
of power between trade-centred and agricultural-centred kingdoms continued, although slightly complicated by the way
Western influence and later domination was superimposed upon
it. The rivalry between Dutch and English for spheres of influence
finally divided the two sides of the Straits of Malacca, so that a
political boundary cut across an economic area. The balance has
swung to and fro between the land power of Java, based on
agriculture and a relatively large work force, and the maritime

commercial power of rival systems centred around the Straits of Malacca. Both have struggled and continue to struggle to control the rest of the archipelago.

Even at the height of the power of Madjapahit, or its heir the Dutch East Indies, Java has never exercised complete power over Sumatra. Atjeh, for example, has seldom been completely subdued. Even at the height of the commercial-based empires' power, Java has never been completely eclipsed. These long-standing rivalries still continue within the present unitary state of the Republic of Indonesia and in her relationships with her immediate neighbours.

Underlying all the differences outlined above are certain similarities of outlook. It would be as wrong to imply that Javanese and Batak, Dajak and Timorese, are completely different types of society as it would be to imply that stresses and strains, and differences of outlook between one district and another, do not exist. Increasingly these differences are being overcome, as Indonesians from different parts of the archipelago have more opportunities to meet each other. Initially the differences arose because small communities were effectively isolated from their neighbours by the jungles and mountains of which we have spoken.

The younger generation is setting aside cultural and ethnic differences. Even intermarriage between people from different islands and districts, once comparatively rare, is becoming common (though less common, still, than marriage within ethnic groups and village communities). The first President, Sukarno, was the son of a Javanese father and a Balinese mother; he urged publicly that young people should consider such cross-cultural marriages as a contribution to the growing unity of Indonesia.

PRELIMINARY READING

As a substitute for an actual visit to Indonesia, the best introduction to a study of her history is to read all you can about contemporary Indonesia, particularly books of travel, less for the information contained (for travellers do not necessarily have all their facts straight, and the authenticity of travellers' tales is traditionally somewhat suspect) than for their general impressions of Indonesia and Indonesians. The books listed here can be read simply for recreation and enjoyment; but try, at the same time, to decide what kind of a person the writer is, and how valid the picture of life in Indonesia given in each book is likely to be. Remember to take careful note of the date when the book was written as this may help in your assessment. Remember too that the most important asset of the would-be historian is a curiosity as insatiable as that of the Elephant's Child in the *Just So Stories*.

[This bibliography is arranged, as any good bibliography should be, in alphabetical order according to the surname of the author. The annotations should give you some idea of which book is most likely to appeal to you. They would all be valuable additions to a school or municipal library. These are suggestions for *preliminary* reading; a fuller bibliography appears at the end of the book.]

Attenborough, D.   *Zoo Quest for a Dragon*. Pan Books: London, 1961. 1st publ., 1957. This quest took the author to Java, Bali, Kalimantan and finally to Komodo, a tiny island in the Lesser Sundas, and the home of the huge lizard which he sought. He collected a variety of other animals during the journey.

Coast, J. *Recruit to Revolution*. Christophers: London, 1952. An adventure story by an Englishman who decided to help the Indonesians in their fight for independence. The book is a good introduction to several Indonesian leaders, and their struggle to maintain the independence which they proclaimed in 1945.

Coast, J.   *Dancing Out of Bali*. Faber and Faber: London, 1954. The story of an overseas tour by a Balinese dancing troupe, this also tells a lot about life in Bali. It becomes tedious when the author starts to defend himself in a one-sided account of a dispute which must certainly have had two sides, but you could easily skip that part.

Epton, N. *Islands of the Sunbird*. Jarrolds: London, 1954. This is a writer's account of her travel through Java, Sumatra, Sulawesi, Maluku and Bali.

Epton, N. *The Palace and the Jungle*. Oldbourne Press: London, 1956. The writer returned to explore some of the contrasts found on the island of Java, from the royal palace of the Sultan of Jogjakarta to a meeting with the Badui tribe, West Java, who traditionally keep themselves to themselves and have practically no contact with outsiders.

Grant, B. *Indonesia*. Penguin: London, 1966. 1st Publ., MUP, 1964. An Australian journalist and political scientist introduces various important aspects of contemporary Indonesian life and society to his own people. He writes as a sympathetic outsider.

Mossman, J.   *Rebels in Paradise: Indonesia's Civil War*. Cape: London, 1961. Another journalist gives an account of his adventures, often exciting, sometimes comical, during the 1958 rebellions in Sumatra.

Schreider, H. & F. *The Drums of Tonkin.* F. Muller: London, 1965, USA, 1963. An American couple visit many of the lesser known islands of Indonesia, travelling by amphibious jeep and having some narrow escapes. The line drawings and illustrations, some of which originally appeared in the *National Geographic,* add to the enjoyment.

Smith, D. C. *The Land and People of Indonesia.* Lippincott: Philadelphia, 1963. This is a sympathetic brief introduction of Indonesia to an American audience. It covers quite a range of material in 119 pages.

Southall, I. *Indonesia Face to Face.* Lansdowne Press: Melb., 1964. The story of young Australians who were privileged to work in Indonesia as members of the Volunteer Graduate Scheme for Indonesia gives their impressions of life as members of the Indonesian government service.

Southall, I. *Indonesian Journey.* Lansdowne Press: Melb., 1965. The writer develops around his journey to eastern Java an account of Indonesia today. Perhaps a good introduction to introductory reading.

Williams, Masslyn. *Five Journeys from Djakarta.* Collins: Sydney, 1966. Journeys to Sulawesi, Bali, Sumatra, Java and Irian Barat by an Australian who was anxious to make his own assessment of life in modern Indonesia.

Wright, R. *The Colour Curtain.* Dobson: London, 1956. An American Negro journalist gives his account of the Afro-Asian Conference held in Bandung in 1955.

Other Introductory Material

Ministry of Information, Indonesia. *Arts and Crafts in Indonesia.* Pertjetakan: Djakarta, 1953.

"Prapantja" (ed.). *Wedding Ceremonials.* Prapantja: Djakarta, ND.

Simatupang, R. O. *Dances in Indonesia.* Jajasan Prapantja: Djakarta, ND.

Tanah Air Kita: A Book on the Country and People of Indonesia. Van Hoeve: The Hague and Bandung, 5th Edn., ND. A pictorial introduction to the diversity of Indonesian life.

CHAPTER TWO

Problems of Studying Indonesian History

The main task of any student in any field of knowledge is to ask a great number of questions and then to set about trying to answer them. The answers are very rarely, if ever, final and conclusive even in the exact sciences. They serve as a basis for further questions which may lead, in their turn, to further discoveries. The historian asks questions about the past, in the light of his own situation in the present. He wants to know what happened in the past and why it happened as it did. In some ways his work is very like that of a detective. From the evidence left behind by the participants (the clues), and from the accounts given by observers of the events (the witnesses), both historian and detective try to work out what happened at a given time in a given place and why it happened as it did. Both historian and detective need to try to understand why the people involved acted as they did and how these actions may have influenced other events.

In studying Indonesian history we may find that Indonesians seem unpredictable to us. If so, this may merely be because we expect them to react in the same way as we do, whereas they have their own way of looking at things, and become quite predictable once this is taken into account—or, at least as predictable as any group of human beings ever can be.

One very important question, then, is: *How do Indonesians view the world in which they find themselves?* When we go on to ask: *Why do they view it in this way?* we are asking a question whose answer is largely historical. In answering it, many problems arise. One is lack of evidence for the early period of Indonesian history. The record of human existence in the area has been traced back to at least 40,000 B.C. In the region of Surakarta (Solo) in Central Java, there lived one of the earliest races of mankind, known as *Pithecanthropus erectus* or Java Man. The

discovery of part of a skeleton in 1890 and several other frag-
ments between 1931 and 1941 are our only evidence about his
way of life. Another problem is the diversity of the archipelago.
Instead of one history, we are dealing with a great many. Each
region has its own history, although in many cases such a history
is still waiting to be discovered and written. These regional
histories are all part of the overall history of the Indonesian
archipelago, and when some of them are compiled they may alter
the general account we now have of Indonesia's development.

At present our main interest will be centred on the trade-
based area surrounding the Straits of Malacca, and the agricul-
ture-based civilization found in Java. Just as most histories of the
British Isles concentrate their attention on England, and within
England on London, with only brief mention of Scotland, Ire-
land and Wales, so we will focus our attention on this area. The
great majority of Indonesians do live in Java (though not all of
them are Javanese) and the record of Javanese civilization,
although incomplete, is more complete than that from other
areas. Yet you need to be constantly aware that 'Indonesia' and
'Java' are *not* interchangeable terms.

The historian works mainly from *written sources* and here
several problems arise. First there are the various related but
distinctive languages in the archipelago itself. The national
language, Indonesian, has only been used as the official medium
of instruction since 1942. To be able to study all the available
written material, we must understand all these regional
languages. Even if we limit our main local inquiry to Java and
Sumatra, there are nine main languages in which relevant
material could be written. In addition for many Indonesians the
national language is actually a second or third language—which
they learnt as a foreign language when they were already adults.
It is sometimes difficult even for other Indonesians to understand
their meaning, especially in written work.

The second problem arises because the Indonesian climate is
not kind to perishable articles such as paper, or the *lontar* leaves
used for many early books. These are specially prepared palm
leaves with the writing cut into the leaf, which is then rubbed
with a particular ash. The leaves are threaded together rather
like a Venetian blind: but once the thread rots through, unless
great care has been taken, the leaves may be reassembled out of
their original order. Even inscriptions on monuments of stone
become worn and difficult to read after several hundred years in
the open air. Where the inscriptions are not too worn to decipher
they present other problems. They may have been written in a

special language which is hard to translate. And as they were not written with the needs of future historians in mind, they often give no indication of the date of the event they commemorate.

Another problem related to this question of language is that much information about Indonesia comes, not from Indonesians themselves, but from accounts given by visitors of various kinds —pilgrims, traders, adventurers, colonizers. Before the sixteenth century there are no known local sources describing the trading principalities centred on the Straits of Malacca. We have to depend on foreign reports. Before the eighth century most dated information for Java and all for Bali comes from Chinese sources.

It is difficult to know how accurate their information is about such remote places as the islands of south-east Asia. It is often very difficult even to locate the various places described. Indian writers, who were not interested in historical or geographical writing, referred to the various islands by descriptive names which could be translated as the 'Island of Gold' (perhaps Sumatra, perhaps Sumatra and Java, perhaps the whole archipelago), 'The Camphor Island', The Coconut Island' and the 'Island of Cardamom'. This makes it even more difficult to identify the particular places concerned, which can only be attempted when the Indian account contains enough information for a modern geographer to recognize the description of the place. The Arabs were more interested in practical information related to sailing routes and products than in describing the lands and people they visited.

With the arrival of European voyagers, from Marco Polo onwards, we are again faced with an array of languages, Portuguese, Dutch and English. Much material concerning Indonesia still awaits exploration in Portuguese archives; and a tremendous and increasing volume of material in Dutch has accumulated during the three hundred years of their contact with the archipelago. Though we may sigh with relief when at last we meet accounts written by English voyagers, it is dangerous to rely simply on English accounts: they incorporate English prejudices, many of which we may share, and should be compared with accounts from other European travellers with different national bias.

When we turn to Indonesian historical sources, there is some fragmentary material going back to about the tenth century. We also have the *Babad Tanah Djawi,* or Javanese State Chronicles, but scholars disagree about how far these are truly historical accounts and how far they represent legendary mythology. Like the Indian writers, the Javanese do not share our conception of

Peasants plough the ricefields with ploughs whose design has changed very little, if at all, over the past thousand years or so

This lumbering ox-cart is drawn by zebu, whose leather-soled 'shoes' look like carpet slippers. The sides and roof of the cart are of woven bamboo

This holy stone on Mount Bromo (East Java) still receives regular offerings from some Tenggerese villagers as it did when animism was the predominant religion (see p. 7)

The *pikulan* or car
ing pole has been u
for hundreds of years
a means of transport
goods. The first man
transporting earth
ware pots used for c
ing and storing wa
(p. 275)

historical writings. To examine this question in any detail we would first need to study ancient Javanese, which is even more difficult than modern Javanese.

For many Javanese these writings are less important for their historical content, their record of past events, than for their prophecies. You may have heard of the prophecy attributed to Djoyoboyo that after the White Buffalo (the Dutch) had ruled in Java for some time they would be defeated by the 'yellowish little chicken' (the Japanese), which would then rule in Java for the lifetime of the maize plant, after which the *Ratu Adil*, the Just King, would rule Java. This hope sustained the Javanese during the Japanese Occupation which at first they believed would last three and a half months, the time from the planting to the harvesting of the maize. At the end of that time the Japanese were still firmly in power, but the prophecy of Djoyoboyo was not doubted. Instead it was argued that the life of the maize plant must extend from one planting to the next. An extra eight months was added to the original estimate. The Japanese defied this new interpretation, and stayed for three and a half years. Again the interpretation was changed rather than the prophecy doubted. Their departure was seen as fulfilment of the prophecy because, it was argued, a maize cob stored for one year will grow well; after two years it will still grow, but not so well. After it has been stored for three and a half years it will no longer germinate. And those who believed that the departure of the Dutch and of the Japanese fulfilled the old prophecy believe with equal faith in the coming of the Just King.

Javanese histories perhaps had magical connotations for their readers, providing legitimacy for the ruler. The Malay historical writings, going back at least to the fifteenth century, are similar to European writings of the time in serving religious interests. History is seen as a branch of theology. The *Sejarah Melayu* has been described as 'a mixture of truth and legend, fantasy and fact, entertainment and instruction'. We must sift truth from legend and fantasy from fact.

In southern Sulawesi there are chronicles, 'the things concerning the people of former times', much closer than either Javanese or Malayan writings to the writing which we regard as historical. They contain legendary material, usually recognised as such by the writer's comment, 'according to the story'. These chronicles, although they seem to be in chronological order and arranged to a set plan, contain no specific dates. Other writings also exist: historical diaries, something like our modern desk calendar, with days and months written down in advance and particular

events recorded. Several of these have been preserved, but most
are not yet edited and published. By working from chronicles
and historical diaries together it should be possible to date the
various reigns in relation to events in other parts of the archipelago.

These southern Sulawesi historical diaries present a fresh problem, for in trying to relate them to happenings elsewhere in the
archipelago, we must first discover what calendar they used. In
the West we use only one calendar, divided into B.C. and A.D.
and based on the twelve months with which we are so familiar;
but even in present-day Indonesia at least four calendars are
still in use. The Moslem calendar dates from the year in which
Mohammed, the Prophet of God, went from Mecca to Medina,[1]
and consists of twelve lunar months, based on the waxing and
waning of the moon, and shorter than our solar months. A.D.
1965 was roughly equivalent to the Moslem year 1385. Older
than the Moslem calendar is the Javanese calendar, a lunar-solar
calendar related to the Indian calendar and dating from A.D. 78.
It has twelve lunar months, but from time to time it is adjusted
according to the solar year. The fourth, even more ancient
calendar is the Chinese calendar, also lunar.

Because we do not know which calendar the Buginese and
Makasarese used in their historical diaries we cannot date with
certainty any events prior to 1511, the year when the Portuguese
captured Malacca. This event is recorded in the south Sulawesi
writings, so that, from that point, it is possible to calculate events
on our own time line.

These problems remind us that history is not a mere listing of
established facts, but is more like the piecing together of a jigsaw
puzzle. Often we have to guess the shape of missing pieces until
they turn up—if they ever do. White ants, and damp and mould
in Indonesia's moist, humid climate are the enemies of the
historian.

For the student just beginning the study of Indonesian history
there are other problems. Proper names of individuals may be
unfamiliar and difficult to remember. Many Javanese names
begin with 'Su' and end with 'o'. Sukarno, Suharto and
Subandrio are examples. Again many Indonesians have not a
given name and surname, but merely one given name. Sukarno,
for example, is merely Sukarno. In some districts, by contrast,
there is a family or clan name as well as a given name. The
Batak and Mendeling people of Sumatra have a clan system and
use their clan name as a surname. Thus Abdul Haris Nasution,

[1] See below, p. 55.

from Mendeling, has two given names and a clan name. At least we can be grateful that not all Indonesians' names are as complicated as that of King Sri Bhuwaneshwara Wishnusakalatmakadigdawidjaja Parakramottunggadewa Lokapala known for short as Rakai Kajuwangi.

But the language problems go much deeper than this. The language in which we think can alter the *way* we think about many issues. Where we distinguish between the words 'hope', 'expectation' and 'reliance', the Indonesian word 'pengharapan' is used in all three senses, not because Indonesians make one word do the work of three, but because they do not always make the distinction we make between hoping and expecting. If they hope, they expect the hope to be fulfilled, and until it is they may continue hoping and expecting, as the Javanese did in the case of the Djoyoboyo prophecy. Nor do they make our sharp division between thinking and feeling. A word derived from the Arabic (*pikir*) means 'thought' or 'opinion'. Another word (*rasa*) means 'feeling' or 'opinion'. The verb derived from it means to think as well as to feel, thus emphasizing something which the English language tends to obscure, the extent to which thinking and feeling are interdependent rather than independent activities.

We are also handicapped in understanding the way Indonesians react to events both past and present because our society is the product of Western ideology and religious belief. 'Religion' to most Australians means Christianity, including the Jewish tradition from which Christianity developed but ignoring other religions—Hinduism, Buddhism, Islam—even though we do know that such religions exist. Most of us have little idea of what their adherents really believe, or how such beliefs affect their behaviour. Our own Western tradition makes European viewpoints easier for us to understand than Asian ones. Therefore we need to make a greater effort of the imagination to understand this more alien viewpoint. Understanding a viewpoint different from one's own and accepting it, are different things, of course; but until we have understood it we are in no position to reject it either.

These problems should make the study of Indonesian history more of a challenge. It illustrates one of the most important lessons of history: that, while the problems presenting themselves to different communities of people may be basically very similar in nature, the solutions they have worked out may vary tremendously.

PART II

Indonesia before the Eighteenth Century

CHAPTER THREE

Early Indonesian History

The First Man

'Bengawan Solo, ancient your history's span,
Linking present close to past, linking life of soil and man.
In the summer's heat sluggish your stream and slow,
In the rainy season's height, far afield your banks o'erflow.
At your source the deep springs of Solo
In Gunung Seribu prisoned fast.
Now you flow on through fertile ricefields
Down to the sea at last.
Here are ships of trade, and when your journey's o'er,
Sailors brave the ocean wide, seeking some far distant shore.'

This is a free translation of a well-known Indonesian song written about the river Solo in Java. It rises in the mountains near the south coast, flows north past the city of Solo (or Surakarta), then gradually winds north and east, entering the sea opposite the island of Madura off Java's north-east coast.

The 'ships of trade' linked its history with the mercantile kingdoms of Java's north coast; its 'fertile ricefields', along with those of the Brantas valley further to the east, helped support the splendour of some of Java's ancient inland kingdoms; but its history's span is even more ancient than either of these. Along the banks of the Solo river, near the town of Trinul, scientists have unearthed part of the skeleton remains of a creature commonly known as Java Man. Scientifically he is referred to as *Pithecanthropus erectus* (upright ape-man), one of the oldest man-like creatures yet discovered. He is even older than a possible relative of his, Peking Man (*Sinanthropus*), discovered in China, although perhaps younger than the recently discovered African man. Solo Man, a more highly developed ape-man than these, also camped in prehistoric times by the river Solo at least 35,000 years ago. His younger brother, Wadjak Man, was unearthed near the south coast of Java and is the earliest example of *homo sapiens*, the scientific name for the zoological species to which we all belong as members of the human race. He

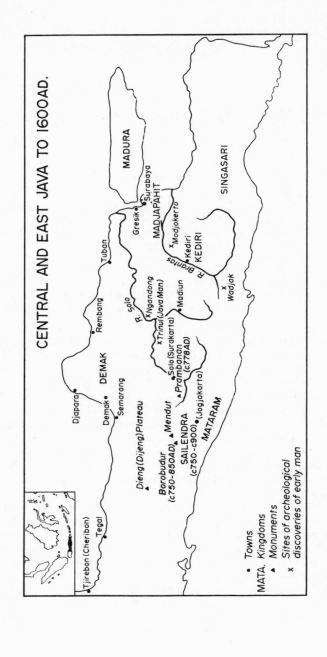

CENTRAL AND EAST JAVA TO 1600AD.

MADURA

Surabaya

Gresik

MADJAPAHIT

Tuban

×Modjokerto

R. Brantas

Kediri

KEDIRI

Rembang

R. Solo

SINGASARI

×Ngandong

×Trinil (Java Man)

×Wadjak

Madiun

Djapara

DEMAK

Dieng (Dijeng) Plateau

Demak

Semarang

Solo (Surakarta)

Prambanan (c778AD)

Mataram

Borobudur (c750-850AD) ▲Mendut

SAILENDRA (c750-c900)

(Jogjakarta)

MATARAM

Tegal

Tjirebon (Cheribon)

• Towns

MATA. Kingdoms

▲ Monuments

× Sites of archeological discoveries of early man

and his fellows probably lived about twelve to thirteen thousand years ago.

In this period of prehistory the jigsaw puzzle of the past has many more pieces missing than we can ever hope to locate. Even for Java Man, Solo Man or Wadjak Man we have not the whole skeleton of any one individual but just a few odd bones from which scientists have attempted to reconstruct the shape and size of their original owners, and to develop a hypothesis about the relationship of these reconstructions to each other. One such hypothesis claims these as the original inhabitants of Indonesia and Australia.

EARLY MIGRANTS

It used to be held that Indonesia's earliest inhabitants came from north-west India or Burma, and that later migrants came from southern China and the areas bordering on China. This theory could explain some differences observed between the hill tribes of many Indonesian islands and the coastal dwellers. Initially it was argued that the migrants from south China came in two waves, first the Proto-Malays and later the Deutero-Malays. More recent investigations and theories favour the idea of a gradual movement south over several thousand years, and suggest that the differences between the groups formerly described as Proto- or Deutero-Malays arose from intermarriage between the Deutero-Malay and later immigrants or trading groups. The Proto-Malays, as the people of the later Stone Age were called, left very few traces, but are believed to have become cultivators rather than food gatherers and to have domesticated such animals as the pig, the ox and the buffalo rather than depending on hunting.

Three methods have been used for learning more about these early settlers. The first is the comparative study of language. By comparing the words used for different household things in early Malay and related languages with those used in other languages, scholars have attempted to discover what words belonged to the earliest original Malay language and what words were borrowed from elsewhere. They argue that, where the words are found in the original Malay language, the objects they described must also have been known, but that where the words are borrowed, the objects they represent were probably borrowed along with the name.[1]

[1] For example, the Indonesian/Malay word for "eye" (*mata*) is found in many local languages in Indonesia as well as in Tagalog (the language of the Philippines) and in Tongan. The word for "fish" (*ikan*) is also widespread.

From this it has been argued that by the early bronze and iron age in Indonesia, before there was known contact with either India or China, the Indonesians already knew how to irrigate their ricefields, to domesticate animals, to use some metals, to navigate in outrigger canoes, and to fish. They were organized in villages whose pattern of life was linked to the irrigation of their ricefields and whose houses were rectangular ones built on piles.

The second method is through digging up the past. Stone Age workshops have been found in various parts of Java, and one has so far been found in Sumatra. Some implements discovered have been made of precious and semi-precious stones and are believed to be for ritual purposes rather than for everyday use, because they have not been worn down as ordinary implements would have been through usage.

In various parts of mainland south-east Asia, and in islands of Indonesia as far east as the island of Flores, there are the remains of bronze drums also believed to have had ceremonial uses. A stone mould found in Bali suggests that some of them may have been locally made. Others may have been imported from the mainland where the first such drums were found, near modern Tonkin. These drums, and the particular motifs with which they have been decorated, have given their name to the Dong'son culture in the period from about the seventh century B.C. to the first century A.D.[2] This culture marked the bronze age, when men discovered how to use metal not only to cast the ceremonial drums but also bronze axes and other objects, many of them made in stone or clay moulds. They could thus make more elaborate and more efficient weapons than the simple stone age implements.

Such archaeological evidence is difficult to evaluate, and archaeologists can only hope to find non-perishable remains. Very few substances can survive for over two thousand years. It has been argued that the Stone Age people were familiar with the art of weaving for, although woven material would have perished, ancient receptacles have been found with the imprint of woven fabrics on them.

These early Indonesians were perhaps familiar with wood work, both carpentry and carving, because although—as with weaving—no traces have survived from that period, their tools include adzes for working wood, and small adzes suitable for

[2] This seems an appropriate place to suggest that F. A. Wagner, *Indonesia: The Art of an Island Group* (Art of the World Series No. 11, Methuen: London, 1962), would make an excellent addition to any school library as well as showing what can be learnt about the past from a study of past (and present) art forms.

more delicate woodwork; while the Indonesian forests contain an abundance of wood suited to carving.

The third method is by working back from the present. The people on the island of Nias, off the west coast of Sumatra, preserved their Stone Age culture until before the Second World War. The megaliths, or giant stones found in many parts of the world—in England (Stonehenge), in Ancient Egypt, and elsewhere—are also found in Nias and still revered there by some older people. William Marsden, in the late eighteenth century, reported that these men of Nias were skilled in handicraft and carpentry, perhaps additional evidence that their ancestors knew how to carve wood with their adzes.

In the neighbouring Mentawai islands to the south of Nias, a dance is still performed similar to that in which it is believed the Dong'son drums were used. Another example of this, from a later period, is the continuation as a living tradition of the Hindu-Balinese religion and culture in the island of Bali.

Arguing back from the present to the past is risky, because we may include in our picture elements which belong to a later period. But Frits Wagner argues that we can work back from the present in the case of present-day stone age cultural groups because this was essentially a static culture, likely to remain unchanged unless influenced from outside. The tribes uninfluenced by Hindu, Buddhist or Moslem newcomers have preserved, in essentials, the style of art and way of life developed two thousands years ago. Various Indonesian ethnic groups who *were* influenced by these new religions have often retained older cultural elements and adapted new elements which could be successfully blended with the old.

From a combination of these three methods scholars have attempted to work out the religious beliefs of these early inhabitants of Indonesia. From the evidence available, it has been argued that these early Indonesians were animists, believing that all animate and inanimate objects have their own particular life force or *semangat,* their soul. Some have greater life force than others—particular places, particular objects and particular people may be specially endowed. The life force is also concentrated in a person's head, and this underlies the practice of headhunting and of cannibalism where these have been practised. (This is possibly connected with the present-day respect for a person's head. It is an insult to an adult for someone to touch his head, even accidentally.)

Supernatural forces are believed to be responsible for what we would regard as natural events, and evil spirits must be placated by offerings and by various rites and ceremonies. In a country where earthquakes, volcanic eruptions and torrential rainstorms are common natural events, a belief in malevolent spirits is hardly surprising. Cock-fighting in Bali is believed to be part of its ancient indigenous culture, a ritual ceremony held during temple feasts.

Certain people, including the village or tribal leaders, had more *semangat* than others. They also included those who could control the spirit world—known as *shamans,* or priests with magical powers—and people with special artistic talent, musicians, dancers, sculptors.

There also seems to have been a dualism in early Indonesian thinking—the mountain on the one hand, the sea on the other; winged beings and water beings; men of the mountain and men of the coast; heavenly gods and the gods of the earth.

Ancestral spirits were also revered and placated, for their *semangat* could continue to help the living. It was thus the custom to bury equipment that would be useful to the dead person on his travel to the afterlife. This explains the collections of ancient weapons and utensils found when ancient tombs have been excavated.

At least one scholar connects the Javanese *wayang* or shadow puppets with primitive Javanese ancestor worship, evoking the spirits of the dead, even though the *wayang* stories which have come down to us are more closely linked with later Hindu mythology. The *wayang purwo* (the oldest or the first *wayang*) is also known as *wayang kulit* (*kulit* means skin, hide) because the puppets are beautifully made from buffalo hide parchment, painted with gold and other bright colours. The *dalang* or puppet master sits behind a white screen and a light behind him casts the shadows of the puppets on the screen as he narrates the story. The audience sees the shadows rather than the puppets themselves. These puppets are stylised representations of humans and gods with elongated slender necks and arms whose faces are designed to reveal certain attributes and characteristics rather than individuals. The arms, skilfully jointed, can be moved by means of long, slender rods attached to the hands.[3]

At the beginning of the Christian era, then, according to present interpretation of the existing evidence, it is believed that

[3] For a more detailed account of *wayang,* with some beautiful colour illustrations, see F. Wagner, *op.cit.,* pp. 126-49.
For some of the *wayang* stories adapted from the Hindu legend of Ramayana see Sunardjo Haditjaroko, *Ramayana: Our National Reader* (Djambatan: Djakarta, 1961). This has black and white illustrations of several *wayang* characters.

various villages and tribal groups lived in the Indonesian islands possibly with little contact with each other or the outside world. Where the soil and climate were suitable, particularly in central and east Java and in Bali, village communities based on irrigated rice cultivation had developed. In less favoured areas rice was cultivated by the *ladang* or dry ricefield method. There were workshops where stone implements were chipped out of appropriate rocks. Weaving and wood-carving were perhaps among their skills.

To sum up the character of early Indonesian history we can say that the original inhabitants were probably animists, worshipping the god of the soil, the spirits of heaven and earth, mountain and sea; and they may also have worshipped their ancestors and have had special respect for the *shaman*, or priest, the person with sufficient knowledge of magic to control the spirits around them. Some of them may already have traded with overseas merchants; others, in the inland or away from the trade routes, may have known no world beyond the limits of their own village or tribal lands.

Very soon these early cultural patterns were to be influenced by the arrival of foreign traders particularly from China and India, and later from Arabia, who brought with them not only material goods but also new cultural and religious influences.

TRADERS, PRIESTS AND PILGRIMS: SECOND CENTURY A.D.—A.D. 414

The first written evidence concerning south-east Asia comes from Chinese sources. Chinese court annals go back to the Han dynasty (200B.C.-A.D.600). These and the biographies of famous men provide evidence of contact with the Roman Empire, with India, and with south-east Asia—although this last seems to have been established mainly through the arrival of envoys from these countries. We cannot always identify with any certainty the places or the people in these Chinese references, yet it is clear that, from very early times, China had important diplomatic and commercial connections with south-east Asia. The bulk of the early trade between the Indonesian islands and China was probably initiated by Indonesians and carried on in Indonesian ships. The Chinese reports seem secondhand, probably from information provided by envoys in tribute-bearing missions. This allowed plenty of scope for misunderstanding, vagueness and misinformation.

Chinese records list the arrival of tribute-bearing missions from different parts of Indonesia. We need not take too seriously the political implications of this tribute. To the Chinese, it was a symbol of the submission of the barbarians of the south to the Emperor, who held the mandate of heaven to rule the world. To the tribute bearers it involved mutual recognition between rulers, courtesies exchanged by one powerful ruler with another even more powerful. Their rare and costly gifts were reciprocated with even more magnificent ones, as befitted the generosity of the overlord to his subordinates, so the tribute bearers usually did quite well out of the exchange, which was almost a form of barter trade. Han Dynasty pottery remains, found in various places in the western part of Indonesia, provide evidence of Indonesian trade with China in the second and third centuries A.D.

In the following two centuries the Huns in central Asia disrupted the internal trade route and the Chinese were pre-occupied with internal troubles. This period saw the Gupta Empire rise in northern India, and Indian culture reach its highest peak. The Indians were also affected by the disruption of the inland trade route, and when, in addition to this, the Roman Empire was not anxious to continue exporting gold to India, Indian traders turned more to south-east Asia and the islands of gold. Rumours of their existence had reached as far as Alexandria, where they were incorporated in the work of the geographer Ptolemy as early as A.D.165.

Indonesia is at the southern apex of a triangle whose base lies along the overland route from India to China, and whose sides are formed by the sea routes. From earliest times, Indian as well as Chinese influences have made themselves felt in the archipelago. On the whole the Indian cultural influence seems to have been the stronger and more enduring. Why should this be so?

First the Chinese view of the world was China-centric; China was the centre of the universe. This is not unusual. Most countries regard themselves in much the same way for most of the time; but the Chinese took their assumptions further than many other countries have been prepared to do. Moving out from the heart of the Empire, the territory of the Son of Heaven, to that of the Emperor's feudal lords and beyond that again to the lesser nobles near the frontier, the Chinese regarded all non-Chinese people beyond these borders as barbarians of little interest to the civilized world. Because the Chinese had no desire to civilize barbarians there was little contact at the level of ideas.

Contacts with India—both trading contacts and cultural contacts—seem to have been much more a two-way affair and while the earlier Hindu religion was in many ways exclusive, based on rigid caste divisions, the later Buddhist religion, which developed from it, was essentially a missionary religion, whose influence was felt, not only in Indonesia, but also in China itself.[4]

The evidence of Hindu-Buddhist influence is clear enough in different parts of Indonesia where there are Sanskrit inscriptions dating back to the fifth century A.D., and many Hindu and Buddhist shrines and statues have been found in the archipelago. Although in India Hinduism and Buddhism are clearly differentiated it is difficult to disentangle them in Indonesia, particularly as their acceptance usually involved the blending of Hindu and Buddhist teachings with older religious beliefs current in Indonesia. Hinduism was more exclusively a courtly system with an emphasis on caste and the social relationships of the different castes to each other. It emphasized the role of the god-king, upon the correctness of whose behaviour depended the safety and prosperity of his kingdom.

Buddhism, on the other hand, is less institutional and more personal. The attainment of salvation or Nirvana (a state of nothingness) is possible to each individual, not limited to those of noble birth. It involves meditation, fasting and good works. The form of Buddhism which came to Indonesia—Mahayana—emphasized good works and the building of temples and monuments. An individual who has obtained salvation, and stands on the threshold of Nirvana, may renounce this ultimate reward in favour of other creatures. For this he becomes a Bodhisattva. These embryonic Buddhas were the object of veneration.[5] Because Buddhists are concerned not simply with their own enlightenment but with showing others the path of enlightenment, Buddhism is a missionary religion but it is doubtful whether its impact penetrated to the village level.

Up to about the seventh century A.D., very little evidence exists about the nature of Indian influence. Yet many theories have been put forward to explain the spread of Hindu-Buddhism and the relationship between Indian and Indonesian states in this period. One of these was that early Indian princes, defeated in India, may have migrated to the islands of south-east Asia and established kingdoms on the Indian model with the support of their followers. Its main weakness is that no evidence of such conquests has yet been found either in India or in Indonesia. Another theory suggests that Indian adventurers established

[4] F. Wagner, *op. cit.* Ch. VI has a brief, clear account of the development of Hinduism and Buddhism, and their relation to Indonesia.
[5] See below, pp. 38-9.

themselves at trading posts and later married into Indonesian aristocratic families, founding or usurping kingdoms and passing on their Hindu religion. Again the evidence is lacking.

These early theories all assume that the initiative in spreading Hinduism and Indian culture came entirely from the Indian side. Dutch historians saw it as a pattern of colonization similar to their own; Indian historians saw it as part of the Greater India movement, the extension of Indian influence throughout the Indian ocean, which bolstered their national pride when they suffered under British colonial rule.

More recently some Dutch historians began to wonder whether the spread of Indian culture was necessarily a result of Indian activity. They were writing in the period when Indonesian nationalism was developing and they asked whether the Indonesian role was simply the passive acceptance of cultural influence from India or whether the Indonesians themselves may have taken an active part in transferring and transforming Indian cultures. Indonesian historians have also stressed the role played by Indonesians in transferring culture, and this is at present the most widely accepted theory. Indonesian princes, impressed with stories of the splendour of Indian courts, invited Brahmans to come to their own courts, hoping perhaps that the more powerful magic of these Indian *shamans* could strengthen their own position. Certainly the elements of Indian culture which seem to have had the greatest influence in Indonesia were to do with courts and government: the Indian concept of royalty, the god-king; the use of Sanskrit as the language of religion and of courtly literature; the introduction of Indian mythology, in particular the stories in the Ramayana and Mahabharata, and its acclimatization in an Indonesian setting; and the introduction of the Hindu legal system.

So we would expect this religion to be mainly a courtly one. Some philologists argue that the art of *wayang*, the *gamelan* orchestra which accompanies it, and the printing of *batik* cloth were all indigenous. *Wayang* has been linked with Javanese ancestor worship, and even if it could be shown, as some writers believe, that the technique and repertoire of the *wayang* were known in India, it is significant that, until very recently, *wayang* has been an exclusively courtly art. The same is true of *batik*-making. This is a process by which cotton cloth is dyed after the pattern has first been 'written' on the cloth with warm wax. The wax remains impervious to the dye. Several waxings and dyeings may be necessary before the process is completed, and to produce one piece of *batik* cloth may take up to six months' work.

Once again the use of wax on cloth was known in Coromandel, one of the areas of trade with Indonesia; and it has been argued that the Javanese could have learnt this art from the Tamils. It is less important to decide whether this was so than to know the art of *batik*-making was also closely associated with the courts and courtly culture. Even when *batik* was no longer exclusively made by the Javanese aristocracy certain patterns were reserved for aristocrats and could not be worn by others.

This too suggests that the influence of Indian ideas and Indian culture was felt at the court level and among aristocrats rather as the English court of Shakespeare's time looked to Italy or the Russians of Napoleon's time looked to France.

Once Buddhism reached China as well as Indonesia, Chinese pilgrims went to India to search for more accurate copies of the Buddhist scriptures than they possessed. One such pilgrim, Fa-Hsien (Hien) journeyed to India and Ceylon by the overland route, leaving China in A.D.399, and returned by the sea route in 414. He spent five months in Ye-po-ti waiting to trans-ship and recorded that 'various forms of error and Brahmanism are flourishing, while Buddhism in it is not worth speaking of'. For us this is a rather unsatisfactory account of a five-month stay about whose location the experts are not even in agreement, some arguing that it was in Java, perhaps near Djapara on the north coast, others that it was more likely to have been in eastern Kalimantan, where inscriptions from the fifth century suggest a Hindu kingdom may have existed.

We can learn a little more than this from his vivid account of the voyage. He travelled in a large merchant ship carrying two hundred men. They sailed in fear of pirates and were beset by storms. 'In the darkness of the night, only the great waves were to be seen breaking on one another and emitting a brightness like that of fire, with large turtles and other monsters of the deep [all about] . . . The sea was deep and bottomless and there was no place where they could drop anchor.'[6] The return journey from Indonesia to China, though expected to take fifty days, in fact took over seventy. Trade was a hazardous business.

So in the period up to about the seventh century A.D. we have some evidence about merchants and sailors and other travellers who made the perilous voyage from India to Indonesia and back, or between Indonesia and China, and about Brahmin priests in the service of Indonesian rulers. The inscriptions in Sanskrit from this period are evidence also of the spread of Indian

* J. Legge, *A Record of Buddhistic Kingdoms* (Dover, N.Y. 1965. 1st pub. O.U.P. 1886) , pp. 111-3.

influence in the upper ranks of Indonesian society. We also catch
a fleeting glimpse of Indonesia through the eyes of a Buddhist
pilgrim returning from the holy land of India to his native China.

If Fa-Hsien had made his pilgrimage three centuries later in
some re-incarnation of his former self he might have been more
impressed with the barbarians of the southern islands, for by the
eighth century, partly as the result of Indian influence, there
had begun to emerge certain political patterns which were to set
the course of Sumatran and Javanese history. In south Sumatra
a great maritime empire—Srividjaya—had appeared, depending
on its control of sea routes and its advantageous position on
Sumatra's east coast. In Java a series of kingdoms based on control
of irrigated rice lands became powerful. The first of these,
Mataram, in central Java, held sway in the eighth century. After
its fall the centre of power moved to east Java where a series of
kingdoms—Djanggala, Kediri, Singhosari and Madjapahit—in
turn were powerful. Between Srividjaya and these successive
kingdoms there was continuing rivalry.

The Javanese kingdoms have left us the most magnificent
material remains. Between A.D.750 and 850, there was built in
Central Java one of the most impressive Buddhist monuments
to have survived to the present day, the temple of Borobudur
which expresses in architectural form the Buddhist concept of
the universe and, in the miles of bas-relief carvings which adorn
the four galleries, tells the story of the life of Buddha.

Borobudur survived the intervening centuries of Moslem
supremacy in Central Java partly because it was blanketed in a
thick layer of volcanic ash and hidden by tropical vegetation.
In 1814 Sir Stamford Raffles sent Lieutenant Cornelius of the
British Army to explore the area in which, according to tradition,
an ancient monument was located. He came upon the ruins, and
reported what he had found. Between 1907 and 1911 a Dutch
archaeological team began to restore the monument which otherwise might have 'melted away' as other smaller ones have done
either because the villagers have used the stones for such mundane
purposes as paving roads or because collectors have removed
statues to add to their hoard. In 1896 the Dutch colonial government presented eight cartloads of sculpture to the visiting King
of Thailand.

An aerial view of the sanctuary shows that it is built in the shape of a large dome or *stupa* around a hill, symbolizing the universe as seen by followers of Buddha. Below the base of the monument are a series of sculptured bas-reliefs representing the world of passion or desire where the good are rewarded by reincarnation as some higher form of life and the evil are punished by a lowlier reincarnation. Strangely the builders, having carved these reliefs, then covered them with stone to hide them from view.[7]

The four galleries, which rise above this in terraces, depict the world of form. If we turn to the left from the central staircase we walk round each of the four terraces in a roofless corridor with a balustrade to the left and, to the right, carved along the inner wall, a 'sermon in stone' with thirteen hundred illustrations of the life of the Buddha in the various stages of his search for enlightenment. After this three-mile walk we emerge from the world of form to the world of no-form represented by three unenclosed circular terraces with a total of seventy-two lattice-work stone *stupa*, arranged in concentric circles around a much larger central *stupa*, and we look across a green valley to the encircling ring of mountains, a magnificent setting.

The smaller *stupa* contain images of the Buddha and the visitor is invited to thrust a hand through the latticework to touch either the hand or the foot of the Buddha inside, while a guide recites appropriate prayers. The larger central *stupa*, representing Nirvana, is symbolically empty.

There are two smaller buildings in the same complex; Tjandi Mendut, a shrine where the nine Bodhisattva are said to represent the nine former kings of the Shailendra dynasty under whose tenth king the complex was begun; and Tjandi Pawon, believed to have been a place for making burnt offerings as purification before entering the sanctuary of Borobudur.

The Borobudur has been seen, not only as a representation of the Buddhist cosmos, and of the ten stages on the way to ultimate Nirvana, but also as having links with the terrace pyramid of earlier times, so that Borobudur itself is not a *stupa* in the original sense of the word—a place in which is enshrined some relic of the Buddha—but the burial place of the Shailendra kings who were cremated and buried at the earlier stages of the building, linking the Buddhist shrine with the older ancestor worship and the indigenous Indonesian terrace pyramids of a pre-Hindu-Buddhist era.

[7] Supomo Surjohudojo, 'Borobudur and the Quest for Ultimate Reality', in *Hemisphere*, Vol. 11, No. 7, July 1967, pp. 18-24, is not only well worth reading but is lavishly illustrated.

Yet we know very little of this Shailendra Dynasty, whose title means 'Kings of the Mountain'. Some scholars have linked the rise of this central Javanese dynasty with the mainland kingdom of Funan in Indo-China, where the same title was used. Funan declined in importance toward the end of the seventh century at about the time of the founding of the Javanese Shailendra Dynasty. It has been surmised that a princess of Funan married into the Javanese family, thus linking the two dynasties.[8]

Later still, not long after the completion of Borobudur, the Shailendra Kingdom of central Java seems to have disappeared, but we find the ruling house of the sea-based Sumatran Kingdom of Srividjaya using the title Shailendra. Between 850 and 860 a Sumatran Shailendra ruler founded a Buddhist centre of study in Bengal. Again one theory is that the Sumatran Shailendra Dynasty's link with the earlier one in central Java may have resulted from a marriage alliance.

Other architectural remains from this period have also been found. The Prambanan complex[9] and the earlier Shivaite temples on the Dieng Plateau[10] have led to speculation as to the number of central Javanese kingdoms existing at this period, and their relationship to each other and to dynasties in other parts of Indonesia. At Prambanan, north-east of Jogjakarta, a Shivaite Hindu mausoleum has been discovered and restored. It consists of 156 shrines arranged around 8 major temples, and possibly erected by King Daksha of the Mataram Dynasty in about 915; although more recent theories give its date as about A.D. 778, suggesting that two important dynasties existed during the eighth and ninth centuries in central Java—one predominantly Hindu, and one predominantly Buddhist. The most important of the central *tjandi* or monuments is dedicated to the Hindu God Shiva, Destroyer of the World. It is flanked by two *tjandi*, one dedicated to Brahma, Creator of the World, the other to Vishnu, the Guardian of the World. These three make up the *trimurti* or trinity of gods honoured by the Hindus.[11] Now the restored mausoleum, burial place of the kings of Mataram, is used as a magnificent open-air setting for the *wayang wong* performances in which human dancers take the place of the *wayang* puppet figures. Behind them, carved in stone, are representations of the Ramayana stories on which their dances are based.[12]

[8] Vlekke, *Nusantara,* pp. 31-4.
[9] Vlekke. pp. 35-7.
[10] Vlekke, p. 30.
[11] Wagner, pp. 116-20.
[12] Southall, *Indonesia Face to Face,* ch. 19, gives a description of the monument and the performance.

By the end of the tenth century, the centre of power in Java seems to have moved from central to east Java. It is wise, though, to remember that evidence is scanty and that much of what is presented as the early history of Indonesia is, in fact, conjecture.

World Trade and Commercial Empires—Srividjaya. c.A.D.450-c.A.D.1300

If these conjectures about the Shailendra are correct then they link the continental kingdom of Funan, whose prosperity depended largely on its proximity to the trade route from China to India via the Kra isthmus, with the central Javanese inland kingdom—based on rice-growing and a relatively abundant workforce having some obligation to work for the ruler—and with the sea-based Srividjaya Empire, whose power depended on controlling the Straits of Malacca and the shipping using this route. The Shailendra ruled over the strong Buddhist kingdoms, but our knowledge of these kingdoms is disappointingly fragmentary.

A map of Sumatra shows running along its west coast from north to south, a high mountain range reaching 10,000 feet in places. From this range a number of rivers, with their tributaries, flow down across low-lying plains to the eastern coast. These plains are not particularly fertile and in many places are covered with mangrove swamps. Palembang, on the River Musi, is about forty-five miles inland from the coast and Djambi, on the River Batang Hari, is about sixty miles from the coast. (This was the 'favoured coast' rather than the west coast of Sumatra, more exposed to seasonal storms.) These two rivers can be navigated in small boats for a considerable distance inland. The Indragiri River farther north is open to ships of up to twenty tons as far as the borders of Minangkabau, one of the chief Sumatran gold-bearing areas, centre of the fabled isles of gold known to the Roman Empire. North-east of Palembang and north of Djambi lies present-day Singapore at the entrance to the Straits of Malacca, and north-west of that again is the city of Malacca, also on the peninsula side of the straits.

Control of these straits meant control of international trade. They form a natural channel, at some points less than forty miles wide. When any one harbour principality was strong enough to control other smaller principalities it could also exercise control over the shipping passing through the straits and could insist that ships call at its market and pay dues for the privilege of so doing.

Trade was 'a thin but golden thread binding the Asian world

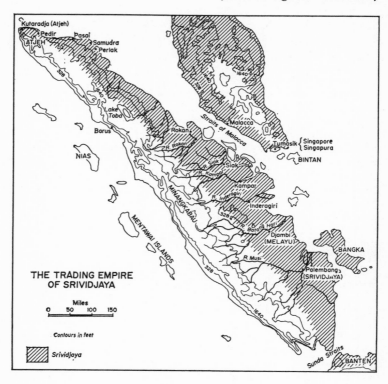

Kutaradja (Atjeh)
Pedir   Pasai
ATJEH   Samudra
              Perlak

Lake
Toba
Barus   Rokan.
                         R. Rokan
NIAS   Siak
                         R. Siak
                         Kampar
                         Kampar
                         R. Indragiri
                              Inderagiri
MENTAWAI ISLANDS
MINANGKABAU   Baru Hari
                         Djambi
                         (MELAYU)
                         R. Musi   BANGKA
THE TRADING EMPIRE
OF SRIVIDJAYA   Palembang
                                 (SRIVIDJAYA)
          Miles
    0   50   100   150

       Contours in feet
                                                    BANTEN
//// *Srividjaya*   Sunda Straits

Malacca
Straits of Malacca
Tumasik { Singapore
         { Singapura
              BINTAN

across great distances'.[13] The bulk of it was probably originally
carried on in short stages from one maritime principality to the
next, a shuttle service of small craft carrying travelling pedlars
to and from neighbouring markets; but an increasing number of
ships, arranging their sailing schedules to take advantage of prevailing monsoonal winds, undertook long-distance voyages. We
know from the pilgrim, Fa-Hsien, already quoted, that merchant
ships with up to 200 people aboard were making the trip from
Ceylon to Indonesia or from Indonesia to China as early as the
fourth century.

Palembang, generally believed to have been the first capital of
the Srividjaya empire, is on the favoured east coast of Sumatra.
With the river Musi giving it access to the hinterland, it was well
situated for trade. Very probably the products of the mountain
areas were brought downstream on small rafts of rough timber,

[13] Van Leur, p. 78.

or of bamboo lashed together, and probably included gold dust as well as forest products—benzoin, the balsam or resin of a tree native to the area, used for incense as well as medicinally; damar, a resin from a species of pine which oozes out and can be gathered in lumps from the ground and used in place of pitch to render ships watertight; camphor, found in the natural crevices of the camphorwood tree; and later, when supplies from India could no longer satisfy the market, pepper.

Although the coastal cities were an outlet for the rare products of the hinterland, their main importance was as market places where merchants from Arabia, Persia, or India brought goods to exchange both for local products and for various goods brought from China or the Spice Islands. Silk, porcelain and Chinese rhubarb (distinguished from our ordinary rhubarb by its medicinal properties) came from China in return for ivory, tortoise shell, rhinoceros horn (believed to be an antidote to poison); spices such as cloves, cardamom, and pepper; precious wood, especially ebony and camphorwood (as well as the camphor itself), pearls, coral, amber and the dull reddish-white precious stone known as cornelian or chalcedony; and perfumes. To Arabia were shipped aloes for medicinal uses; forest products such as camphor, sandalwood, ebony and sapanwood (from which a red dye is made); ivory; tin; and spices.

The staple was not limited to luxury goods, although these seem to have predominated. By the early thirteenth century woollen and cotton cloth were also part of the merchant's stock-in-trade, as well as other bulk commodities such as iron and rice. The import of rice suggests that the swampy hinterland could not supply sufficient rice to feed the inhabitants of the coastal cities.

In this 'splendid and trifling' trade in rich silks, rare spices and drugs, expensive and rare woods, exotic birds, and precious gems profits could be made because such articles were scarce in the places to which they were exported, possibly making them worth several hundred per cent of the merchants' original investment. Many small merchant-pedlars, whose stock-in-trade was limited but valuable, took a passage on the merchant ships, owned in some cases by the ruler of the principality, and hazarded their fortunes on the perilous journey. In some cases the ruler may not only have owned the ship but may also have had a part-interest in the merchandise aboard it.

Srividjaya's ruling dynasty maintained its power by military and maritime force. In 1178 a Chinese writer reported that 'in fighting on land or on water none surpass them in impetuosity

of attack . . . If some foreign ship, passing this place, should
not enter here, an armed party would certainly come out and kill
them to the last.'[14]

The distinction between this royal compulsion and plundering
or piracy is a rather fine one. While one principality was strong
enough to control would-be rivals and to enforce its own right
to customs duties and port dues, levied through royal officials,
its royal authority remained strong, and it could maintain tribu-
tary overseas possessions as Srividjaya seems to have done on the
Malay Peninsula and possibly in western Java as well. Some
writers believe that, at the height of its power, it also exercised
control over west Kalimantan and central Java with possible
sovereignty over the settlements along the rivers of the hinterland.

Apart from such levying of toll and the provision of outlets
for its products there was probably little connection between the
hinterland and the coastal ports. Without their levy on passing
traders the coastal principalities of the loosely-structured Srividjaya Empire would most likely have remained small subsistence
villages instead of becoming glittering jewels strung along the
thin gold thread of international trade.

Probably the palace of the Buddhist rulers of Srividjaya was
erected on elevated ground, justifying the title King of the
Mountain (the mount presumably signifying Mount Meru, the
sacred mountain). The monarch, the nobility and the Buddhist
priests may have had little contact—apart from the levying of
taxes—with the merchants of a dozen different nations who frequented the market squares, or whose ships lay at anchor in the
Musi river. Yet the trading profession was approved for Buddhist
believers because it involved no risk of sacrificing insect life as in
agriculture, slaughtering animals as in husbandry, or killing silk-
worms as in silk manufacture; and the Buddhists revere all life
as sacred.

As early as the seventh century, Srividjaya was a centre of
Buddhist learning. I-Ching, a Buddhist monk from China, spent
seven months there learning Sanskrit grammar in a community of
over a thousand monks. Through the monarch's good will he
then spent two months at Mo-lo-yu (Djambi), in 671. In 685 he
returned from India and spent another four years at Srividjaya
translating Buddhist texts. He recommended that fellow Buddhist pilgrims from China should plan to spend up to two years
there, perfecting their knowledge of Sanskrit before continuing
on to India. In the early eleventh century a Srividjaya king was

[14] Chou K'u-fei, quoted in B. Schrieke, *Indonesian Sociological Studies*, I, p. 15.

Local fishing boat with square sail, the simplest and earliest design to catch and utilize the winds as a means of transport

This fishing boat has a triangular sail similar to the sails on Arabian ships designed for long distance sailing into the wind

Top: Aerial view of Borobodur showing the sphere of desire (the outer base platform), the sphere of form (the five terraces), and the sphere of formlessness (the three circular platforms with their *stupas* around the central, empty *stupa*)

Above: Indonesians and tourists making their way to Borobodur as Buddhist worshippers and saffron-robed monks used to do in the ninth century

Right: The Buddha shown in the incomplete *stupa* of the foreground is similar to those enclosed in the other *stupas* behind it. To touch a carved hand or foot of the Buddha through the latticework brings blessing

(See pp. 38-9)

Part of the Hindu temple complex at Prambanan (see p. 40)

Bali still retains as a living culture the old Hindu-Buddhist religion. This is a decorated funeral pyre on which the body of a dead warrior will be cremated according to the custom of Hindu Bali (see p. 52)

This shows some of the bas-relief carvings on the front of the Temple dedicated to the god Shiva

Above: The members of this *gamelan* orchestra are wearing traditional Javanese court dress. Notice the *kris* each man wears in his belt, and the *batik* cloth in the headdress and 'skirt' (see pp. 113-14)

Below: These *wayang golek* are a few of the many characters in the stories of the *Mahabharata*. The wooden puppets are representations of more stylized shadow puppets made from buffalo hide, and are found mainly in West Java (see p. 32)

responsible for the erection of a Buddhist temple (or place of
learning) on the Indian coast, and shortly after that we learn
from Tibetan sources that Atisa, a reformer of Tibetan Budd-
ism, spent twelve years studying in Srividjaya.

For the merchants the focal point of the town was the market
where person to person bargaining went on, trading that
ve been on the basis of barter, or may have involved
ving scope to the activities of money-changers. In
ets were merchants of different nationalities, perhaps
from their home port or perhaps spending several
g for a connecting ship and a favourable wind to
ther afield, or to their port of origin. It was a
lation, where local people lived either on rafts
n stilt houses not so very different from those
forbears or their more modern descendants.
pire is in many ways more vulnerable than one
e. Local wars and natural disasters can dis-
the former is sensitive to events anywhere
e. Events in China, in India or in Arabia
rupt the flow of trade on which the stapl-
their wealth. Closer to home, attacks on
es could weaken the maritime strength
ower of the empire depended. It seems
s kind existed between the east Java

ched from the Coromandel coast of
dom of Chola was at the height of its
Palembang, Djambi, Atjeh, and
and Burma. They aimed at sup-
nesian rulers who levied taxes on
ina. From the Srividjaya point of
ul sovereignty over the Malacca
e weakened their control of the
King Airlangga, then ruling
o attack Srividjaya from the
narriage alliance between the
in the face of the Indian
en Srividjaya and Chola.
's power seems to have
e trading principalities of
utstripped that of Srivi-
century emigrants from
h on the Malay Penin-

sula, creating a rival centre of power across the Straits, while the increasing importance of the spice trade with eastern Indonesia strengthened the position of the northern Javanese ports.

By 1292 when Marco Polo, the Italian trader for many year in the service of the Great Khan of China, made the voyage fror China to India, he spoke not of Srividjaya but of 'an island kin dom called Malayur', so it seems that, by the end of the th teenth century, if not earlier, the centre of power had mov from Palembang to Malayu (Djambi) further north. His acco also suggests that the once powerful Kingdom of Srividjaya disintegrated into eight Sumatran kingdoms, each with its crowned king. Marco Polo found also, to his disappointm that the fabled unicorns of western mythology existed in S tra but that 'they have the hair of a buffalo and feet li elephant's. They have a single large black horn in the mid the forehead . . . They spend their time by preference wall in mud and slime. They are very ugly brutes to look at. Tl not at all such as we describe them when we relate that themselves be captured by virgins, but clean contrary notions.' How sad to have to substitute the reality of th ceros for the fantasy of the unicorn.

By the fifteenth century the centre of power had mo south-eastern Sumatra to south-western Malaya where th centre of Malacca was reaching the height of its power

Perhaps it is to the commercial empires of the Malacca that Indonesia owes one of its strongest unify —its national language. The use of Malay as the lin of trade owes much to the stapling ports whose wealt on their domination of the straits, and this is the basi Indonesian.

THE KINGDOMS OF EAST JAVA. c.1000-c.15

In the lands adjacent to the straits of Malacca th a number of small maritime principalities acknov kind of allegiance first to the ruler of Srividjaya and later to Malayu (Djambi). In Java where the seemed to move from the central to the eastern er at about the end of the ninth century there we kingdoms, sometimes rivals and sometimes allie was based on the fertility of the soil and whos was centralized on the *Kraton* or palace of the

For this period there are written records as w to help with the task of piecing together what past, and some were written, not by outsiders

One, the *Pararaton* or Book of Kings, has been discovered in a sixteenth century version, although parts are believed to date back to the fourteenth century. The *Nagarakertagama*, a long narrative poem, was written in 1365 by Prapantja, a court poet at the height of the kingdom of Madjapahit's power, to glorify his master the king. With both of these works it is difficult to decide how far their contents are historical and how far they are myths and legends. Sometimes it is possible to check against inscriptions, but the inscriptions themselves are not always easy to read or to interpret. We can compare these writings in places with the stories of King Arthur and the knights of the Round Table, although rather more is known of some of the persons mentioned in the *Pararaton* and *Nagarakertagama* than about King Arthur. Even if at times the stories themselves may seem unlikely to be true we can learn much about Javanese attitudes and values from the stories about past heroes.

We have already referred to Airlangga, ruler of eastern Java, who possibly took advantage of the Chola raid on Srividjaya to launch his own attack, but who seems later to have made an alliance with Srividjaya, perhaps in face of the threat from India. Airlangga was the son of a Javanese princess and a Balinese prince. He spent several years in hiding with a group of hermits before being able to claim the throne. (Some people have even argued that he may have been an usurper, but according to legend he was the rightful heir, strengthened for taking his position by the meditation and religious observation undertaken in hiding.) Under his government eastern Java became united and powerful. In 1030 he married a princess from Srividjaya and the court poet Mpu Kanwa wrote the epic poem *Ardjunawiwaha* in which the story of Ardjuna is used as an allegory, with Ardjuna representing Airlangga.[15] This is still one of the most popular of the *wayang* stories.

Before his death Airlangga retired to undertake further religious activity and, according to the legend, divided his kingdom between his two sons, with the river Brantas dividing the two kingdoms, Djanggala to the east, and Kediri to the west. We know nothing of Djanggala but Kediri seems to have risen to power.

At the beginning of the thirteenth century Kediri's pre-eminence seems to have passed to Singhosari under the leadership of the usurper, Ken Angrok (1222-27), a man of extraordinary violence. He came to the throne by murdering the former ruler of Singhosari and marrying his wife. Legend says that Ken

[15] Wagner, pp. 92-3.

Angrok, impatient with delay, tried out the murder weapon on
its maker, who cursed it with his dying breath, saying that seven
rulers would die by it. As might be expected, the curse was fulfilled, despite Ken Angrok's efforts to avert it. The ruler of
Kediri at that time, Kertadjaya, seems to have aroused the opposition of the priests by demanding an act of submission which
it had never been traditional for them to make. Rather than
accept such tyranny, they supported Ken Angrok who thus
obtained control over Kediri. His title as ruler was Ranggan
Radjasa.

The last ruler of Singhosari was King Kertanegara (1262-92).
According to one theory, he unified East Java and then set out
to conquer other parts of Indonesia. According to another he
was a skilful diplomat seeking diplomatic alliances with other
Indonesian rulers in face of the threat to the whole archipelago
from the excursions sent out in the late thirteenth century by
Kublai Khan (in whose service Marco Polo had spent so many
years), demanding that homage be paid to China.

In 1292 a Chinese embassy arrived at Kertanegara's court, but
the king refused to do homage to Kublai Khan. The insulted
envoys returned to China. Meanwhile King Djayakatwang, ruler
of Kediri, rebelled against Kertanegara. During the fighting,
Kertanegara was killed, and Djayakatwang came into power.

Meanwhile the offended Chinese were preparing a punitive
expedition to avenge the insult to Kublai Khan's former mission.
By the time news of the insult had reached China, the expedition
had been prepared, and the fleet had made the long return
voyage to east Java, Kertanegara, the guilty party, was already
dead. The Chinese held his successor, Djayakatwang, responsible
—after all *someone* had to be punished—and attacked him,
joined by Widjaya, son-in-law of Kertanegara, who paid homage
to China. Once Djayakatwang had been removed from the throne,
Widjaya and his men turned on the Chinese and drove them out.
The only result of the punitive expedition was to restore to the
throne the son-in-law of the man the Chinese had set out to
punish!

To establish his own legitimacy more firmly, Widjaya, or
Kertaradjasa Djajawardhana, to give him his royal title, is said
to have married the four daughters of Kertanegara, although
some writers doubt whether such a quartette ever existed. They
suggest that he actually made marriage alliances with Bali,
Malayu, Madura and Tandjungpura (north of Deli in Atjeh).
He was the first ruler of the Madjapahit empire, the most famous
of all Javanese kingdoms.

Most countries have their Golden Age, the period of past greatness to which, above all others, they look back with pride. For most Indonesians, Madjapahit represents the Golden Age. Some historians have argued that, at the height of its power, Madjapahit's territory was at least co-extensive with that of the modern Republic of Indonesia, perhaps including parts of present-day Malaysia too. Others say there is little evidence that Madjapahit, at its widest extent, controlled any more territory than eastern Java, Bali and Madura, and that she probably had insufficient naval strength to extend her authority outside Java except in the most nominal sense.

One characteristic of a Golden Age is that what actually happened becomes less important than what people believe happened. Certainly there was a Kingdom of Madjapahit, which, at the height of its power in the second half of the fourteenth century, was ruled by a young King Hajam Wuruk (or Radjasa-nagara), guided by his powerful First Minister, Gadjah Mada.[16]

Prapantja's writings give some idea of life in the *kraton* of Madjapahit, the tasks of the various *kraton* members, the activities of the ruler. There are occasional glimpses of some of the common people, whose main contact with their ruler, apart from taxes or labour service, was during his ceremonial tours and festivities. The poet describes the people crowding the open, calmly waiting for their Prince to pass by in royal splendour; some of the women who lived further away running agitatedly to find a place in the crowd and, in order to see, being forced to climb coconut palms so that 'dangling in bunches from their branches were girls, old and young, like luxuriant fruit'.

The Patih, keeper of the country, Gadjah Mada, had general oversight of the affairs of state and the special privileges attached to his office included a yellow state sunshade (usually reserved for royalty only), a red palanquin, a gold betel-chewing set, and the right to be accompanied by a band of musicians. The chief justice, the members of the priesthood, the commander-in-chief, the chamberlain (in charge of hunting and fishing parties, transport arrangements and entertainments), the chancellor (in charge of state ceremonies and state guests), the aide-de-camp and the master of guards all had their special duties and privileges.

The *kraton*, surrounded by a thick, high wall of red brick with watch towers at intervals, and huge ornamental iron gates, was like a miniature walled city within the larger city. The Ruler

[16] The first national university to be established after Indonesian independence was named after Gadjah Mada. It was housed in the *kraton* of Jogjakarta in central Java. See footnote, p. 236, below.

had his private residence in the inner private courtyard and there was also accommodation for relatives, Shivaite priests, Buddhist priests and their respective shrines, and possibly ancestral shrines, as well as accommodation for palace servants.

At intervals the Ruler, with his royal entourage, went on royal progress, visiting different parts of his realm. The carts and wagons of the different members of his party were distinguished by the designs painted on the side, emblems often of gold or silver. The Royal highway was one vast traffic jam, crammed with loaded carts which blocked the way, while throngs of serving-men on foot swarmed around among the elephants and horses pulling the wagons. To honour the occasion, the local people were expected to outdo each other in providing food for the visitors, and in return the Ruler scattered largesse in the form of clothing and other rewards.

The Ruler, with his attendant priest, through the ceremonies and rituals in which they took part, acted on behalf of his realm, preserving the order and balance, the peace and harmony which denoted a well-governed state. The *kraton* was both palace and shrine and the Ruler was believed to be either the incarnation of one of the gods, or their descendant. An usurper such as Ken Angrok emphasized his incarnation, because the matter of his descent was better left unemphasized.

In the *kraton's* inner sanctuary were kept the *pusaka* or emblems of sovereignty, possession of which symbolized possession of the kingdom, rather like Henry VII at the Battle of Bosworth plucking the crown from a thorn bush. In addition the Ruler, by virtue of the fact that he *was* a ruler, possessed supernatural power or *kesaktian,* a notion similar to the divine right of kings in English history. Again, for an usurper, the fact that his usurpation was successful showed that he must indeed possess *kesaktian,* while a ruler's defeat suggested a loss of his *kesaktian,* or its defeat by a stronger one. And whenever such a break in continuity occurred, attempts were made to explain it away and to emphasize the succession's underlying continuity. Descent along the female line was one important way of doing this, and was perhaps the origin of the story of King Kertaradjasa (Widjaya) and his marriage with Kertanegara's four daughters. It explains also the importance of marriage alliances contracted between different south-east Asian states.

The Javanese ideal was one of order. 'Orderly are the villages all over the country, giving wealth' wrote Prapantja in praise of his ruler. Everyone had his appropriate duties and his appropriate privileges. 'The Shivaite's son shall be a Shivaite, the

Buddhist's son shall be a Buddhist, the Radja's son shall be a Radja, the common layman's son shall be a common layman, the commoner's son shall be a commoner, and all classes shall follow their own avocations (and ceremonies)', wrote the poet. Anyone who constituted himself an ordained priest was to be tortured to death because this would lead to disorder in the world. Such a pretender would be 'an incarnation of the Great Annihilation'.

It was a hierarchical and static social order. 'As to property it should honour its master, the master should honour the headman, the headman should honour the minister of state, the minister of state should honour the Ruler, the Ruler should honour the ordained priest, the ordained priest should honour the gods, the gods should honour the holy spirit and the holy spirit should honour the Supreme Non-Entity.' Here we have a hierarchy stretching from inanimate property through the various ranks of human kind and beyond to the centre of the universe.

It has been argued that Hindu influence in Java failed to introduce any rigid caste system, as in India. Some students of Balinese history have argued that there may have been castes in Hindu Java, because traces of a caste system remain in Bali, whose Hinduism came via Java without any known direct contact with India. Caste may have been less rigid than in India because of the smaller number of upper caste people and the relatively greater number of the merchant caste.

History was seen as a falling away from the perfection of an ordered state into a period of chaos, symbolized in the story of Airlangga's division of his kingdom, which in turn would be overcome by the appearance of a Just Prince, the restorer of unity. Coupled with this was a widespread Javanese belief that a *kraton* would not last more than a hundred years, or ten *windhu* (a Javanese period of eight years, hence not more than eighty years). In the light of such beliefs, what is known of Javanese history suggests that Airlangga was the tenth century restorer of unity; Ken Angrok, for all his violence, was the Just Prince of the twelfth century; while Kertanegara, for the thirteenth century, and Hajam Wuruk (Radjasanagara) for the fourteenth, filled a comparable role. In the twentieth century, the first president of the Republic of Indonesia can be seen as the modern restorer of unity. Some awareness of this pattern of history helps explain the way in which many Javanese have viewed President Sukarno, and the myths on which he has been able to call, in working towards Indonesian unity.

Madjapahit's greatness did not outlast its hundred years. Its decline is usually linked with the rise of Islamic trading principalities along the Javanese north coast, although Balinese tradition explains it in terms of a demon-induced disease. Other factors were probably the empire's chronic internal weakness, due partly to inadequate communications, the fact that Madjapahit was peripheral to the main centres of trade, the rise of Thailand and Malacca on the mainland, and the expansion of China under the Ming dynasty.

As Islam spread through Java, Hindu-Buddhist priests and their followers took refuge in Bali and Lombok, taking with them the literature, and sacred books of Madjapahit. The manuscript of the *Nagarakertagama* was found in Lombok, and without it we would know almost as little about the court of Madjapahit as we do about the earlier *kraton* of Singhosari or of Kediri. Instead we catch a glimpse of Hajam Wuruk, in his jewel-studded lion-throne palanquin, shaded with a sunshade of peacock feathers, attired in clothes glittering with gold, preceded by booming drums and noisy conches and trumpets; or going on royal procession in an open wagon, ornamented with gold and jewels, its radiant rays sparkling in the tropical sunshine, and preceded by his retinue of 400 carts, elephants, horses and crowds of servants; or seated in his reception hall in ceremonial sitting position, his Brahmins and priests in front 'maybe one finger lower than he', with incense, and with 'harmonizing pairs of maidens' to carry the yellow state sunshade, the golden betel-chewing set, the treasure boxes, the golden fans, the red and white royal regalia, and the sacred *kris* or sword of state. Even allowing, as of course we must, for a certain amount of poetic licence on the part of Prapantja, the splendour of Madjapahit is revealed to us.

Village life in Java

The wealth of the kingdom came from the products of the soil, in particular the rice crops produced by the villagers from their irrigated fields. As well, from charters of the fourteenth century, we catch an occasional glimpse of other village artisans. One charter refers to 'the ferrymen of the whole island of Java', reminding us of the important role they played in transporting goods and people along the rivers which were the main highways of the island and which were deeper and less silted up than they are today. Another charter exempts certain tradespeople from taxation, including merchants, tappers of sugar-palms (or toddy-tappers who drew off the liquid from the sugar palm to ferment it into toddy), butchers, bleachers of textiles, dyers with indigo, millers of oil-mills, noodle-makers, and lime-burners, suggesting some of the other activities which went on in the villages.

Compared with the Srividjaya harbour principalities, the east Javanese kingdoms had greater manpower resources on which to draw; but compared with modern-day Java, the kingdoms of Java of the eleventh to fourteenth centuries were sparsely populated, with much untouched forest land, and with riceland available for all villages. Once a village reaches a certain optimum size it tends to divide off and form new village communities when there is still enough land available.

From the charters exempting certain villages from taxes, we obtain an idea of the taxes levied on the unexempted villages. They include payments resembling the feudal dues of medieval Europe, connected with ceremonial occasions—massaging on the occasion of a birth; wedding celebrations; services for the dead; entertainment of guests of high rank. There were also compulsory purchase of 'pepper, capsicum, cubeb, cardamom, iron, iron pans, dishes, rattan, cotton', and various contributions of building materials; as well as compulsory labour—earthing the roads; keeping ports in order; making various contributions to royal works and ceremonies.

The village has been the basic Javanese social unit since time immemorial. Sometimes the income from a village was given as a reward to faithful servants. Sometimes, in lieu of taxes, a village was appointed caretaker of a sanctuary. The village headmen linked village and court. They were responsible for supervising bridges and roads, irrigation dikes, and the sacred monuments. Much of the village work was probably planned and executed on a communal basis, and present-day Indonesians look to this village tradition when seeking the origin of indigenous democracy and *gotong royong,* or mutual self-help, a system whereby certain agricultural tasks are undertaken jointly.

The village population probably shared little in the cultural values of the *kraton* but had their own culture. Their main link with the central authority was through their tax and labour obligations, and their occasional participation in the festivals or royal processions, as spectators.

The relation of the ruler to his people was seen as that between the lion and the jungle. The lion must protect the jungle, but the lion's protection is the jungle. During wars, the villages suffered through disrupted communications and the destruction of crops. Apart from that the villages probably had a greater sense of identity with their village community than with any supra-village authority.

CHAPTER FOUR

The Coming of Islam

The decline of Madjapahit has been linked with the growth of trading principalities along the north coast of Java. This growth, in its turn, was connected with the revival of trade in Asia in the fifteenth century, particularly through the Straits of Malacca. The city of Malacca, which depended for its wealth and prosperity on trade links stretching halfway round the world, developed as a new centre of power controlling the Straits of Malacca.

The city was established at the beginning of the fifteenth century. According to legend, its founder, Paramesvara, was a Shailendra prince of Palembang whose wife was a Madjapahit princess. He fled, possibly after an unsuccessful revolt against Madjapahit in the 1390's, first to Tumasik (the site of present-day Singapore) where he took control of the settlement from his host after assassinating him, then later, when driven out, settled at Malacca. This gradually developed from a pirate settlement to a trading centre able to rival both the developing ports on the north-east coast of Sumatra, and Tumasik and the older Sumatran ports to the south. In the words of the *Malay Annals*, 'the fame of Malacca was spread abroad, from above the wind to below the wind'.

The rise of Malacca and of the Javanese north-coast trading ports coincided with the spread of Islam throughout the archipelago, until Islam replaced the former Hindu-Buddhist religion in many places (with the notable exception of the island of Bali which retains its own form of Hinduism to the present), and had become amalgamated with it in Java to form a new variant of traditional Islam.

THE NATURE OF ISLAM

What was this traditional Islam, the faith which, during the following two centuries, spread from Atjeh in northern Sumatra, to Makasar in Sulawesi and the Spice Islands of eastern Indonesia? Many writers, some of whom should know better, talk about 'Mohammedans' and 'Mohammedanism' instead of about 'Moslems' or 'Muslims' (the people who follow the religion) and 'Islam' (the religion itself). Moslems do not like to be called 'Mohammedans'. This implies a false analogy with Christians, rather like calling Christianity 'St Paulism'. Christians worship Christ but Moslems do *not* worship Mohammed. They believe that God sent twenty-five great prophets, including Abraham, Moses and Jesus, all of whom the Moslems respect and honour, but that the last and greatest prophet sent by God, the twenty-fifth, was Mohammed. Through him God revealed His message in the Koran, the sacred book of the Moslems. A person enters the community (*ummat*) of acceptors or submitters—the literal meaning of Islam and derived from a word meaning 'surrender' (*u salim*)—by making the affirmation of faith: 'There is no God but Allah[1] and Mohammed is His Prophet.'

Moslems date the beginning of the Moslem era, not from Mohammed's birth (about A.D. 571), but from A.D. 622 when Mohammed and his followers fled from the city of Mecca (Mekah) to Medina, that is, from the founding of the community of believers. In Medina, Mohammed established an administration able, within eight years, both to effect the conversion of Mecca and to unite virtually the whole of Arabia under his leadership. He died in A.D. 632, and in the following century Moslems conquered the surrounding countries and moved as far north as Spain and southern France where they were halted by the armies of Christendom.

Meanwhile Arab Moslem traders, like their non-Moslem predecessors, continued to follow the trade routes to India and beyond. Some evidence suggests that, as early as A.D. 674, Moslem Arabs may have settled on the north-west coast of Sumatra at the camphor-producing port of Barus. By A.D. 758 Arab traders in southern China were strong enough to sack the city of Canton. But although the first Moslem inscription in Java dates back to the beginning of the eleventh century and although there may even have been Arab settlers in the city of Madjapahit at the zenith of its power in the mid-fourteenth century, it was not until the fifteenth and sixteenth centuries that Indonesian rulers turned to Islam and it became the state religion.

The Five Pillars of Islam outline the religious requirements laid down for members of the community (*ummat*) of Islam. First is the affirmation of faith, already mentioned—'There is no God but Allah and Mohammed is His Prophet'—the central pillar of the faith. Second is prayer. Moslems should pray five times a day, within specified times and after ritual cleansing, and,

[1] Literally 'the God'; that is, 'the one God'.

as well as this private prayer, they should attend, when possible, the public prayers at the mosque on Fridays where all men are shown as equal in God's sight. Their third obligation is to give alms to the poor (*zakat*). Fourthly, in the ninth month of the Moslem year, the month of Ramadan, they should fast from sunrise to sunset neither eating nor drinking nor indulging in other pleasures during that time.[2] Finally they should, if possible, make the pilgrimage to Mecca, the Holy City, at least once in a lifetime.

These Five Pillars—the affirmation of faith, prayer, almsgiving, fasting and the pilgrimage—represent for many Moslems the ideal rather than the actuality. As in all religions, there is a gap between what the religion itself teaches and what most of its adherents actually do. Islam as it has developed in Arabia, in Persia, in India and in Indonesia has assimilated to the different societies in which it has established itself, and adopted some of the local customs. In Indonesia, where the *adat* or customary law of the different districts was already quite strongly developed before the arrival of Islam, the two have blended together so that it is often difficult to know what derives from *adat* and what from Islam. The same process occurred in Arabia in the early years of Islam and many overseas Moslems who look to Arabia as the Holy Land, do not always distinguish between the local customs there and the teachings of their religion.

Two aspects of Islam which contrasted with the older Hindu-Buddhist religion of Srividjaya and Madjapahit were the emphasis on the importance of the individual in direct relationship with and submission to God, and the emphasis on the world-wide community, in which all believers were brothers. In Islam there is neither church nor priesthood. The mosque is not an organizational institution but a place of worship, more like the Quaker meeting house than the churches of the older Christian

[2] During the fast the strict Moslem rises before sunrise at about 4.30 a.m. to have his last meal before 6 p.m. and then in the intervening period, however hot the day or hard his work, he has neither food, drink nor cigarette. The less strict Moslem may perhaps weaken and have a secret snack, but once he does this he has broken the fast period. He may, if he is a traveller, be exempted from fasting. The nominal Moslem may fast on the first and last day of the fast month, but even the most nominal Moslem will nevertheless join in the festivities and celebrations which mark the end of the fast, the Lebaran feast. The actual date of this feast is determined by the start of the new lunar month, and so people wait anxiously for the first sight of the new moon, the crescent which has long been a symbol of Islam, and then, after prayers, the festivities begin. People, even down to the youngest member of the family, have new clothes for the occasion. Special dishes are cooked. Families reunite to share the Lebaran meal, to ask forgiveness from each other for all sins of omission and commission during the year, and to pay their respects to the senior members of the family.

denominations. The religious teacher may in practice be specially respected in the community, but public worship can be led by any believer whom the community in a particular place appoints. It thus differs from Hindu-Buddhist worship, where the priest performed certain rituals on behalf of the people and the special priestly caste was entrusted with the responsibility of ensuring the safety of the realm by the correct performance of these rituals, in which the ruler too was often required to participate as someone himself part divine. Hinduism was suited to a settled, hierarchical agrarian community. Islam, perhaps, was more suited to the life of the trader.

The trader hazarded his life and fortunes upon the wide ocean, and put himself at the mercy of winds and tides. He moved from community to community depending on his own initiative and judgement to make or lose a fortune. He was perhaps more pre- pared to take individual responsibility for his own eternal life, fulfilling the obligations laid upon him by Islam and also finding himself a member of a world-wide community, a brotherhood of man. Like the earliest Moslems, he too was a nomad. Yet we should remember that, although at some points Islam was a religion suited to the trader, there were many Moslems who were not traders and there continued to be many traders who were not Moslems. Simply because these aspects of Islam harmonized with the trader's way of life, this in itself cannot explain the spread of Islam, although the unity of Islam, its belief in the equality of all men in the sight of God and its comparative simplicity of ritual and doctrine were important in encouraging its spread.

ISLAM AND THE STATE

While certain aspects of Islam may have appealed to the trad- ing community, whose status under the Hindu caste system was low, we might wonder why a Hindu-Buddhist ruler should wish to change from a religion which recognized him as part divine to one which claimed equality of all believers. The author of the *Malay Annals*[3] records the conversion of the Sultan of Malacca as follows. The King in a dream was taught the Moslem faith by Mohammed the Prophet Himself, and woke reciting the creed in Arabic, 'to the astonishment of all the women-attendants of

[3] This is an account written not long after the fall of Malacca to the Portu- guese and is a mixture of tradition, legend and history recorded so that following generations 'may be conversant with the history and derive profit therefrom'. See D. F. Lach & C. Flaumenhaft, *Asia on the Eve of European Expansion* (Spectrum Books, 1965), pp. 81-92, for translated extracts from these annals.

the palace', who did not know what language this was. In due course, as the dream had foretold, a ship arrived with a Moslem scholar, Saiyid 'Abdu'l 'Aziz. (The title 'Saiyid' implied that he was a direct descendant of the Prophet and hence an Arab rather than an Indian Moslem.) The ship berthed at the time for afternoon prayer. The prayer of a Moslem involves not only the speaking of certain words but also the performing of certain actions, standing, bowing, kneeling, prostrating oneself on the ground, sitting and then standing again. After the ritual cleansing, the new arrival began to perform his prayers. 'And all who saw him were astonished at his behaviour and said, "What means this bobbing up and down?" and there was a general scramble to see him, the people crowding together so thickly that there was not a space between one man and another and there was such a disturbance that the noise of it came to the ears of the Raja inside the royal apartments of the palace. And straightway the Raja set forth on his elephant escorted by his chiefs and he perceived that the Makhdum's behaviour in saying his prayers was exactly as in his dreams'. So he took the Makhdum on his elephant, a sign of great honour, as places on the Raja's elephant were allotted strictly according to precedent. They returned to the palace where the King and his chiefs embraced Islam 'and every citizen of Malacca, whether of high or low degree, was commanded by the Raja to do likewise.'[4]

This demonstrates the point made earlier. The writer of the *Malay Annals* is more concerned with edifying his Moslem readers than with any explanations in terms of non-religious factors which may have affected the conversion of the Hindu-Buddhist Malayan rulers of Malacca to Islam. It does suggest two points though. First this account, as well as the one in Portuguese sources and derived from local oral tradition, suggests that the act of conversion was a deliberate break, publicly acknowledged. Second, it suggests that, as in sixteenth and seventeenth century Europe, the subject followed his ruler's religion.

In many north coast Javanese towns the struggle for independence from Hindu-Buddhist Madjapahit may have encouraged the rulers to accept Islam, particularly in those places where the rulers were perhaps merchant adventurers who, like the original ruler of Malacca, moved from open piracy to a more respectable version of it—the compulsory levy of import duty and harbour dues. In a religion such as Islam, again in contrast to the Hindu or Buddhist religion, all members were expected to be propagators of the faith, not only the members of a priestly

[4] *Malay Annals*, pp. 53-4.

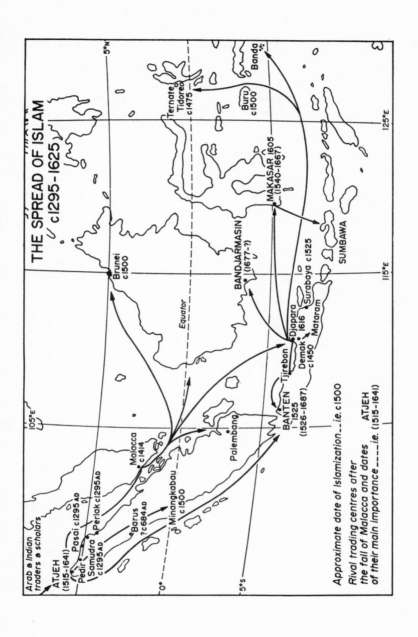

THE SPREAD OF ISLAM
c1295-1625

Arab & Indian
traders & scholars

ATJEH
(1515-1641)

Pedir
Samudra
c1295AD
Pasai c1295AD
Perlak c1295AD

Barus
?c684AD

Minangkabau
c1500

Malacca
c1414

Palembang

Brunei
c1500

Equator

BANDJARMASIN
(1677-?)

Ternate
Tidore
c1475

Buru
c1500

Banda

MAKASAR 1605
(1540-1667)

SUMBAWA

BANTEN
1525
(1526-1687)

Tjirebon

Djapara
1616
Demak
c1450

Surabaya c1525

Mataram

Approximate date of Islamization __ i.e. c1500

Rival trading centres after
the fall of Malacca and dates
of their main importance ___ i.e. (1515-1641)   ATJEH
(1515-1641)

5°N

125°E

115°E

105°E

0°

5°S

caste. Wealthy Moslem merchants, settling in these cities, built
mosques for themselves and their fellow Moslems. Then Moslem
teachers entered the country and helped to establish still further
the *ummat Islam*. Possibly as the Moslem trading communities
grew in size and prosperity, the rulers, through contact with leading and wealthy traders, felt that adherence to Islam gave them
greater legitimacy than they could otherwise claim from their
somewhat shady pirate origins.

THE SPREAD OF ISLAM

Islam spread through Indonesia from west to east, following
the trade route. During the thirteenth century it had become
firmly established in India, and by the end of that century we
have the first record of a Moslem state in the archipelago, Perlak,
on the north-east coast of Sumatra. According to Marco Polo
'the people of Ferlec [Perlak] used all to be idolators but owing
to contact with Saracen merchants, who continually resort here
in their ships, they have all been converted to the law of
Mohammed. This applies only to the inhabitants of the city.'

Once Moslem communities had been established, the shipping
along the trade routes was also used by pilgrims undertaking
the pilgrimage to Mecca, providing direct contact between Indonesian Moslems and Arabia.

There were similarities between Islam as it developed in Indonesia and the older Hindu-Buddhist religion which it replaced.
In every part of the archipelago, Islam had to come to terms
with older existing tradition and customs, just as Christianity in
northern Europe had incorporated some of the older pagan mid-
winter and spring festivals into the celebration of Christmas and
Easter. The more fully the two are blended, the more difficult it
is to decide where the influence of one begins and that of the
other ends. Certainly such similarities helped the assimilation of
Islam where it became established.

The Moslem idea of *keramat,* holiness or supernatural power
attached to outstanding individuals, was familiar to Hindu-
Buddhist thought in which the idea of *kesaktian* was already
held.[5] The person who was *keramat* was 'miraculously revealed
as the chosen friend of God.' Just as the concept of *kesaktian*
drew on the even older idea of *semangat*[6] the special power in-
nate in people, objects and places, so the concept of *keramat*
drew on that of *kesaktian*. Just as the ruler was seen to be especially endowed with *kesaktian,* so *keramat* was an attribute of the

[5] See p. 31 above.
[6] See p. 50 above.

Islamic ruler, who was held to be 'the shadow of God upon earth'. So, despite its emphasis upon the equality of all men in the sight of God, Islam could also give legitimacy to a ruler, for 'a just prince is joined with the Prophet of God like two jewels in one ring. Moreover the Raja is as it were the deputy of God.'[7]

It has also been claimed that Islam was spread partly through the missionary activity of members of the Sufi brotherhoods. These brotherhoods were societies within Islam whose members practised certain forms of mysticism and could thus confront the mystics of the earlier religion. They were also more tolerant of some aspects of *adat* law which, on a more strictly literal inter-pretation, might have been seen as conflicting with Islamic doctrine.[8]

Because there had been no firmly established caste system in Indonesian Hinduism there were fewer problems associated with the expansion of Islam in Indonesia than there were in India. On the whole, Islam spread peacefully throughout the archipelago rather than, as in east Asia, north Africa and India, predomin-antly through dynastic wars. Its spread to east Indonesia was closely associated with the trade rivalry which developed in the archipelago after the arrival of the Portuguese and their capture of Malacca in 1511.

During the rest of the sixteenth century, the Portuguese attempted to consolidate their strongholds along the trade route —Goa in India, Malacca in south-east Asia, Macao near China —and to establish control of places further east in order to mono-polize the trade of the Spice Islands themselves, and their precious crops. As they moved farther east so did Islam, a rally-ing point for those who opposed the intruders. And as the Portu-guese sought to concentrate all trade on Malacca, rival trading areas sprang up, first in Atjeh (1515-1641), then in Banten (1526-1687), in Makasar in southern Sulawesi (1540-1667) and later again at Bandjarmasin from 1667 onwards. Here Moslem traders came to avoid the Portuguese, and later the Dutch monopoly, or attempted monopoly of trade. Trade rivalries were sharpened by religious differences.

So the spread of Islam was a gradual process. Although it may

---

[7] *Malay Annals*, p. 118.
[8] Some traces of such brotherhoods still exist in parts of Indonesia and are described by C. Geertz, *The Religion of Java*, pp. 182-3. Geertz says that part of their meditation involves the counting of beads, so it seems likely that John Davis, who visited Atjeh in 1599, was speaking of members of the Sufi brotherhood when he said that 'In religion they [the Atjehnese] are Mahometists, and pray with Beades as the Papists doe.' (quoted in B. Schrieke, *Indonesian Sociological Studies*, II, p. 393.)

have been known in Indonesia within thirty-five years of Mohammed's death, few traces remain of its existence before the late thirteenth century. By then it had spread to India and to China. During the fifteenth century it became established in Malacca, which, with its widespread trading contacts, provided avenues for further Moslem penetration. With the fall of Malacca and the continuous rivalry with Portuguese Christian traders, Islam spread quite rapidly through the archipelago to other trading principalities, although at this stage it still had not penetrated to the interior of the larger islands. With the rise of Mataram in central Java and the rule of Senopati from 1586 Islam penetrated to the *kraton* of Java, when the northern coastal states, with their trade routes disrupted by Portuguese intervention, were no longer centres of power in Java.

MALACCA, THE MEETING PLACE

It is easier to reconstruct life in Malacca at the height of its power than it was for the kingdoms of Srividjaya and Madjapahit, because there are accounts by Malay writers and contemporary Chinese sources as well as reports from the increasing number of Europeans visiting Malacca after its capture by the Portuguese. Tomé Pires has left a detailed account. He was resident in Malacca in 1513-17 and later became Portugal's first ambassador to China. This was a posting as perilous then as in more recent times. As a reprisal for his fellow countrymen's activities in south-east Asia, he and his attendants were imprisoned, and he died in China. His *Suma Oriental* (Account of the East) reported on the trade and commerce of Malacca and the area which centred on it.[9] There are also the lively but chronologically unreliable *Sejarah Melayu* (Malay Annals) from which we have already quoted.

Malacca soon seems to have outstripped its rivals on the Straits of Malacca. Tomé Pires reports that it was ten times the size of Pasai in northern Sumatra. Palembang, centre of the earlier Srividjaya Empire, had declined from its former glory to become a haunt of pirates under a Chinese chief. Malacca was a more sheltered port than the Sumatran ones and, unlike another potential rival, Tumasik (Singapore) in the south, it was free from dangerous shallows.

Malacca's rise to power coincided with the renewed interest of China in southern trade. In this period the eight to ten trading junks which normally set off from Canton to Malacca usually terminated their voyage in Malacca rather than travelling east

[9] See the excerpts in Lach and Flaumenhaft, pp. 19-31.

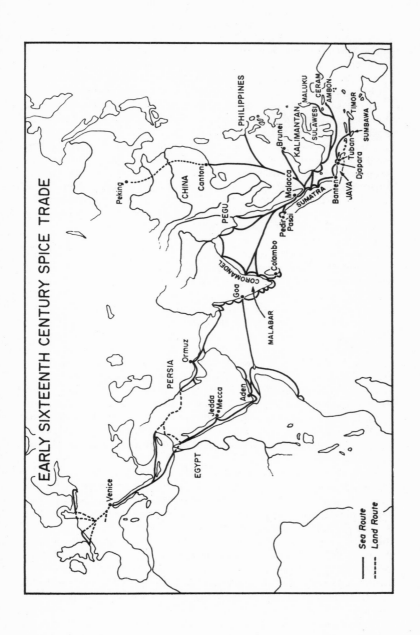

EARLY SIXTEENTH CENTURY SPICE TRADE

Sea Route
Land Route

to the Spice Islands, as earlier traders may have done. The higher spice prices in Malacca were compensated for by the shorter and therefore less hazardous voyage, and the Malacca spice market could supply the requirements of the Chinese merchants.

In the west there were also set stages in the voyage to Malacca. It became increasingly common for Arab and Persian traders to travel only as far as India in their own lighter, faster but less seaworthy ships, which, despite their speed, could not make the whole voyage during one monsoon. These ships returned to Arabia or Persia while passengers for ports further east transshipped and voyaged across the Indian Ocean aboard ships from Gujrat and Coromandel. Although some of these traded directly with the north and north-west Sumatran ports of Pasai, Pedir, Atjeh and Barus, the majority traded through Malacca.

The Javanese ports rose to prominence because they served as staging ports for the spice trade with the eastern islands—Ternate and Tidore, the clove islands, and Banda, home of the nutmeg and mace. The local people had no trading ships of their own and depended on the ships from Java for foodstuffs and material for clothing, for which they bartered their spice harvest.

Nowadays we can buy spices pre-ground and pre-packaged—nutmeg to sprinkle on junkets or egg flips, cloves to add to stewed apples, mace for potted meat, pepper to sprinkle on tomato sandwiches, cinnamon as a topping for tea cake. They are little more than an optional extra to be added or omitted according to taste, and it is perhaps hard to understand why the spice trade could have formed the basis of a whole network of trade from Indonesia north to China and west from Indonesia to Arabia and beyond to Europe, or why at a later date Europeans were so anxious to venture into unknown seas in order to obtain spices directly.

First, these spices were found only in tropical climates. The rarest of them, nutmeg and mace, which come from the same tree—the former the actual seed, the latter its fleshy seed-casing—and cloves, the dried flowers of another tree, are natives to the few small islands already mentioned. Ternate and Tidore were the clove islands, Banda was the home of nutmeg and mace. Pepper, which grows as a small cluster of berries on a vine, was more widespread, particularly in western Java and in parts of Sumatra as well as in India. Then there were other spices, some of them less familiar to most of us today—cinnamon, coriander, cardamom, cummin, ginger, turmeric, chilli—derived from the bark, the seeds, the fruit or the roots of different trees and shrubs.

The spices were used not simply to flavour but also to preserve food, added not as an afterthought but cooked long and slowly with meat, fish, poultry and other foods which decayed quickly in the tropical heat. Even in the milder climate of Europe the preservation of meat was a problem. Spices served this purpose in the days before refrigeration, tin cans and instant soups. In addition to that they have medicinal properties and these were more important too in the days before the development of the modern pharmaceutical industries. Oil of cloves, before the days of dentists, was a remedy for toothache. Both oil of cloves and oil of cinnamon are germicides more powerful than carbolic acid.[10] Many of these spices were also prized as ingredients in cosmetic preparations and perfumes.

So we should think of the spice trade as a combination of the modern pharmaceutical, cosmetics and perfume industries, as well as a substitute for refrigeration, canning and other more modern food preservatives. For the trader himself a small consignment of spices in terms of actual freight space could yield an enormous profit, and if carefully dried and then securely packed for the voyage they did not deteriorate on the long journey from the Spice Islands to their distant destination in China, India or Arabia and, in later years, the even longer journey to Europe.

Gresik, the easternmost Javanese port, opposite the island of Madura, was, according to Tomé Pires, who visited it from Malacca, 'the great trading port, the best in all Java, the jewel of Java in trading ports where the ships at anchor are safe from the winds, with their bowsprits touching the houses. Among the Javanese it is called the rich people's port, and under Patih Sushuf's patronage many foreign merchants have settled in the country.' The westernmost port, Demak, at the height of its power, controlled various other Javanese and south Sumatran ports, and each year sent about forty junks with foodstuffs to the markets at Malacca. North of Demak was Djepara, which was subordinate to Demak, though according to Pires, almost as powerful. Between Gresik on the one hand, and Demak and Djepara on the other, lay the older port of Tuban, dating back to the eleventh century, the outlet for the produce of Madjapahit, and quite closely linked to the inland Hindu-Buddhist state. Pires reports that its ruler was Moslem but 'no firm believer in Mohammed'.

With the probable exception of Tuban, whose rulers seem to have been indigenous landed nobility, the other cities were governed by newcomers, merchants risen to political power. Some

[10] See H. Day, *The Complete Book of Curries* (Kaye and Ward, 1966), pp. 17-20, 134-7.

of these new arrivals were from China, especially the settlers in Gresik and in Semarang (south of Demak), although those who rose to political power seem to have been from India, Arabia or even from Malacca. Although they may have introduced Islam into these ports, those foreigners who had lived in Java for a long time gradually adopted the manners and customs of the old Javanese nobility whose role they had usurped.

Finally we turn to Malacca itself, the meeting place of the nations, with trade routes radiating north to China and Pegu (in Burma), east to Brunei, the Philippines and the Spice Islands, south to the ports of Java and southern Sumatra, and west to the Indian ports of Coromandel, Gujrat and Bengal, linked in their turn with Arabia and Persia, further west again. 'And from below the wind to above the wind Malacca became famous as a very great city . . . so much so that princes from all countries came to present themselves before Sultan Muhammad Shah, who treated them with due respect, bestowing upon them robes of honour to the highest distinction together with rich presents of jewels, gold and silver.'[11]

Malacca's trade can be divided into several categories. Most vital to Malacca itself was the importation of foodstuffs upon which its very survival depended. The country round about was poor agricultural land, and the indigenous inhabitants, Malay fishermen, produced little else but fish. Foodstuffs were imported from Bengal in India; from Pegu in Burma; from Siam, when hostilities between the two did not prevent trade altogether; from Palembang; from Kalimantan; and, above all, from Java itself. Rice was the staple, then as now, and other foodstuffs included sugar; dried and salt meat and fish; onions; garlic; preserved vegetables, fruit and salt.

There was also considerable trade in textiles from India, and in other high value products, including not only spices and medicaments, but perfume, jewels, ivory, precious metals and the plumage of rare birds. There was also quite a brisk market in slaves, hardly surprising when we remember the trading pattern developing at much the same time in the West Indies.

In Malacca the various communities each appointed their own *shahbandar,* the official through whom negotiations were made between the ruler and the merchants. Malacca had four of these officials: the most senior dealt with the Gujrati traders; a second was for other Indian traders, and those from Pegu (Burma) and northern Sumatra; a third looked after traders from the island ports east of Malacca from Palembang to the Spice Islands, in-

[11] *Malay Annals*, p. 59.

cluding the Philippines; and a fourth acted for the Chinese community. The captain of a newly arrived ship contacted his *shahbandar* who in turn presented him to the Raja's highest official, the *bendahara*, a combined treasurer-cum-prime minister who often held more real power than did the Raja himself. The *shahbandar* allotted the captain warehouse space for his cargo, arranged for payment of customs duties according to the scale applied to his particular nationality, or arranged instead for the gift which some traders gave instead of duty. The *shahbandar* also supplied the ship's captain with transport, in the form of elephants, perhaps the first example of a state-subsidized transport system or perhaps a forerunner of the more modern hire-a-car service for present-day businessmen.

Although Islam itself is a more austere religion than was the Hindu-Buddhist religion preceding it, its introduction did not seem to bring about a more austere court ritual. The *Malay Annals* reflect great concern with court ceremonial and with the importance of precedent both in court dealings and in international relations. When a chief was installed he came to court by elephant, on horseback or on foot according to his status. A yellow umbrella indicated someone of equivalent rank to a prince; a purple or red one, a courtier or war-chief; a blue one a person of lower status again. The robes of installation and the number of trays on which they were carried to the ceremony also depended upon and signified the recipient's status. The newly-installed chief was then taken home in procession: in some cases the only instruments used were the drum and clarionet, in others the trumpet was added, and in yet other cases there were the kettledrums and white umbrellas as well, though in former days it cost money to get white umbrellas and kettledrums; even yellow umbrellas and trumpets were hard to procure.[12] The wedding of Sultan Mansur Shah (1459-77) to a Javanese princess involved forty days and nights of feasting, 'and the music of every sort of instrument was heard and solemn and awe-inspiring was the sound of the music—gongs, drums, clarionets, trumpets, kettledrums' so that the chronicler remarks, understandably, that 'the noise thereof was unimaginable.'[13]

Beyond the royal palace stretched the city, with the warehouses and residential areas of the various nationalities separated from each other. At the mouth of the river was the food market, probably a series of stalls not unlike the modern *pasar* or open air market, where a conglomeration of tradesmen sit or squat

[12] *Malay Annals*, p. 57.
[13] *Ibid.*, p. 80.

beside their respective stalls, calling their wares. This food market was run by the Javanese, the main supplier of foodstuffs.

At its heyday the population of Malacca probably included
between ten to fifteen thousand traders. At any one time up to
a thousand Gujrati might have been resident in the city, while
another three to four thousand of them were coming or going
along the trade routes. The busiest period in Malacca was
between December and March when ships from both western and
north-eastern Asia were usually in port loading or unloading.
Then the whole city resembled one vast fair.

Into this world of rich and complex interinsular and inter-
continental trade Vasco da Gama found his way when, in 1498,
at the height of Malacca's greatness, he reached Goa by way of
the Cape of Good Hope.

CHAPTER FIVE

Early European Penetration

Early European penetration of Indonesia from the sixteenth to the eighteenth centuries, initially at least, was the penetration of European individuals and organizations into the complex trading network already described. The Portuguese Empire, even at the height of its power, was only a number of fortified positions through which the Portuguese sought to control the whole network of trade. Their control of the sea guaranteed their rather precarious control of these strategic trading ports, and they controlled the sea mainly because they had faster, more manoeuvrable ships and more efficient armaments, although partly because their various opponents did not develop any effective alliance against a common foe.

D'Albuquerque, Portuguese viceroy at Goa in India, was responsible for the Portuguese capture of Malacca. He reported that 'if once Portugal should suffer a reverse at sea, your Indian possessions have not power to hold out a day longer than the kings of the land choose to suffer it'.

Everyone knows that Vasco da Gama and his crew were the first Europeans to make the sea voyage from the Atlantic coast of Europe to Asia round the Cape of Good Hope. The second stage, from the east coast of Africa to Calicut, on the south-west coast of India, was assisted by Ahmed ibn Majid, a prominent Gujrati seaman who became their pilot. In 1498 the Portuguese fleet arrived in Calicut to be welcomed without much cordiality.

Within a few years of their arrival in Goa the Portuguese pushed further east again and a Portuguese trading ship arrived in Malacca from Goa. According to the *Malay Annals*, 'the people of Malacca . . . came crowding to see what the Franks [Portuguese] looked like; and they were all astonished and said, "These are white Bengalis!" Around each Frank there would be a crowd of Malays, some of them twisting his beard, some of them fingering his head, some taking off his hat, some grasping his hand.'[1]

[1] *Malay Annals*, p. 157.

The Portuguese success in establishing themselves along the trade route in south-east Asia—by 1510 they had conquered Goa on the east-central coast of India, by 1511 Malacca was in their control, by 1512 they had reached the Spice Islands—encouraged explorers of other European nations and their sponsors and financial backers, usually the monarchs of the newly developing nation states. The Spanish monarchy backed Ferdinand Magellan, one ship of whose original fleet of five, with a handful of its crew, became the first to circumnavigate the globe. The clove shipment sold at 2500 per cent profit. The English concentrated on the search for a north-west passage, although in 1577-80 Sir Francis Drake and his crew became the first Englishmen to circumnavigate the globe, visiting both the ruler of Ternate and the island of Java major, where they 'found great courtesie, and honorable entertainment'. Dutch merchants followed up the routes pioneered by others both to the east and to the west.

Only later did the Dutch in Indonesia, the Spanish in the Philippines and the English in India and Malaya find themselves gradually involved in government and administration as well as in trade. They penetrated beyond the coastal areas, seeking to control not only the seaways but also the land-based economy and the apparatus of government. The Dutch first became heirs to Srividjaya and later they became heirs to Madjapahit as well. The Portuguese empire never developed beyond the stage of a sea-based, far-flung string of possessions along the trade route to the Spice Islands.

Against this general outline, let us examine the growth of Portuguese influence in Indonesia during the sixteenth century. 'Indonesian history is an international history' according to the Dutch historian van Leur, and during this period the trade routes put a girdle round the earth.

POINTS OF VIEW

You may feel relieved to meet familiar names at last; but we will be viewing these explorers from a point of view different from the one most familiar to you. In the past, you have looked over their shoulders, putting yourself in the place of explorers of the unknown who brought back rare and valuable cargoes, and tales of strange and wonderful places, of hardship and endurance, and of new worlds waiting to be conquered. Now we must consider the point of view of the people being 'discovered'. They were not at all desirous of being conquered. We must ask different questions from those we consider when viewing the voyages of discovery from the European end.

Why did Europeans discover Asia? Why did Asians not attempt to discover Europe? Europeans usually answer the first question by stressing the greater intellectual curiosity of the European, his initiative, his spirit of adventure, as well as his hope for gain, his desire for spices, and for cheaper spices at that. The answer to the second question, as to why Asians did not discover Europe, is probably that they had no incentive to try. Their own world provided all their immediate needs. The small trickle of European goods which found their way to Asia aroused no great demand. China, who had already shown ability to undertake long-distance voyages, had also shown little further interest in the world beyond her border. No population pressure drove Indonesians to search for new land; no European items of trade drove them to search for direct routes to the source of such goods. Chinese porcelain was superior to anything which Europe then offered; Indian cottons were more appropriate textiles for Indonesia than European woollen cloth.

Let us look briefly at the traditional accounts of the voyages of discovery, made from over the shoulder of the explorers and their sponsors.

The struggle between Moslems and Christians was familiar to the Portuguese, who, with the Spanish, were in its European front line. The Atlantic seaboard countries had experienced a gradual rise in spice prices when the overland route from the Persian Gulf was dislocated by the advance of the Ottoman Turks, who, in 1453, had conquered Constantinople. A direct route to the spice islands would circumvent the Venetian middleman in the Mediterranean, and, more important, the Arab middleman behind him again; spices would be cheaper, profits would come to Portugal rather than to the middleman, and a blow would be struck for God's greater glory by defeating the Moslem.

The traditional European accounts of the voyages of discovery often suggest that the attempt to outflank the Moslems was a continuation of the Crusades of the twelfth, thirteenth and fourteenth centuries, which European nations saw as a Holy War to defeat the enemies of Christendom and to recover the Holy City, Jerusalem, from the Saracens (Arabs). Here the writers are looking over the Crusader's shoulder and they do not always realize that for the Moslem, this was equally a Holy War against the infidel attacking the community of Islam. Islam and Christianity have in common both their love of peace and their missionary zeal. Christians stress the peaceful elements in their own creed while emphasizing, and often misunderstanding, the Moslem teaching about the *jihad* or Holy War, which is sanctioned only when it is a defensive one. Of course, neither side always adheres to its own creed; nor is it easy to decide when a defensive war becomes an offensive one. Certainly this element of religious rivalry was important in the Portuguese expansion. That they could serve God and at the same time grow rich at the expense of their trade rivals, who were one and the same with their religious enemies, seemed a special dispensation of Providence.

The Portuguese explorations and the profits won by explorers, pirates and traders stimulated Portugal's European rivals, who wished to prevent her having uninterrupted control of the spice trade at the European end. Spain, with papal blessing, sailed west to search for spices; Portugal, also with papal blessing, sailed east. Holland and England, by the mid-sixteenth century, no longer accepted the papal ruling. Dutch merchants sailed both east and west, stimulated by the closing to them of the port of Lisbon—the capital of Portugal and hence the centre of the spice trade in Europe—once the crowns of Spain and Portugal had been united in 1580: for Spain was their enemy in their struggle for independence. The British, continuing their rivalry with the Spanish, sailed west rather than east. The Dutch and the English were themselves trade rivals, and much European activity in south-east Asia (and indeed elsewhere in the world) is best explained in terms of the European situation from which the participants had come. Yet the world of south-east Asia was more than a colourful backdrop against which these brawling, buccaneering traders fought out their rivalries.

How far did the arrival of the Europeans actually affect the society into which they had intruded? Were they simply one more group of traders, 'white Bengalis', or did they introduce new methods, new techniques, new concepts into the world of trade?

The older colonial histories of Indonesia claim that the arrival of the Europeans marked a distinct break with the older way of life. With the arrival, first of the Portuguese, later of the Dutch, the historian's attention became focussed on the activities of these newcomers, largely because these are well-documented, in letters written home, in accounts of their travels, and in the minute books and other records of the trading companies. Also these colonial histories were written in the colonial period before the emergence of newly independent Asian states. For both these reasons they saw Indonesia only in interaction with the newcomers. The history of south-east Asia became the history of expanding European trade.

The Dutch historian J. C. van Leur was one strong critic of this Europecentric point of view, in which Indonesian history became the history of Portuguese and Dutch expansion, a history of Europeans in Indonesia rather than a history of Indonesia and Indonesians. The book in which he expressed this point of view appeared in 1934 and van Leur himself died while still quite young in 1942, on active service during the war, before the events of the next few years marked the end of the colonial period.

Van Leur pointed out that Dutch histories of Indonesia, for the centuries preceding the Dutch arrival, adopt an Indocentric viewpoint, 'but with the arrival of ships from western Europe, the point of view is turned a hundred and eighty degrees and from then on the Indies are observed from the deck of the ship, the ramparts of the fortress, the high gallery of the trading-house.'[2] He argued that 'it is incorrect to make a break in describing the course of history upon the arrival of the first scattered seafarers, merchants, and privateers from north-west Europe and change over to the point of view of the small, oppressed European fortress, the stuffy trading-house, and the armed ship riding at anchor'[3], and he also asked why the Indonesian world was 'only seen as the antagonist; why does it all remain so grey and undifferentiated?'[4]

In referring to the arrival of the Portuguese, he argued that 'the Portuguese colonial regime, built by and upon war, coercion, and violence, did not at any point signify a stage of "higher development" economically for Asian trade. The traditional commercial structure continued to exist . . . Trade did not undergo any increase in quantity worthy of mention in the period.'[5] The Portuguese, according to van Leur, were simply another group of traders, numerically small, who used the same methods as earlier traders and whose activities did little to alter the traditional ebb and flow of trade. He points out that, even in the 1530s, while an annual 20 tons of spices went via the Cape to Europe, 320 tons went via Hormuz to Arab countries and to the traditional sources of distribution in the Mediterranean, via Venice and overland across northern Italy.

Van Leur is anxious to restore some balance to the account of the first European arrival. It is a temptation to look back with the knowledge born of hindsight, to exaggerate the importance at the time of some new element in the situation. Numerically

[2] J. C. van Leur, *Indonesian Trade and Society*, p. 261.
[3] *Ibid.*, p. 270.
[4] *Ibid.*, p. 153.
[5] *Ibid.*, p. 117-8.

the new arrivals were small compared with traders from other
parts of the world; culturally they were not at all superior to
their Asian merchant counterparts; politically the establishment
of Portuguese rulers at Goa, Malacca and the Spice Islands was
similar to the process by which merchant families came to power
in some north Javanese ports. Even their technological advantages—more advanced naval and military tactics[6], more accurate
and reliable artillery—were not really apparent until they had
managed to capture and to defend their land bases. These were
always vulnerable, because they depended on support, or lack of
opposition, from the ruler of the hinterland. They depended
also, especially in Malacca and bases in the Spice Islands, on
inter-island trade to supply them with food, and on the trade
with Portugal itself to supply such essentials, unavailable locally,
as wine, olive oil and Dutch cheese.

But of course the foreigners did have superior power and their
trading ventures were conducted on a larger and more systematic
scale. Their influence was, therefore, significant.

PORTUGUESE PENETRATION. 1511-1641

According to the *Malay Annals* the first Portuguese attack on
Malacca was unsuccessful[7] but, after obtaining an armada from
'the Raja of Portugal', the Portuguese returned. In the
chronicler's words: 'the noise of their matchlocks was like that
of frying nuts popping in the pan'. The men of Malacca were
driven back from the shore and the Portuguese bore down on
the bridge in their ships. As a result of this Portuguese assault
in 1511, the city of Malacca fell, the Sultan and his forces withdrew, and the Portuguese occupied the city. They built a fort,
using stones from the mosque, and by the superiority in arms
which had enabled them to conquer Malacca, they maintained
control, if at times precariously, of this great entrepôt.

The Sultan of Malacca established himself first on an island
off the Malayan coast and then on the mainland at Johore.
Although Johore Sultanate was never strong enough to rival
Malacca, it could harass the conquerors when occasion arose.

There is no evidence to suggest that the trading communities
of Malacca were involved in the struggle for power and they
seemed prepared to reach agreement with the new rulers and to
continue trading in the shadow of the Portuguese fort, just as
they had traded previously in the shadow of the Raja's palace.
The trader, unless forced to do so, takes little notice of political

[6] J. H. Parry, *The Age of Reconnaissance.*
[7] See Lach and Flaumenhaft, pp. 90-1.

boundaries and allegiances when these do not interrupt the flow of trade. The logic of international trade had made Malacca a great port, and it remained one until the seventeenth century, when the Dutch blockade effectively restricted its usefulness. Under Portuguese control therefore it remained a centre of Asian trade. 'The country hath nothing of itself,' wrote van Linschoten, 'but all things are brought thither in great abundance.' Yet, the Portuguese conquest of Malacca, with the attempt to reserve special products as a monopoly of the Portuguese crown, and the known hostility of the Portuguese to Moslem traders, meant that, while the local Asian coastal trade in foodstuffs continued, long distance trade, especially that in Moslem hands, tended where possible to seek alternative ports of call to avoid Portuguese customs officers and Portuguese monopoly enforcement.

THE PORTUGUESE IN EAST INDONESIA. 1522-1668

After the conquest of Malacca, the next stage in Portuguese penetration was their endeavour to obtain a monopoly of the spice trade by establishing strongholds in the Spice Islands themselves, cutting out *all* intervening middlemen, a logical if ambitious extension of the original programme. By 1522 they were established in Ambon, spurred on by the arrival of Magellan's ships there in 1521. The clove islands of Ternate and Tidore were rivals who both invited the Portuguese to make their headquarters, a fortress with permanent garrison, in their respective territories. Oddly enough the Portuguese allied themselves with Ternate, the more fanatically Moslem of the two, and this alliance brought them into conflict with Tidore. Their treaty with Ternate gave them, as far as they could enforce it, the monopoly of the clove trade, because the trees were native to these two islands only. Their presence in the area encouraged the planting of cloves on other islands, such as Ambon and Buru, although, as the period from planting to first flowering is about twelve years, this did not immediately increase the clove supply.

Ambon, where the Portuguese had established a small fort, was not rich in spices, but it served as an important port of call where ships could replenish their water after the long journey east from Malacca, and it was conveniently placed particularly in relation to Banda, home of nutmeg and mace, and also to the cloves of Ternate and Tidore.

The fortresses at Ambon and Ternate were the outposts of the farflung Portuguese empire, precariously held against local hostility and increasing European rivalry. The governors of such remote outposts were seldom either the most able or the most diplomatic men in the Portuguese service. With one exception, Antonis Galvas (1536-40), none won any respect from the Ambonese or the other local people. Francis Xavier abandoned his missionary activities in Ambon (1546-8) because they were nullified by the rapacity and greed of his fellow countrymen, particularly the Portuguese sailors, who had rarely been selected either for their adaptibility or for their spirit of adventure. When signing up crews for such long and perilous voyages their ultimate destination was often concealed until the ships were upon the high seas and desertion out of the question.

By 1565 they had aroused the hostility of Sultan Hairun of Ternate, their former ally, who attacked the Christian communities, but was opposed by a fleet from Goa. Peace was restored and a fortress was built at Ambon. Then the Portuguese attempted to keep more than the share of the spice trade profits stipulated in the agreement made between them and Ternate. When Hairun resisted this, further war seemed inevitable, but a solemn treaty was made, Sultan Hairun swearing on the Koran, the Portuguese on the Bible, and, the following day, when the Sultan visited the Portuguese fortress he was murdered, which did nothing to establish the good faith of the Portuguese or the sanctity of an oath sworn on the Bible. Hairun's son, Sultan Baabullah, swore to avenge his father and, after four years of seige, the fortress on Ternate fell in 1574. During that time no help had arrived from either Malacca or Goa.

Shortly afterwards Sir Francis Drake arrived in the Moluccas (Maluku), via Cape Horn. He received a cordial welcome from the Sultan of Ternate as a prospective ally against the Portuguese. It was evident to such visitors that the Portuguese hold was precarious. It became more precarious with the uniting of the throne of Portugal to that of Spain in 1580, because Spanish interests usually had precedence over those of Portugal in the united kingdom.

THE SIGNIFICANCE OF THE PORTUGUESE PERIOD

From the European point of view the Portuguese were the pioneers who opened up the sea routes to Asia and showed that these were practicable, if perilous, and also paying propositions. It was said that if five out of six ships were lost on the voyage it was still possible to make an overall profit on the sale of the cargo of the sixth. Older European writers have seen them as forerunners of European global expansion; more recent writers have seen them as simply one group of traders, rather better equipped and armed than their rivals, but otherwise not easily distinguished from any other group. From the Indonesian point of view they were a new group of traders among the rich variety of merchants from different countries who found their way to the markets of the east at the centre of the known world. In the seventeenth century their position was to be challenged successfully by the Dutch.

Today if we look at Portuguese overseas possessions on a map of the world we can still see the last remaining fortresses along the trade routes to China and the Spice Islands. Angola, in west Africa, is still precariously Portuguese. Mozambique, in east Africa, is still held by force against local opposition. Goa, in India, was retained until India reclaimed it in 1961. Part of Timor is still a Portuguese possession, and it was there that the Portuguese fled when finally evicted from Makasar, Banten and Malacca. On the China route Macao is still in Portuguese hands.

THE DUTCH

From the first arrival of Dutch ships in 1596 to the final declaration of independence by the Indonesians in 1945 was a period of almost 350 years. Indonesian nationalist historians speak of 350 years of suffering under Dutch colonialism; Dutch nationalist historians look back with pride on 350 years of Dutch colonial empire. Both overlook the fact that at first the Dutch position in Indonesia was quite as precarious as that of the Portuguese during their century of power. The English controlled Dutch holdings in Java and Sumatra from 1811 to 1816. Uprisings against the Dutch continued throughout the whole period of their residence in the area, and Dutch assumption of direct control outside Java was still incomplete well into the twentieth century. Not until 1919-20 did the Dutch assume direct control of Vogelkop (Bird Head) in West Irian. (The name should help you to locate it easily on a map of New Guinea.)

After the successful exploratory journey of the first Dutch fleet in 1596, a further five expeditions set out in 1598. Thirteen ships came via the Cape of Good Hope and twelve arrived safely. Nine ships set out via South America, only one of which arrived. It is hardly surprising that the Dutch then decided to concentrate on the former route. Dutch ships had reached Maluku by 1599 and in 1600 the Dutch concluded a treaty with Ambon, giving the Ambonese protection from other foreigners in return for a trade monopoly and the right to build a fortress there.

Initially the Dutch arrival stimulated Asian trade, by providing new customers competing with former ones and with each

other to outbid rivals, particularly European rivals. But in 1602
the various rival Dutch companies and private ventures were
combined into the United East India Company (usually referred
to as V.O.C. from its Dutch initials), which had a monopoly of
Pacific and Indian Ocean trade and the power to make treaties
and to build forts or factories[8] at strategic points. The monopoly,
as granted by the Dutch government, was, of course, only as effective as Dutch sea power and military might could make it, but
the Dutch, unlike the Portuguese, dealt effectively with their
own private traders, and with Portuguese and English opposition in the area. Ultimately, they also dealt effectively with their
Asian trade rivals.

Yet, for many years it was a precarious foothold which the
Dutch had in their growing string of fortresses. William Dampier describes one such fortress, Pulau Dinding, established to
preserve the Dutch monopoly of the tin trade from nearby
Bangka island. Dampier visited this fortress in the late 1680s.
The Dutch were the only inhabitants of the island and imported
all their supplies from Malacca (which had fallen to them in
1641), not because the island was barren but because 'they dare
not trust them [the Malayans] so far, as to be ranging about the
island in any work of husbandry'. This small fortress, with a
force of twenty to thirty soldiers, and a governor, had thick
stone walls about thirty feet high, and from each of the four
squares of the fort twelve to fourteen guns looked out.

Dampier describes a visit paid by the ship's captain to the
governor's house below the fort for a dinner engagement. As
they sat at the table set with silver dishes and plates and a
brimming silver punch-bowl, waiting to be served with freshly
caught and cooked fish, 'one of the soldiers cried out, Malayans,
and spoil'd the entertainment; for immediately the governor,
without speaking one word, leapt out of one of the windows, to
get as soon as he could to the fort.' He was followed by his
officers and servants. 'Every one of them took the nearest way,
some out of the windows, others out of the doors, leaving the
three guests by themselves, who soon followed with all the haste
they could make, without knowing the meaning of this sudden
consternation.' A Malayan canoe full of armed men had set on
Dutch soldiers catching further fresh fish for the banquet. Such
a life of constant suspicion and fear of attack can hardly have

---

[8] But do not think in terms of modern industrial factories. If you check in
the dictionary you will find that the word has an older meaning, referring to
a merchant company's foreign trading station. A factor was a merchant
buying and selling on commission, a company agent attached to the factory.

been a pleasant one, despite the silver plate and the fine food and drink.

The Dutch maintained their precarious hold by their naval supremacy. Their ships were lighter and thus more easily manoeuvrable, yet more heavily armed, than those of the Portuguese, who as we have already seen, were themselves better armed than their Asian rivals. The Dutch also had better trained sailors than did the Portuguese. Dutch ships were usually manned by Dutch crews, while the Portuguese, who suffered increasingly from lack of population in Portugal itself, were often forced to use foreign sailors, including those recruited in Asia. This shortage of sailors is hardly surprising when we think of the mortality rate aboard these trading ships. Heat and scurvy and other diseases claimed many victims, and even when ships made the voyage safely they often arrived with only half the original complement of crew.

The Dutch were most noticeably superior to the Portuguese in their financial backing and in the development of an effective form of centralized monopolistic trading. Interlopers and private traders found their activities in the region increasingly risky. Nor could Dutch employees in the early days of the V.O.C. engage in private trade as a lucrative sideline, as had been the case with the Portuguese. Penalties were severe, and strictly enforced. Christopher Fryke, ship's surgeon with the V.O.C. in 1680-86, reported that pepper was so plentiful in Indonesia that it was sometimes used as ballast, or shiploads were either thrown into the sea or burnt, 'yet dares no man in the service of the company take one single corn of it'. He also recorded the fate of pirates in the Sunda Straits when captured by two men-of-war belonging to the V.O.C. and brought to Batavia for trial. 'Of the whole one part was broke upon the wheel, some were quartered, some were whipt, some had their ears and noses cut off, and some were burnt in the forehead. The three Hollanders were hang'd; the two Danes beheaded: and a great number of others were sent to several islands; to burn lime, hew stone, and, etc., and there to remain slaves all their lives. Their wives and children were served after the same manner, that it might more effectively prove a terror to others.' (Perhaps it should be pointed out that in inflicting such penalties the Dutch were neither more nor less severe than their Asian counterparts nor other European nations of the time, and that at least one of these barbarities— hanging—has survived to the present day in many nations which regard themselves as civilized.)

The Dutch, especially after the establishment of the V.O.C., had greater home support and greater powers against pirate traders and other rivals than the Portuguese had. They also had greater capital resources and more business-like management of their affairs, and about five times the number of ships available to the Portuguese. They were the attackers rather than the defenders, so the initiative lay with them. And where the Portuguese had been fortified by a sense of mission, which did not always work in well with the interests of traders, the Dutch were not involved, initially at any rate, in any missionary activity and so could give their single-minded attention to the pursuit of trade.

EARLY DUTCH PENETRATION

Early in the seventeenth century the V.O.C. established a foothold in Jakatra or Sunda Kelapa, the site of present-day Djakarta. They named their fortress-city Batavia and they selected it as their headquarters partly because local opposition was weaker there than at Banten or at Johore where they also had factories, partly as a potential rival to Portuguese Malacca, for, according to van Linschoten, a sixteenth century Dutch geographer, 'The principal haven in the island [Java] is Sunda Kelapa'. They had established connections with the Spice Islands to the east, extending their original treaty with Ambon (1600) to one which recognized Dutch suzerainty (1605). They benefited in this area from the rapacity and unpopularity of their predecessors, the Portuguese, and made an alliance with Ternate in 1607 as well as virtually occupying Banda during the period 1609-21. This gave them control of the source of both cloves (Ternate) and nutmegs (Banda) and, as their power in the area extended, they used similar tactics in the pepper trade. By forcible reduction of production they kept European prices high and ensured greater profits for themselves. That in cutting down the clove and nutmeg trees they ruined the livelihood of the local inhabitants, whose trees they were, seems to have concerned them not at all.

In 1611 the first Governor-General of the V.O.C. was established in Banten, on the Sunda Straits, and the Dutch managed to squeeze out their English rivals with trade connections there. By the mid-seventeenth century the central Javanese kingdom of Mataram had attempted unsuccessfully to drive away these newcomers, now firmly entrenched at both Batavia and Malacca, which they had captured from the Portuguese (1641). The Dutch had also established factories at Banda and Ternate in east Indonesia, Gresik on the north coast of Java, Patani and Johore

on the Malay Peninsula, and Banten in western Java. By the end
of the century they had intervened successfully in Makasar,
ensuring the expulsion both of their Portuguese rivals in 1660,
and their English ones in 1667, as well as 'continuous residency'
for the Dutch in a fortress established for the purpose. (They
had had a factory there since 1609.) The Governor-General had
also made an alliance with the central Javanese state of Mataram
(1677) granting the V.O.C. an import monopoly, and had been
able to make use of civil war in Banten to gain virtual military
and financial control of the rulers there. The V.O.C. was no
longer simply a company of traders but a potential rival to the
existing rulers in the area. This new city state, founded on the
pattern of the other north Javanese ports by newcomers,
threatened the existing powers within the area.

Yet despite the extended area of influence in Java at the end
of the century, the V.O.C. was still one trading group among
several others, although its methods of organization, its financial
support and its military strength made it a formidable trading
rival. Initially the V.O.C.'s interference in local politics was
simply an attempt to eliminate its European competitors, but
increasingly the company became a challenge, both to other
European traders, and to the traditional pattern of trade in the
area.

INDONESIAN KINGDOMS OF THE SIXTEENTH CENTURY

Already, as we turn to the new arrivals and their bids for
power and trading advantages, the Indonesian protagonists are
in danger of becoming 'grey and undifferentiated'. Apart from
the first comment of the Malay chronicler, we scarcely know how
they viewed these new arrivals. Yet it is partly because of the
variety of interests in the area that the foreigners could gain,
maintain and extend their influence. The Portuguese capture
of Malacca was one factor in the growth of the Sultanate of Atjeh
during the sixteenth and seventeenth centuries as an alternative
port of call and entrepôt. Along with Banten in western Java,
and Makasar in southern Sulawesi, it became a trading centre for
Moslem merchants avoiding the Portuguese.

(a) *The Sultanate of Atjeh.* 1515-1700

Even before the fall of Malacca to the Portuguese, the port of
Atjeh had been Malacca's trade rival: a role intensified when
trade rivalry was reinforced by religious hostility, for Atjeh was
one of the earliest centres of Islam in the archipelago, and many
traders driven from Malacca turned to Atjeh instead. During

the sixteenth and seventeenth centuries Atjeh's power extended along both west and east coasts of Sumatra. The city itself became an important centre of Islamic learning, the 'gateway to the Holy Land', the nearest point of departure from Indonesia for Moslem pilgrims on pilgrimage to Mecca.

When van Linschoten was in Indonesia, in the 1580s, he reported that the king of Dachem (as he called Atjeh) was the principal king of the island of Sumatra and was 'very mightie and a great enemie to the Portingals', having often besieged Malacca and attempted to divert shipping from the straits. William Dampier was there in the 1680s and described Atjeh as 'the largest and best peopled' of the many small Sumatran kingdoms, giving a vivid description of the city of Achin (as *he* called Atjeh). He was struck by the city's lack of walls, 'nor so much as a ditch about it'; a contrast to fortified Malacca or Batavia. He estimated that there were about seven to eight thousand houses in the city, and a sizeable merchant-stranger population of English, Dutch, Danes, Portuguese, Chinese, and Gujrati. Of these, the two largest groups were the Gujrati and Chinese. He also mentioned that 'the Dutch free-men may trade thither, but the Company's servants are deny'd that privilege'. The English seem to have had special privileges in regard to customs duties, dating back to the interchange of letters between the Sultan of Atjeh and the English Tudors and Stuarts.

Some Chinese merchants lived there all the year round but others came in the annual fleet of ten to twelve ships, arriving in June and taking up their residence in the Chinese Camp. Several craftsmen, including furniture and toy makers, arrived with the fleet and immediately set to work making furniture and toys for sale. For two months to ten weeks the Chinese quarters were like a vast fair, selling both the goods imported from China and the goods being manufactured on the spot. As their goods were sold off they made use of fewer houses, and as business fell off because nothing was left to sell, they took to gambling. They would even sell some of their ships if they could return as passengers on one of the unsold ships, which left at the end of September.

The local country people, living in pile houses of woven bamboo, thatched with palm leaves, bred cattle and fowls, with various fruits and other food for the weekly market. An increasing amount of rice was also being grown. The wealthiest working people were the fishermen; and a Jesuit monk *en route* to China in 1698, describing the city of Atjeh, obscured among the trees by the river, said that 'nothing is more delightful than to see in the morning, an endless stream of little fishing boats which leave the river at daybreak and only return in the evening at sunset. You would call it a swarm of bees returning to the hive laden with the fruits of their labour.'

The main trading was in the hands of Gujrati merchants, 'the chief men that keep shops here', and most traders bringing materials, or other imports, sold them to Gujrati shopkeepers for the retail trade. When foreign merchants sold their rice, usually direct, they hired a broker, mostly a Gujrat, who was responsible for checking that the money paid in was good and of the right weight. If not, the broker stood the loss.

Atjeh's main exports were pepper and gold, both obtained from the hinterland. Dampier reported that, 'I made some enquiry concerning their getting gold, and was told that none but Mohammedans [Moslems] were permitted to go to the mines: that it was both troublesome and dangerous to pass the mountains before they came thither; there being but one way, and that over such steep mountains, that in some places they were forced to make use of ropes to climb up and down the hills. That at the foot of these precipices there was a guard of soldiers, to see that no uncircumcised person should pursue that design [all Moslem men were circumcised at a special ceremony at puberty] and also to receive custom of those that passed either forward or backward'; an account which was probably designed to be discouraging to a buccaneering Englishman, however enterprising, since trade with the interior was a prerogative of the Sultan.

Dampier was struck by Atjeh's devotion to Islam, commenting that the Atjehnese are 'very superstitious in washing and cleansing themselves from defilements' as part of their preparation for prayer. Indeed, to the amazement of this seventeenth century Englishman, whose fellow countrymen regarded bathing as a risky business, 'some come on purpose to wash themselves, for the pleasure of being in the water'.

Dampier was in Atjeh when the last of four women rulers occupied the throne. 'The Queen of Achin, as 'tis said, is always an old maid, chosen out of the royal family', he reported, adding that he did not know who did the choosing, though he believed it was the council of twelve Oronkey (*orang-kaja*—rich men), in whose hands the actual power lay. Some English residents believed that the government of Atjeh had always been in the hands of a Queen, perhaps a descendant of Solomon's Queen of Sheba. Unfortunately for such a theory there are records of kings before this time.

In 1699, on the basis of a legal recommendation from Mecca which condemned rule by a woman as contrary to Islamic practice, the fourth woman ruler was deposed and replaced by a government headed by religious leaders, an early example of the conflict between religious leaders and local *adat* (customary law) which is a continuing theme of history in Atjeh and elsewhere in the archipelago.

The Queen's palace was a large one 'built handsomely with stone', according to Dampier, although he added that he could not get inside it to give any further account. 'Tis said there are some great guns about it, four of which are of brass, and are said to have been sent hither as a present by our king James the First.' The Queen herself seldom appeared in public, 'except that once a year she is drest all in white, and placed on an elephant, and so rides to the river in state to wash herself'. Here we can see how the *Nagarakertagama* and the *Malay Annals,* written from inside the court by a court official, contrast with the traveller's account written from outside the castle walls with no knowledge of the court ritual and activity except from local rumour. Dampier can tell us a lot about the life of the market place, and describes it very vividly, but can only give us hearsay and gossip, some of it demonstrably wrong, about the government and the life of the court.

The Kingdom of Atjeh, during the seventeenth century, was powerful enough to deal with both Portuguese Malacca and Dutch Batavia as an equal, and within the realm of Atjeh, could exclude the V.O.C.'s servants from its trade. Yet, as happened in 1700, it could be forced to negotiate by a determined nine-day blockade carried out by three English ships. Moreover, chiefs in revolt against its suzerainty could take advantage of alliance with the Dutch to resist Atjehnese control. In 1662 the Minangkabau leaders of the central west coast of Sumatra put themselves under Dutch protection.

The Sultan of Atjeh sent ambassadors to Turkey in the late sixteenth century; in return, the Turks sent craftsmen skilled in casting cannon. He had corresponded with the rulers of England, and continued contact with the Moghul Emperors of India, at the height of their power in the second half of the seventeenth century. Atjeh in the early seventeenth century was a formidable rival both to Portuguese Malacca and to Dutch Batavia, a centre of Islamic culture, and 'gateway to Mecca' for Indonesian Moslems from other areas. Even toward the end of the century it remained independent.

(b) *The Rise and Fall of Makasar.* 1605-1667

For Atjeh the two peninsular settlements, Malacca and Johore, were potential rivals, which prevented any alliance between Atjeh and Johore against Malacca. The long-standing rivalries of these principalities provided the background to which they fitted new rivals on the scene. It was the the same in other parts of the archipelago. Traditional hostility between neighbouring principalities could be exploited by the newcomers to their own advantage. Portugal, Spain and the Netherlands had each done this in the case of the traditional rivalry between the clove islands of Ternate and Tidore. The events leading up to the Makasar war are an even clearer example of this.

Makasar benefited indirectly through the fall of Malacca, and like Atjeh, though later, it became a Moslem state. The Makasar annals record the exact date and month in 1605 in which the King embraced Islam. His conversion being recorded so precisely suggests that it was seen as a matter of state, perhaps a political conversion; although there is some doubt as to which of three varying records is correct. Shortly after his own conversion the Sultan of Gowa[9] undertook the forceful conversion of his Bugis neighbours and rivals.

A map of Sulawesi shows it as an island made up of peninsulas. On the south-western peninsula lies the port of Makasar, from which visiting traders, Malay, Dutch or English, named the whole area. In fact it was the chief port of the twin states of Gowa and Tallo, rivals and enemies of the Bugis to the north of the same peninsula. The westernmost of the islands south of Sulawesi, Buton (or Butung), acknowledged Ternate's overlordship and sought alliance with the Dutch as protection against Makasar, which was prepared to dispute with Ternate and Tidore their overlordship of the area. Strategically Makasar could benefit from trade coming via Brunei in northern Kalimantan and through the Makasar Straits, and was a victualling station for ships engaged in the Timor sandalwood trade or the eastern spice trade.

Little is known about Makasar's history prior to the seventeenth century, by which time it had become a port of call for ships on their way to and from the Spice Islands and, by 1606 at the latest, a centre for the propagation of Islam. It was also a competitor of Ternate for dominance of the eastern archipelago. The V.O.C. was given permission to establish a factory there as early as 1609, but not the exclusive permission the Company desired, for in 1613 the English East India Company was made even more welcome when its traders also wished to

[9] In order to avoid confusion between Goa in India and Gowa (sometimes also spelt Goa) in Sulawesi, the Malay spelling 'Gowa' is used for the latter.

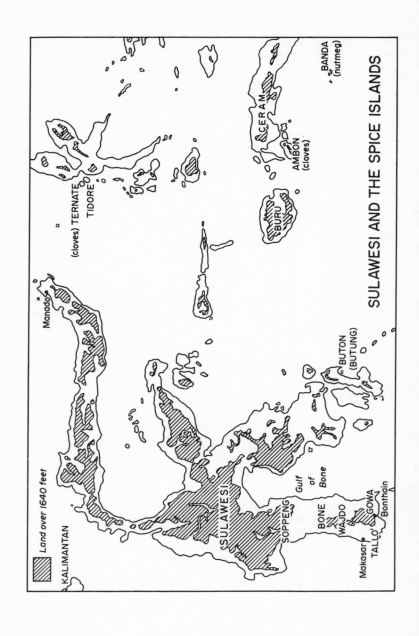

KALIMANTAN

Land over 1640 feet

Manado

(cloves) TERNATE
TIDORE

CERAM

BANDA
(nutmeg)

AMBON
(cloves)

BURU

BUTON
(BUTUNG)

SULAWESI

Gulf
of
Bone

SOPPENG

BONE

WAJO

Makasar

TALLO'

GOWA

Bonthain

SULAWESI AND THE SPICE ISLANDS

establish a factory. The Sultan of Gowa (the senior Sultan of the twin Kingdoms) wanted to attract as much trade as possible, conflicting with the Dutch attempt to gain a trade monopoly. When the V.O.C. requested the Sultan of Gowa not to trade with the Spice Islands, except through the Dutch themselves, he replied: 'God created the land and the sea: the land he divided out amongst men, but the sea he gave to all. No one has ever tried to forbid men the sea. If you do so, you will be taking the bread out of our mouths—and I am not a rich King.' This was the heart of the matter. The Dutch differed from their predecessors (although they only differed from the Portuguese in achievement, not in aim) in attempting 'to forbid men the sea', one of the main reasons for coming into conflict with Makasar.

In 1637 the Dutch Governor-General, van Diemen (the same van Diemen after whom Tasman named the island now known as Tasmania), made a treaty with the Sultan recognizing Dutch interests in the Spice Islands. In 1653, when the Dutch tried to get assurance that the Sultan would recognize the treaty and interpret it as the Dutch wished, the Sultan wrote to the Governor-General asserting that Makasar too had rights in the Spice Islands. When, two years later, the Governor-General sent an ultimatum to the Sultan, the Sultan sent a counterdemand, that the Dutch should destroy their fortifications at Manado, established in 1608. Manado, on the northernmost peninsula of Sulawesi, was a potential rival to the southern ports, particularly as traders increasingly used the route via Brunei.

Meanwhile in 1641, the Dutch captured Malacca, and Makasar became the centre of Portuguese trade. Some Malayan traders probably moved there too. Amin, secretary to Sultan Hasanuddin, and author of a poem commemorating the battle of Makasar (*Sja'ir Perang Mengkasar*) was a Malay of Makasarese descent. The Malay community had a large share in Makasar's trade.

In 1660 a Dutch expedition of 31 ships with 2,600 men defeated the Portuguese and the Sultan's forces. By the terms of the ensuing treaty Buton, to the south of Sulawesi, Manado in the north, and the Spice Islands gained Dutch protection against Makasar's interference; the Portuguese were expelled from Makasar; and the Dutch gained 'continuous residency' rights.

The Sultan now had additional cause for resentment against the Dutch because they were giving assistance to his rebellious subjects, the Buginese. Negotiations broke down and an expedition under Cornelius Speelman was sent from Batavia where he joined forces with Arung Palakka, the Buginese general. After three years of fighting, Makasar finally fell. On this occasion the Sultan of Gowa was supported by the English, 'infidels but gentlemanly infidels' as the poet described them, 'men with razor-sharp minds. Although of course overbearing infidels, they were honest men, unwavering in their determination.'

The Sultan himself summed up the situation when he said: 'What these damned Dutch want is for us to bow the knee.' This his advisers were not prepared to do until forced by Dutch superiority in naval tactics and in arms. The King of Tallo's ship was very beautiful, 'carved in a pattern of drifting clouds and curving lotus leaves . . . stamped with sparkling gold leaf so that it glittered and shone in dazzling fashion'; but although the gold-mounted oars shone like torches, this ship required 260 oarsmen and was no match for the Dutch ships not dependent on oarsmen. The poet early found the moral of his story. 'Listen, sirs, to my advice: never make friends with the Dutch. Possessed of a sort of devilish cunning, no country can call itself safe when they are around.' Yet for the Buginese the moral was the reverse. Together with the Dutch they had proved a more powerful combination than the English and the Makasarese. The main indigenous power in south Sulawesi passed from Makasar to their former vassals the Buginese, under the Sultan of Bone, chief of the four Buginese states around the Gulf of Bone in south Sulawesi, while many Makasarese fled to Madura, north of Java, and lived by piracy.

The 1667 treaty provided for the expulsion of the English and for Dutch control of the fortress of Udjong Padang, 'a strong fortress with a supply of good drinking-water and situated in a healthy locality, possessing moreover a suitable harbour where our ships can shelter from almost any wind, so that it might well be termed a bastion of the valuable easterly districts.' According to the Sultan's secretary, this latter 'request' was granted because he believed it was an arrangement to lease the fort, although the Dutch certainly thought it a fairly permanent sort of 'lease'. They were still there when the V.O.C. was wound up in 1799 and the Netherlands government assumed its debts and possessions.

(c) *The Javanese Kingdoms*. 1500-1700

Before the close of the seventeenth century, the V.O.C. extended its authority to the Spice Islands, successfully evicting its European rivals, the Portuguese and the English, and establishing control over the local rulers and their subjects. Mean-

while the Dutch were establishing themselves in Java, rivals of
both Portuguese (at Malacca) and English (with a factory at
Banten). Again two intertwining histories interact on each
other. One is continuing European rivalry; the other is the local
rivalry of inland kingdom against coastal principality, and
between different coastal principalities.

(i)   Banten. 1526-1684

Banten developed as a trading centre after Malacca fell to the
Portuguese, just as did Atjeh. Banten, in west Java, facing the
Sunda Straits, was a particularly suitable trading entrepôt for
merchants coming via the west coast of Sumatra and through the
Sunda Straits rather than through the Straits of Malacca. It was
also a suitable terminal point for many Chinese traders. When
the early European traders arrived, they found that Banten's
administration was largely in Chinese hands, although these
Chinese advisers owed their position entirely to the Sultan's
favour.

Banten, like Atjeh, was strongly Moslem and a centre of Moslem learning. In 1574 the neighbouring Hindu state of Padja-
djaran, whose port, Sunda Kelapa, had already been captured by
Banten, was forced to become Moslem.

The arrival of Dutch, English and Danish traders at Banten
initially forced up pepper prices. Pepper was the main trade item.
In time the Sultan of Banten also wished to increase customs
dues. When pepper prices fluctuated because of the Sultan's
monopoly of the trade, the Dutch, strangely enough, regarded
this as extortion and corruption, expressing their moral indignation as well as their envy, because the Bantenese were doing
successfully what the Dutch themselves wished to do.

The Dutch Governor-General, initially situated at Banten,
soon decided to move instead to Sunda Kelapa, or Jakatra, where
the fortified trading depot Batavia was established. From
Batavia the Dutch, with their superior naval and military force,
could establish a virtual blockade of the Bantenese, and, by seiz-
ing Chinese junks laden with pepper and forcing them to sell
their cargo at prices determined by the Company, they soon
persuaded many Chinese merchants to transfer from Banten to
Batavia.

When the blockade was at its height, many Bantenese turned to
fishing and growing food crops in place of pepper cultivation.
Some Chinese residents began refining sugar. Banten remained a
troublesome rival to the Dutch until 1683-84, when a dynastic
struggle enabled the Dutch to intervene in favour of one candi-

date. With Dutch support he was victorious, at the price of virtual submission to the Dutch.

With the fall of Banten in 1684 the English merchants set up a port at Bengkulu (Benkulen) in south-west Sumatra. According to William Dampier this was on the invitation of the local rajas who preferred the English to the Dutch, 'but however that were, the English had the good fortune to get hither first: though so narrowly, that the Dutch were within an ace of preventing them, their ships being in sight before our men got ashore.'

(ii)   The North Coast Ports. 1540-1625

The ports along the north coast of Java had become an integral part of the spice trade centred on Malacca, complementary to Malacca yet rivals of it, of each other, and of the inland kingdom of Madjapahit from whom they had become independent during the late fourteenth and fifteenth centuries. With the rise of Mataram, with its *kraton* in central rather than east Java, like the earlier kingdom of that name, the coastal principalities were again involved in a struggle to maintain their independence; more difficult because it coincided with Portuguese and Dutch seaward attacks on their trade.

In 1540 Demak was at the height of its power. By 1546 it had been captured by Djapara. In the third quarter of the sixteenth century Djapara was Portugal's most dangerous rival, because of its important role in the spice trade with Ambon. By 1599 it became Mataram's port, and the outlet for its surplus rice crops.

To the east the port of Gresik, described by Tomé Pires, had come under the control of Surabaya, further to the east again, and the Sultan during the early seventeenth century engaged in a landward struggle with Mataram and a seaward struggle with the Dutch. Surabaya finally fell to Mataram in 1625. The Sultan had earlier resisted the Dutch demand for a monopoly of the rice trade.

The long-term effect of first Portuguese and later Dutch control of the spice trade at its source was the decline of the north Javanese shipping ports and, in the Spice Islands, where the population relied on imported rice from Java, the need to substitute sago as a staple for the rice no longer imported. It is very difficult for a confirmed rice eater to be reduced to eating sago instead.

The long-term effect on the balance of power and the balance of trade throughout the archipelago was considerable. The pattern of trade involved the export of Javanese rice and foodstuffs to Malacca where they were sold and Gujrati textiles bought, some for Java, some to be bartered in the Spice Islands (along with rice and other foodstuffs) for spices, most of which were then sold at Malacca. The Portuguese attempt to monopolize the spice trade made it increasingly difficult for the north Javanese merchants, particularly when the Portuguese began to use the route via Brunei and Sulawesi to by-pass Java. Dutch monopoly was even more serious, as the Dutch headquarters were on Java itself. Malacca remained dependent on the ports of southern Sumatra and northern Java for the bulk of its food supplies, and here too the Dutch blockade of Malacca prior to its ultimate capture by the Dutch in 1641 affected not only Malacca but also former suppliers of foodstuffs along the north Java coast.

(iii)   The Inland Kingdom of Mataram. 1613-1705

Mataram first became established as a land-based power under Senopati, a semi-legendary ruler, who looked back to the glories of Madjapahit and sought to restore the unity of Java. The most striking difference between the new Mataram and the older king-doms was that this heir to Madjapahit had an Islamic ruler, even though many older traditions were incorporated into Islam as practised in the court of Mataram.

It reached the height of its power under Sultan Agung (1613-45). By 1625 Mataram had conquered Tuban (1619), Madura (1624) and Surabaya (1625) and was preparing for an attack on the newly established coastal port of Batavia, whose embassies had been received in 1622, probably as tribute-bearing missions acknowledging the suzerainty of Mataram, but which were rebuffed in 1626 because the Dutch had not assisted Sultan Agung in his attack on Surabaya.

In 1627 Mataram attacked Batavia by sea, but the Dutch narrowly averted defeat and drove off the attackers. Sultan Agung then attempted to lay siege to Batavia. This involved a long, slow, arduous journey from central Java along the north coast 'roads', with elephants, cannon and carts carrying sufficient supplies to maintain the army on the journey. Unfortunately for the Sultan he depended on the sea route to replenish his supplies. The Dutch, with their superior naval strength, des-troyed the supply ships, and so the armies of Mataram, half-starved and decimated by disease, were forced to turn back and Batavia was saved—or lost, depending on one's point of view.

Even after failing to take Batavia in 1629, Sultan Agung was a powerful and implacable rival of the infidel Dutch. Meanwhile he turned his attention to Balambangan, a Hindu kingdom in

the extreme east of Java opposite the island of Bali, conquering
it in 1639 but failing in his attempt to subjugate Bali.

Sultan Agung's achievements were not limited to conquest.
During his reign the *Suria Alam* (literally: Light of the Universe)
or the code of laws for the kingdom was prepared, combining
the influence of *adat* (the customary law) with that of Islam.
The code of law speaks of 'the Precious Stone and that in which
it is set. To these may be compared the Radja and his people.
The former is in a dependent state.' His immediate advisers are
'1. One who possesses his confidence; 2. A scribe skilled in writing; 3. An interpreter well versed in language; 4. A good
messenger; 5. An intelligent doorkeeper; 6. A person who knows
in what a want of manners consists; 7. An experienced general.
Then will the country flourish.'

Sultan Agung encouraged the propagation of Islam within
Mataram and had diplomatic links with the centres of Islam,
Arabia and Turkey. His court poets wrote the *Babad Tanah
Djawi,* a narrative poem part-historical, part-mythical, in the tradition of the *Nagarakertagama,* stressing Mataram's legitimacy and
its continuity with the glorious Kingdom of Madjapahit. Sultan
Agung was probably spurred on in his attempted conquest and
reunification of Java by his desire to restore Madjapahit's former
glories.

Mataram, like Madjapahit, was based on rice cultivation. The
king had supreme authority and held both political and religious
power. The *kraton* was the centre of the kingdom, and the king's
wealth came from taxes levied on imports and exports, tribute
from different parts of the kingdom, and labour services due to
him. These must have been particularly heavy when Mataram
was engaged in wars of conquest.

Such a kingdom was fairly loosely structured. The sultans of
Mataram lived in a constant atmosphere of intrigue. Every member of the royal family was a potential danger to the Sultan
himself. The Sultan tried to insure himself against this danger
by insisting that the most senior government official, the *pangeran,* either lived within the *kraton* or at least paid an annual
visit there. Within each of the districts into which the state was
divided, there was appointed a *tumenggung,* or district ruler,
below the *pangeran* in status, but, in his own district, a very
powerful official, able to make considerable demands on the
villages under his authority.

The villagers, especially in outlying districts, had little contact
with the *kraton,* apart from demands to supply the courts with
rice, or to repair the roads whenever the Sultan wished to

journey along them. If the Sultan should decide to wage war then economic disaster might result. Harvests suffered, either from being trampled down by elephants, cannon, carts and marching armies, or from lack of people to reap the harvest, where villagers had been conscripted for service. Villages were often burnt to prevent them falling to the enemy, leading to depopulation of some areas. Under such circumstances, famine was often prevalent, and disease spread rapidly.

There was little hope of agreement between Mataram and Batavia while Sultan Agung ruled the former and van Diemen was Governor-General of the latter, but in 1645 both died. Sultan Agung's successor was Amangkurat I, during whose reign there may have been a reaction within court circles against the Islamization of Javanese society in the previous reign. As evidence there is the claim that Amangkurat I decreed the death of 6,000 Moslem holy men, which does suggest that he was not a devout Moslem; but he also had a great many other people killed if they chanced to displease him. He has been described as a 'monster of cruelty whose atrocities were on so extravagant a scale as to be scarcely credible'.[10]

Mataram sought to strengthen its position in Java through marriage alliances. There was more opportunity for such alliances because Islam sanctioned polygamy[11], as Hinduism and Buddhism had also done. These marriage alliances could provide alternative claimants to the throne, and one common way of dealing with this was by the destruction of rivals and potential rivals to royal power. This was not always possible, even for someone as bloodthirsty as Amangkurut I is reputed to have been.

In 1674 Trunadjaya, prince of Madura, who claimed descent from the house of Madjapahit, revolted against Amangkurat I, supported by many Makasarese pirates, driven to piracy on the north Javanese coast after Makasar fell to the Dutch and their ally the Sultan of Bone. Trunadjaya burnt and sacked the *kraton* of Mataram and set up his own headquarters at Kediri.

At first the Dutch were reluctant to intervene but they finally did so and, with their help, Trunadjaya was driven out. Amangkurat I had been killed during the fighting and the Dutch reinstated his son Amangkurat II, restoring to him the sacred *pusaka,* the emblems of state, including the crown which, sym-

[10] D. G. E. Hall, *A History of South-East Asia* (London, 1964), p. 301.
[11] This sanction of polygamy has certain provisoes in Islamic law. A man may have no more than four wives, and he must treat them all equally. The first wife should give her consent before a second is taken. These provisoes are not necessarily adhered to by all Moslems, but in that case they are not behaving as good Moslems should.

bolically, was placed on his head by the Dutch commander, who first tried it on himself, an act of desecration long remembered and resented. By the ensuing treaty between the Dutch and Mataram, Amangkurat II recognized Dutch protection. His new *kraton* at Kartasura in the Solo valley was guarded by a battalion of Dutch troops. He also recognized Dutch control of the greater part of west Java.

(iv)   Batavia

The traditional trade of the north Javanese ports was disrupted by Dutch attempts to achieve monopoly of the spice trade at its source. More and more the Javanese were forced to concentrate on the export of rice and foodstuffs to Malacca or Batavia. Jan Peterszoon Coen, the founder of Batavia, was Governor-General of the V.O.C. in 1618-23 and again from 1627 to 1629. He aimed at establishing a series of trading settlements linked by sea power throughout the whole of Asia, and was prepared to be ruthless to achieve commercial monopoly and to crush trade rivals.

By the end of the seventeenth century, unwittingly and perhaps unintentionally, the Dutch had embarked on a policy which was to make them not only a powerful trading nation but which drew them more deeply into Javanese territorial affairs until a trading post developed into a colony and, from being one trading group among many, the Dutch became the masters of a colonial empire centred on their chief trading port at Batavia.

At the end of the century Batavia was still a small settlement carved out of the surrounding jungle where tigers, rhinoceros and bandits were to be found. From the outset Batavia had a considerable Chinese population, whom it was the V.O.C. policy to encourage to attract trade, so the Company could benefit from customs and other dues. Until that was achieved the V.O.C. depended on finance from home, and needed ready cash for trading and for establishing and maintaining forts along the trade routes.

By the 1680s the city was well established and according to one contemporary European writer, finer than Amsterdam itself. It was five or six miles round, with canals 'wall'd up with good square stone, and all along each side of it, there goes a row or two of fine cedar, coco or figg trees, where the freemen use to walk at night under a most pleasant shade'.

The castle, which dominated the city, was strongly fortified and surrounded with a moat. It was a huge stone building in which lived the Governor-General and some of the chief merchants of the Company, along with assistants, bookkeepers and various craftsmen, especially 'gunsmiths, locksmiths, joiners and such like, that are to be employed in any military business'.

The city itself was also walled, 'a strong wall above 40 paces broad', and armed. 'The cannon is always ready to turn, as well upon the city itself, as upon the enemy without, in case of any insurrection or disturbance among the inhabitants, which are of all nations' and far outnumbering the Dutch inhabitants. They included Turks, Persians, Tartars, Siamese, Moors, Japanese, Armenians and Arabians as well as people from Ambon, from Malabar and from Madagascar, many of them slaves, and slave women from Bali and Makasar kept by the Chinese, the latter 'being the chief and greater part' of the inhabitants, but few, if any, Javanese, of whom the Dutch were suspicious especially after the 1627-9 attacks on Batavia.[12]

Shops had a variety of wares, and eating houses were good and reasonably priced. At least one European, the first of many, found the place 'an earthly paradise', even reporting that the 'bissang-figgs', the banana trees, had leaves so large that some people were 'apt to believe they were the leaves which Adam and Eve made their aprons of after the Fall'.

By 1694 Batavia included Semarang, Tjeribon and the mountains of Priangan in west Java within its territory. By 1799 the Dutch had virtual control through treaties over practically all Java but when the Company was wound up in that year it was still primarily a trading company, responsible to the parent body in the Netherlands, and charged with the task of making a profit on the investments of the Company's shareholders.

[12] For a lively description of Batavia and 'Homo Bataviensis', the Dutch settlers there at this time, see B. H. M. Vlekke, *Nusantara* (W. van Hoeve, The Hague, 1959), Ch. IX.

PART III

Deepening Western Penetration

CHAPTER SIX

Indonesia in the Eighteenth and Nineteenth Centuries

By the beginning of the eighteenth century the Dutch East India Company was at the height of its power. It had outsailed, out-fought and outmanoeuvred its European rivals, the Portuguese, and had held its own against later European rivals, the English, French and Danish East India Companies, as well as maintaining trading rights with Japan. Its trading connections stretched from Arabia and India to China and Japan, and, although it had failed in its attempts to achieve complete monopoly control of Indies products (except nutmeg and cloves), it carried on a wide and diversified trade, not only in these spices and in pepper, but also in textiles, especially silk from China, and in Japanese copper. Later in the century, as the European taste for coffee and tea was cultivated and promised to be insatiable, these com-modities, along with sugar, formed an increasing part of cargoes destined for the Netherlands market.

Batavia, headquarters of the Company's eastern trading posts, was no longer a walled fortress carved out of tiger-infested jungle. Territory acquired through Dutch intervention in the disputes of its neighbours in Java, a reward from the victor, meant that the city, although its walls were still 'abundantly provided with cannon', was surrounded now by fertile country abounding in 'rice, sugarcane fields, gardens, and orchards, mills for sugar, corn and gunpowder'. An English captain described Batavia in 1710 as a city not quite as large as contemporary Bristol but more populous, calling it 'one of the pleasantest cities in the world'. Nevertheless it was perhaps symbolic that, during the eighteenth century, the castle built by Coen a century earlier to dominate the city, although it still looked formidable enough, had in fact suffered so badly from assaults and from the weather that the garrison was forbidden to fire too many salutes from the guns mounted on its walls in case the reverberations should cause them to crumble.

By the mid-eighteenth century, although outwardly strong and still believed by contemporaries to be extremely wealthy, the V.O.C. was living on credit and its fortunes were declining. For almost the last fifty years of its existence according to recent investigations it made an overall loss rather than profit. Its trading empire was decaying at the periphery in face of growing competition from the British, and from other European and Asian merchants. The Company's aim was to monopolize certain exports and by restricting their production, to keep up the prices asked for them on the European market, while preventing illicit supplies from reaching foreign merchant rivals.

Not all goods were reserved as the monopoly of the Company, only spices, including pepper; coffee; firearms; opium; rice and wood. On the whole the Company could still control open infringement of monopolies by private traders, but increasingly its own employees, unable to manage on their inadequate salaries, engaged in smuggling. Batavia was developing interests which ran counter to those of the Company in the Netherlands, and as everyone from highest to lowest was likely to be involved in some such private sideline, nobody was available to police such activities.

With trade diversification during the eighteenth century, this policy of monopoly and of adjusting production to European demand became less easy to follow, although the Directors in the Netherlands never quite realized or fully accepted this. They were also handicapped because any instructions sent from the Netherlands would be two years out of date by the time they could be acted on, and this two-year gap between supply and demand reacted against any proposed adjustment of production. Clove trees take nearly twelve years from planting to the first crop of flowers, and nutmegs take ten. It was relatively easy to cut down production by cutting down the trees but when, later in the century, spice prices rose with increased demand it was impossible to meet this demand by extending production. Prices given to the cultivators had been drastically reduced and they showed little enthusiasm about increasing production when European demand rose.

As the emphasis in eastern trade shifted from spices (cloves, nutmeg and pepper) to other commodities such as silk, Japanese copper, coffee, tea and sugar, there was even less possibility of maintaining or establishing a monopoly, for these products were not exclusive to any one particular area, as were cloves and nutmeg. Silk had once been the monopoly of China but by the eighteenth century it was produced also in Persia, India and Italy.

Coffee, tea and sugar were in a different category from other goods. Sugar had been grown, but not processed, in Indonesia, while coffee was introduced early in the eighteenth century as a new crop, and the first experimental consignment was sent to Holland in 1712. These, along with tea, were cultivated in Java so that the Dutch could participate in the growing trade in such commodities without depending on coffee prices at Mocha (Arabia). Even so they found, as the century progressed, that in the China trade they were being outstripped by their European rivals and that their trade with the Coromandel coast of India was being diverted to Madras by the British. Along with other European traders, they met with 'highhandedness and fortuitousness' from local merchants and officials in Arabian and Chinese ports. This was something they naturally preferred to give rather than to receive.

As their trading interests contracted more upon Batavia, the Dutch increasingly played the role of merchant prince, drawing more income from their princely functions through taxation of the inhabitants of Java, than from that of merchant. The stages in this process are difficult to determine because the Company did not distinguish between the two roles, and also made every effort to ensure that nobody, including the Directors themselves, could really find out just what the Company's financial state was.

EIGHTEENTH-CENTURY TRADERS AND MERCHANT PRINCES IN THE ARCHIPELAGO. 1700-99

By the early eighteenth century the V.O.C. controlled the sea lanes of the Indonesian archipelago. Throughout the latter part of the seventeenth century they had managed to exclude their European trade rivals, with the exception of the small British colony in Bengkulu (southern Sumatra) and to destroy the carrying trade formerly in the hands of local merchants from the north coast Javanese ports. By the second half of the century it is possible to distinguish three different areas within the archipelago: eastern Indonesia, where the Dutch influence, following that of the Portuguese, had been intensive and oppressive; Sumatra and Kalimantan, where Western influence had hardly penetrated at all, beyond a few fortress settlements; and Java, where Western penetration extended further and changed in nature as the Dutch acquired more territory.

(a) *Eastern Indonesia*

The main Dutch concern remained the preservation of the spice monopoly and reduction of output if it was large enough to reduce European prices. Ambon had become the centre of clove production rather than Ternate and Tidore whose rulers remained stubbornly independent. Banda remained the home of mace and nutmeg. Makasar, after the defeat of 1667, remained a Dutch stronghold fortified against all comers. Phillip Carteret, no trader but captain of a 'King's Ship' of the British Royal Navy, on a voyage round the world, was forced through delays and misadventures to make for Makasar in December, 1767, to seek supplies and to avoid unfavourable winds. He had over forty sick men aboard, 'the sight of which could not fail to raise a shudder' according to the Dutch officials, because 'they were infected by scurvy to such a degree that the teeth of most men were loose or had fallen out; their gums black and swollen and their legs as blue as lazuli'. Carteret had scarcely enough crew to sail the leaking ship, provisioned only with 'wine, bad salt meat and bread full of weevils'. Yet it took two days, a very close inspection of the ship, and several meetings before the Makasar Council dared set aside the 'very strict and positive orders they had from their honourable masters' to forbid any foreigner to land there.

Carteret reported that 'the Dutch never yet could get this part of the country into their hands' although they had been able to hamper local trading activities by refusing to issue passes, particularly to anyone wishing to trade with the English, 'so that they are obliged to go by stealth', facing severe punishment, even death, if caught by a patrolling Dutch cruiser.

Carteret was allowed to stay in neighbouring Bonthain Bay until the winds were set for Batavia, and to bring ashore the sick, but they could not go further than twenty or thirty yards from the hospital without fear of arrest, and could buy provisions only under Dutch supervision. Two Dutch warships anchored one on each side of the English ship. At the sight of these warships, Carteret and his crew 'resolved if they attacked to sell ourselves so dearly as possible for there was but few on board but what entertained the gloomy thoughts of an Amboina' (Ambon).[1]

The whole incident illustrates very well the mutual distrust between trade rivals, the uneasiness of the Dutch at this trading

[1] In 1623, in what has become known to English readers as the massacre of Amboyna, though the Dutch do not regard it as such, the English were driven out of the eastern archipelago, after eight (or ten) Englishmen were executed for attempting to seize the Dutch fortress at Ambon. It is interesting to compare the account given by Vlekke, pp. 140-1, with that given by Hall, pp. 287-8, as an example of the different viewpoints of a Dutch and an English historian concerning the incident.

outpost, their particular suspicion of the English, the continued hostility of the enemies and rivals of the local allies of the Dutch, and also how difficult it is to catch anything more than a glimpse of the life of the local inhabitants, 'those poor enslaven people' as Carteret called them. Makasar was retained as a stronghold because it was 'the key to the Molucca [Maluku] islands', but to grow export crops there would only have encouraged further illicit trade by Buginese˙ sailors in defiance of the Dutch monopoly. It would be satisfying to know more about the volume of their trade but understandably there is little if any direct evidence available on such matters. Meanwhile the Spice Islands had been reduced to subsistence level—or below—and each year the *hongi* raids set out from Ambon and Banda to visit any islands suspected of having unlicensed spice-trees and to destroy them.

(b) *Sumatra and Kalimantan*

The Dutch had broken the Atjehnese control of the pepper trade and with the consequent loss of wealth and prestige the Atjehnese kingdom was no longer as powerful as in the early seventeenth century. It was, nevertheless, independent. Its merchants still had contact with foreign countries and, although it was no longer a great entrepôt, it still traded throughout the eighteenth century with private European merchants, including Americans, and with Indians from the Coromandel coast, who supplied salt and textiles, in return for gold-dust, raw silk, betel nut, pepper, sulphur, camphor and benzoin. The trade in elephants for the Coromandel coast, carried in specially constructed ships, had died out with the adoption of European-style warfare by the Indian princes, but other branches of trade continued to flourish.

The Sultan of Atjeh was still chief merchant of the capital, attempting to monopolize the trade of the port and holding some kind of suzerainty over the seaboard territories of the west coast as far south as Bengkulu, and parts of the east coast. His palace was surrounded by a moat and strong walls, and near the gate stood the brass cannon sent by James I of England to an earlier ruler of Atjeh.

The incidence of piracy, to judge from reports, seems to have increased throughout the archipelago during the eighteenth and nineteenth centuries, but this may have been less an actual increase than a matter of definition. In the fifteenth and sixteenth centuries little distinction was made between piracy and trade. A trader risked losing his cargo to rivals unless he were swift enough to escape or strong enough to take a rival captive himself. It was sometimes difficult to distinguish between pirate activity and the more respectable process of enforcing a visit to a certain port and demanding compulsory payment of dues to its ruler. Now this distinction was being more clearly drawn, particularly by the Dutch, who claimed the monopoly of trade in the area and saw the trade rivals they had ousted continuing these old-fashioned forms of plunder. They therefore labelled them pirates. They themselves had moved to other more sophisticated forms of plunder.

The Dutch presence had enabled various former vassal states of Atjeh to seek Dutch protection against the Atjehnese. Through such a request the Dutch obtained their fortress at Padang, west coast port for the Minangkabau kingdoms, and their exports of gold and pepper. The Dutch had little contact with the inland kingdom in the fertile mountains. The Minangkabau king, with his seat of government at Pagaruyung, no longer had effective control over the chiefs who owed him allegiance. His orders could be annulled by meetings of village chiefs to whom he had delegated his power. These chiefs depended for their wealth on the produce of irrigated and dry ricefields, as well as the gold produced in the district.

The Palembang and Djambi sultanates on the east coast, formerly centres of the Srividjaya Empire, were vassal states of Batavia, but the Dutch garrison at Palembang could not exceed fifty to sixty men 'without giving umbrage' to the Sultan, which they were not prepared to risk. By a treaty of 1777 the Sultan could trade only with the Company in pepper and tin and must exclude traders of other nations, but local trading vessels from Java, Madura, Bali and Sulawesi still called there with rice, salt and local manufactures. In return for opium, salt and piece-goods traded by the Dutch, they received the products of the interior: rough raw silk, elephants' teeth, sulphur, alum, arsenic, tobacco, dragon's blood (the bright red gum of a palm tree), and gambier. Palembang itself was a city of wooden or bamboo houses on posts, and floating habitations, shops on bamboo-rafts moored in the river. Most of the local commerce was carried on by boat because the surrounding land was marshy and subject to flooding. The population was a mixed one with many Chinese, Cambodians, Siamese, Javanese and Buginese as well as Arabian religious leaders.

The Batak tribes further to the north sought independence from Atjeh to the north and from Minangkabau to the south and so made trade treaties with the Dutch. At the end of the eighteenth century the Bataks were still divided into a number of warring tribes whose life, according to William Marsden[2], 'appeared to be a perpetual state of hostility'. They lived in villages fortified with ramparts of earth and brushwood surrounded by 'an impenetrable hedge of prickly bamboo' which effectively camouflaged their dwelling. In the early nineteenth century they were still cannibals, although Raffles, commenting on this, pointed out that 'however horrible eating a man may sound in European ears, I question whether the party suffers so much, or the punishment itself is worse than the European tortures of two centuries ago', or indeed, as he went on to add, the capital punishment accepted by his own society. And cannibalism was a form of punishment, legally and ceremonially controlled. The flesh of the guilty person, lightly broiled, was eaten with salt and *sambal*, a hot chilli paste.

The Batak women, wives and children, could be sold at will by their menfolk. They worked in the ricefields while, according to Marsden, the men, when not engaged in warfare, 'commonly lead an idle, inactive life, passing the day in playing on a kind of flute, crowned with garlands of flowers' or else hunting deer, horse racing or gambling. Nevertheless Marsden, and later Raffles, commented on the high percentage of the population able to read and write; more than half, according to Marsden, who added that this was 'a qualification seldom observed in such uncivilised parts of the world, and not always in the more polished'.

The English presence at Bengkulu made it difficult for the Dutch to maintain their exclusive right, according to treaty, to handle the export crops of the various kingdoms, although they did attempt to monopolize the tin deposits of Bangka and Billiton, islands off the south-east coast of Sumatra. Bengkulu, the settlement founded when the Dutch expelled the English from Banten, was little more than a toehold, an outer settlement in terms of the British trading establishments firmly centred in India. The presence of two European powers on Sumatra, and the relatively free trading at Atjeh gave the rival tribes in different areas greater flexibility in making alliances.

The English attempted to monopolize the pepper production of Bengkulu and made more or less regular surveys of the pepper gardens to check whether cultivators were fulfilling the treaty obligation to plant a given number of vines per household. Such surveys came up against considerable difficulties. Not only was it

[2] His *History of Sumatra*, written at the end of the eighteenth century, still makes lively reading today.

arduous and dangerous to travel any great distance, but the local custom of changing one's name upon what the British called 'the most trifling incidents' (such as marriage or recovery from a serious illness) meant that, within twelve months, all the cultivators in any one village might have changed names, throwing the survey into complete confusion.

In 1719 the local people drove away the British garrison and not until 1724, when a less onerous pepper treaty was made, were they allowed to return. Joseph Collet, governor from 1712 to 1716, throws some light on this incident in his comment to a friend that 'the Malays are not the brutes they have been represented, they can distinguish between justice and villainy, kindness and cruelty', adding that 'for the English, I had rather drawn a curtain over their past action than relate the particulars. I shall only say that the corruption has been universal'.

The European settlements in Sumatra interfered very little with the traditional way of life. The British lived—and died— in their unhealthy west coast stronghold, attempting by a combination of force and persuasion to encourage a greater output of pepper. To the north the Dutch at Padang did much the same. Dutch contact with Sumatran rulers was limited to coastal areas, no greater in extent and perhaps even less in impact than those of the seventeenth century. Both Dutch and English were more preoccupied with keeping an eye on each other's activities in the area than with extending their territorial holdings, if this had been possible. For each, Sumatra was an outpost, and settlements were retained there more for their strategic importance than their immediate value as trading centres. At the same time we may wish that others besides Marsden had paid more attention to the local people so that we could know more about their everyday activities and ways of life.

In south-east Kalimantan the sultanate of Bandjermasin had succeeded Makasar as the trading depot for non-Dutch vessels; Portuguese from Timor, British from Bengkulu and a few Chinese junks. Throughout the late seventeenth and early eighteenth centuries, Dutch and British traders were often murdered by local rivals, and the same fate befell Portuguese missionaries. The Sultan was strong enough also to defend himself against the pirate fleets operating in this area.

The rest of Kalimantan had little or no contact with foreigners, except for the north-western sultanate of Sambas, which had succeeded in liquidating earlier Dutch garrisons. The Sultan had called in hundreds of Chinese miners to work the gold deposits, and the many thousands of Chinese who followed them had been kept under control by Dyak guardsmen until they revolted in 1770 and set up semi-independent republics of mixed-blood Chinese. The Dutch settlements in Kalimantan were abandoned by the end of the eighteenth century because the trade, due largely to successful Chinese competition, was not sufficiently valuable to justify the expenses of manning and defending such settlements.

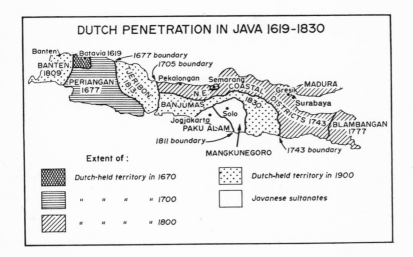

DUTCH PENETRATION IN JAVA 1619-1830

Extent of :

Dutch-held territory in 1670

"   "   "   " 1700

"   "   "   " 1800

Dutch-held territory in 1900

Javanese sultanates

(c) *Java*

In eastern Indonesia the Dutch destroyed the traditional way of life, decimated the population and adversely affected the living standards of the survivors; in the west they barely made any impact at all, except perhaps in the immediate vicinity of their trading posts. In Java, the centre and focus of their eastern trade, they penetrated into the traditional way of life and, without actually destroying it, utilized it for their own ends. Here Dutch penetration was a prolonged and continuous development throughout the eighteenth century. Batavia was the centre of the Dutch trading empire. Here the Dutch first began to play the role of merchant prince, and then to move to the domination of the greater part of the island. By 1750 the Dutch held one-sixth of the territory of Java. By the end of the century this had been extended to three-fifths of the territory, despite strong opposition and at considerable cost both in men and in ammunition and supplies. The wider the territorial sway of the Dutch the more men they needed to staff the administration, and the more money to finance this extension. Sir Thomas Raffles, in his *History of Java,* commented that 'ever since the arrival of the Europeans they (the Javanese) have neglected no opportunity of attempting to regain their independence' and while, from the Dutch side, the eighteenth century was a period of gradual expansion in Java, from the Javanese side it was a continuing struggle against the encroachments of the Batavian city state, most powerful of the North Coast principalities, upon the inland kingdoms. In the process the protagonists exercised considerable influence on each other.

Within Java itself, west Java, with the exception of Banten, was under more direct control not only because it was closer to Batavia but also because much land was ceded to the Dutch, while in central and east Java, the kingdoms became Dutch protectorates. We must also consider the role of the growing Chinese community in Java and its relationship to the Europeans on the one hand, and the Javanese and Sundanese on the other. Finally we shall look at the city state of Batavia at the end of the eighteenth century, when the Dutch East India Company, having declared itself bankrupt in 1793, was finally taken over by the Dutch government.

(i)   West Java

The land around Batavia had been sold to European and Chinese private citizens. The Europeans were often former servants of the V.O.C. who chose, on completion of their contract, to remain in Java. One Dutch visitor remarked in 1722 that 'one may safely affirm of Java, that there is not, under the canopy of heaven, an island more plentiful or more pleasant', and a growing number of his fellow countrymen seem to have agreed with him.

Beyond this again was land under the control of Regents from whose subjects the Dutch demanded tribute. By the treaty of 1677 the Dutch territory included the district of Priangan, stretching from the north to the south coast and separating the sultanate of Banten from the rest of Java. The treaty laid down the tribute required and the terms on which further trade was to be carried out. From the point of view of the inhabitants there was very little difference between the two. The tribute, known as con-tingencies, consisted of payment in kind, mainly the provision of rice, which the Dutch received by right of conquest. The trade, known as forced deliveries, was based on trade treaties, but the forced deliveries were really 'tribute disguised as trade'. The

payment was entirely fixed by the buyer, not by the seller, and
the amount to be delivered was also specified, whether it bore
any relationship to the size of the annual crop or not. Increasingly the Dutch supervised, through the Regents, the cultivation
of produce for the export market, demanding fixed amounts of
different crops at fixed prices. Some of these were crops traditionally grown by the villagers—rice or pepper for example—
but others were new and unfamiliar.

The most important crop which the cultivators of west Java
were forced to grow under this system was coffee. The first consignment of Java coffee was sent to the Netherlands early in the
eighteenth century and up to 1750 attempts were made to
regulate coffee production in accordance with the requirements
of the European market. The constant fluctuation of policy—
high demand one year followed by the demand to cut down
bushes or the refusal to buy the whole of the crop the next—
caused considerable hardship to the cultivators.

The V.O.C. also gradually reduced the price it paid the Regent,
through whom the financial arrangements were made. All that
the Regent could do to maintain his traditional prestige and
relative wealth, was to increase the demands he made on the
villagers over and above what was required by the Dutch.

The villager had even less redress than the Regent, either
against his traditional master, or against his new master, the
Company, of whose existence he was likely to be unaware since
it acted through the Regent. His only possible escape, when the
burden of production became intolerable, was to move somewhere else. This was possible because the peasant in Java,
unlike the serf under the European feudal system, was not bound
to the soil. The only restriction on his movement from one place
to another was his own reluctance to leave the familiar village,
or the availability of land in the area to which he moved. In
west Java, where *sawah* or wet rice cultivation had only recently
begun to replace the shifting *ladang* (slash-and-burn) rice cultivation, the peasant was more accustomed to a semi-nomadic life,
and the limit of the Regent's control over his subordinates was
thus set by the point at which they preferred flight.

It has been suggested that the extension of *sawah* cultivation
in west Java during the eighteenth century shows that although
Dutch rule was oppressive, it had reduced the amount of warfare
in the area (for example by separating Banten from Mataram)
and so encouraged the inhabitants to undertake a more permanent cultivation because of greater peace and stability.

In practice, forced cultivation was uneven in effect. Some crops, such as indigo, took both time and labour out of all proportion to the meagre returns. Coffee caused relatively little hardship, where the land used was not suitable for the cultivation of rice.

(ii)   Central and East Java

The kingdom of Mataram, so formidable an opponent of the Dutch under Sultan Agung, had declined under his successors. The cost of fighting the Dutch was one cause of this decline. Another was the constant rivalry between different branches of the royal family. Polygamy further extended the range of potential candidates for the throne. Initially, even when appealed to by one of the rival candidates, the Dutch intervened reluctantly in such disputes, but the more they intervened the more necessary did they find further intervention.

Early in the century the Dutch were troubled by a runaway Balinese slave, Surapati, who organized opposition in the mountains south of Batavia. When they tried to capture him he fled to the *kraton* of Kartasura, where Amangkurat III, son of Amangkurat II[3], now reigned. When Surapati had outstayed his welcome there he moved to east Java and proceeded to carve out a kingdom for himself from Mataram territory. The Dutch, displeased with Amangkurat for harbouring Surapati at his *kraton*, supported his uncle, Pangeran Puger, as a rival claimant to the throne. With Dutch support he defeated Amangkurat III in what has become known as the First Javanese War of Succession. He was installed as Pakubuono I on the basis of a treaty very advantageous to the Dutch while Amangkurat III sought refuge with Surapati in east Java. By 1706 the Dutch had defeated both opponents, killing Surapati and sending Amangkurat into exile in Ceylon, at that time a Dutch possession. Surapati's followers were not finally subdued until 1772 but for the time being the ruler of Mataram was the vassal of Batavia.

On the death of Pakubuono I in 1719 further disputes arose about the succession. The Dutch again found themselves intervening to support their candidate against rival claimants. In this Second Javanese War of Succession it took the Dutch four years to round up rival claimants and exile them in Ceylon.

In 1740 there was an armed uprising of Chinese[4]. The ruler of Mataram, after some initial hesitation, took this opportunity to encourage the Chinese in opposition to the Dutch, hoping that once the Chinese had got rid of the Dutch, the Javanese could then rid themselves of the Chinese as well, just as Widjaya,

[3] See above, pp. 93-4.
[4] See below, pp. 115-6.

son-in-law of Kertanagara, had done in the thirteenth century. As one of the local leaders put it: 'We are as the people who bear two burdens: the Dutch are on the right shoulder, the Chinese on the left; if we throw off one the other still remains. If we can accomplish it, why should we not get rid of both?'[5] Other counsel was more cautious: 'The Dutch are as iron, the Chinese as tin: therefore it is better to assist the party most likely to be victorious.'

When Javanese support for the Chinese became obvious, which it did once the Javanese had killed the Dutch garrison in Karta-sura, the ruler of Madura joined the Dutch, hoping to shake off Mataram's overlordship and gain his independence.

The ruler of Mataram, realizing that the Dutch were indeed 'as iron', switched sides and made his peace with them, thus losing the support of many followers, who continued their opposition to the Dutch. When finally the Dutch reinstated him, the new treaty obligations were even more onerous than those he had sought to have abolished, and he had to cede the north coast to the Dutch. After this defeat the *kraton* was shifted from Kartasura to Surakarta (Solo). The Dutch ally, Madura, fared little better than its opponents for, instead of gaining inde-pendence, Madura found it had substituted the overlordship of the Dutch for that of Mataram.

Within a few years the Dutch were involved in the Third Java-nese War of Succession partly caused by the tactless intervention of the Dutch Governor-General in a dispute between brothers. It lasted from 1749 to 1757 and in the early years the Dutch were handicapped by being involved, at the same time, in a dispute with Banten and so, up to 1753, were fighting on two fronts. In 1755 the Dutch partitioned Mataram, establishing their own candidate in Solo and recognizing the rival claimant as Sultan of Jogjakarta. The ruler of Solo took the title of Susuhunan (Sunan), rather than the more strongly Islamic title Sultan. This implied also that he was the senior of the two rulers.

In each war of succession the Dutch participated at the invita-tion of one party to the dispute, and were thus able to claim that the favourable terms of the treaty were a reward for services rendered to the victorious party. The Dutch indeed proved themselves to be 'as iron' by the superiority of their weapons and the superior training of their troops under the command of professional soldiers, pitted against the Javanese troops—villagers recruited from their ricefields. The Javanese might occasionally

[5] T. S. Raffles, *History of Java*, 2nd Edn., Vol. II (John Murray, London, 1832), p. 238.

succeed in a surprise attack, as with the killing of the Dutch garrison at Kartasura, but the Dutch were better able to succeed in prolonged warfare. Yet the costs were high, and more effort was required to defeat the enemy as the century proceeded. It caused a severe drain on the treasury at Batavia, and affected the rice production of Mataram on which both Dutch and Javanese depended for food.

After the partition of Mataram in 1755 the Dutch seemed to have achieved their dual aim, the maintenance of internal peace because war was bad for crop production, and because a peaceful peasantry was to be preferred to one skilled in the arts of warfare. The Dutch sought to centralize control at Batavia, but were anxious to preserve the differences between different parts of Java, in the interest of their policy of 'divide and rule'.

A further method of ensuring continued peace was the Dutch policy of hemming Mataram in and as far as possible preventing contact with the outside world, except under Dutch supervision. With the 1703 treaty renouncing Mataram's control of the Tjeribon district and the 1743 cession of the north-east coastal districts to the Dutch, the kingdoms of Mataram were concentrated behind the mountain barrier with their only outlet on the south coast of Java away from the trade routes[6].

Under the new treaty obligations, the Dutch could impose contingencies and forced deliveries upon wider areas. It was easier to take over a long-standing *sawah* civilization where for centuries the villager had cultivated his land and, through the headman, paid services in kind and labour to the Regent and, through him, to the Sultan. The cultivator was less likely to move, because bound by long tradition to one village; although even here, if pressure became extreme, areas might be depopulated. The population increase which began in the eighteenth century was not sufficient to prevent movement to uncultivated land. The Dutch demands, in most cases, became simply one additional rung on the ladder, and as under the former administration each official had absolute authority over those who were under him, the whole structure of government made it relatively easy for an outside power to step in without destroying the general fabric of life.

Again the forced cultivation of crops was uneven in its effects, depending partly on the suitability of the crop to the particular area and partly on the rapacity of the officials in the area. Some crops encroached on *sawah* land, and sometimes the demands

[6] See the map, p. 107, which shows how small an area remained under the direct rule of the royal house of Mataram.

upon labour to cultivate them reduced the labour available for planting and tending rice. In some areas where this occurred, the villagers had to re-allot the *sawah* lands to ensure that labour would be adequately distributed. In practice the cultivator usually bore the losses resulting from a bad harvest or when the Dutch refused to take all the produce available because of a glut on the market.

As all these dealings were carried out through the Regent, very few Javanese, except those in the household of the Dutch Resident of the district, had much direct contact with the Dutch. The middleman's task, in the case of contingencies, was farmed out to the Chinese and the villager was unlikely to be aware of the reasons for his added burden.

The two *kraton* of the divided kingdom of Mataram were cut off from contact with the outside world, and so increasingly, they looked backward rather than forward, preserving the old rituals even when these were cut off from the realities which had given them their meaning. They preserved and stimulated the decorative arts of *batik*-making and armoury. Even at the more conservative *kraton* of Solo these arts no longer included sculpture, as it had in the days of Madjapahit, partly because the introduction of Islam had not only removed the older religious reasons for the creation of carvings and monuments (which continue to be created in modern Bali for example) but had also forbidden representation of humans or animals in art forms because of their links with older forms of idolatry[7]. Furthermore there was now no surplus labour available for the task of monument building; the villagers were working instead to pay the tribute demanded from the Sunan and Sultan by the Dutch.

Within the *kraton*, a city within a city, the traditional art of *batik*-making was encouraged. As explained earlier, *batik* patterns are produced by covering certain areas of cloth with wax and then soaking the whole length of cloth in dye. Afterwards the wax is scraped off revealing an undyed pattern on the cloth. Originally such *batik* were made in patterns of white on deep blue, the blue dye coming from the indigo plant. Later patterns incorporate a rich, earthy brown, a dye made originally from the bark of a palm tree. For each dyeing the area to remain impervious to the dye must first be covered with wax on each side of the cloth[8].

[7] This led to more stylised *batik* patterns in those designs in which animal and bird forms continue as the basis.
[8] See F. Wagner, *op.cit.*, pp 154-61 and especially the illustrations on pp. 159 and 163. For an account of the technique of *batik* work and its present-day application see N. Krevitsky, *Batik Art and Craft* (Reinholt Publications Corp., New York, 1964).

During the eighteenth century the *tjanting* was invented, a small lamp-shaped implement with a bowl in which the wax could be warmed to keep it molten and a fine spout through which the molten wax could be more easily 'written' on to the cloth. This gave greater flexibility of design, and, although patterns were largely traditional, individual styles of 'writing' were developed within the traditional framework.

The armourer's art also developed within the *kraton* walls. The *kris,* the traditional wavy-edged sword, part weapon and part talisman, was produced by the *kraton* armourers, men of high status within the *kraton* hierarchy. The intricate patterns etched into its blade or carved on its polished wooden handle, were mystical symbols which went back, in many cases, to pre-Islamic days. The shape of the *kris* represented the *naga* or snake of Hindu mythology. The handle often represented a *raksasa,* the demon guardian of earlier temples, although so stylised, out of deference to the teachings of Islam, that it was hard to distinguish the original human figure. But the armourer's craft became increasingly associated with court ceremonial rather than with the practical arts of war.

Court dancing and its accompanying *gamelan* music also developed during this period, as did court literature, particularly the semi-sacred, semi-historical writings, the chronicles of Java.

The court of the Sunan of Solo, whose rulers had been more dependent on the Dutch for support, was the more conservative. Although the Dutch were able to keep the balance of power between the two *kraton* they never really won more than the nominal allegiance of the Sultan of Jogja. They did prevent one eventuality which, situated as they were between Banten and Mataram, had always seemed a potential danger to them, an alliance of Moslem sultanates against their settlement. From early in the century they preferred to support the *adat* or customary rulers against Islamic leaders. As early as 1717 the Resident at Tjeribon reported that: 'I always made the judges of Tjeribon follow the customs of pre-Islamic times and opposed the interference of the priests.' Although the Dutch were not as fanatically opposed to Islam as the Portuguese, there was fear of the potentially unifying force of Islam leading to alliance with the more conservative *adat* chiefs whose adherence to Islam was often only nominal.

(iii)   The Role of the Chinese

We already know that from earliest times the Chinese came to Indonesia as traders. We know too that, when the Dutch first arrived at Banten, there were Chinese merchants and advisers in the court of the Sultan. One of the initial aims of the Dutch blockade on Banten was to persuade these Chinese to transfer to Batavia. From the earliest settlement at Batavia, the Chinese quarters were the centre of much of the city's commercial activity, and the Chinese population by far outnumbered the Europeans.

They were middlemen in several fields especially the rice trade of east Java, where they had had trading contacts long before the Dutch arrived. By the early eighteenth century, they numbered about 10,000 including craftsmen, wealthy landholders, sugar cultivators and tea traders. Tax collection was sometimes farmed to Chinese.

With the growth of the tea trade with Europe, the Dutch encouraged the import of tea to Batavia for trans-shipment to Europe, and each year a fleet of fourteen or fifteen junks arrived laden with tea. In 1714 the Dutch lowered tea prices. Although they succeeded in forcing the lower price on the Chinese in that year, the Chinese tea merchants retaliated by staying away from Batavia in 1715. Indeed, from 1718 to 1722, upon orders of the Emperor of China, no junks came, and the Dutch, having offended the Chinese, were hesitant to venture to China in search of tea. Clearly the Dutch could not force price reductions on the Chinese.

By 1740 the Chinese community had grown considerably, and included many unemployed Chinese. The Dutch, concerned about this, limited the number of immigrants through a quota system. This was fairly easily circumvented by bribery of under-paid Company officials. Then the Dutch began deporting unemployed Chinese to Ceylon or the Cape of Good Hope. Batavia was still a city on the defensive and, as friction between these two groups grew, so did all sorts of wild rumours. It was rumoured among the Dutch that the Chinese planned to revolt and to capture Batavia, and among the Chinese that, once aboard the deportation ships, they would be thrown overboard. In such an atmosphere, trouble was inevitable and the government was unable (or perhaps unwilling) to stop the ensuing massacre of several thousand Chinese. Revolts of Chinese occurred in several of the north-east coastal towns and it was at this point that the Javanese were faced with the problem of whether to support the Chinese or the Dutch, with the results already discussed.

The massacre had a serious effect on the sugar industry. Sugar had been grown in Java for many years but not processed there until quite recently. The Dutch demand for sugar led to forced deliveries of this crop, milled by the Chinese prior to export. Because of its bulk it was often used as ballast in the ships bound for Europe. It also had a wide sale in inter-Asian trade. As early as 1710 there were 130 sugar mills in the Batavian lands as well as others in neighbouring Tjeribon and Banten owned by Chinese, and in the 1740s, sugar production came almost to a standstill.

By the end of the century the Chinese were re-established as middlemen in the economy. They were as indispensable to the Dutch as Dutch rule was to them. They came as immigrants at a period when the Dutch were still there primarily as merchants and traders. They came to improve their economic position and they remained, on the whole, in separate communities retaining their own customs even after several generations. As immigrants seeking a niche for themselves in an alien environment they were industrious and energetic, contrasting—in the minds of Europeans, themselves in a similar category—with the more settled and leisurely existence of the Javanese villager secure in his traditional role within the village community. So there developed the myth of the industrious Chinese and the lazy Javanese or Malay, on which was built the whole edifice of forced delivery. The Javanese was regarded as lazy because he found insufficient incentive in the low and dwindling payment given for growing crops unfamiliar to him, not for his own needs but to satisfy the capricious requirements of foreign overseers.

By the end of the eighteenth century, the place of the Chinese entrepreneur was firmly established in the Javanese economy, and was one factor preventing the development of a significant indigenous middle class. Much of the trade of the north-east coast from which Javanese merchants had been excluded fell into the hands of Chinese merchants.

(iv)   Batavia at the End of the Eighteenth Century

By the end of the eighteenth century, Batavia was no longer regarded as 'one of the pleasantest cities in the world' but rather as a place to be avoided at all costs. Ships still called there but, by the 1730s, it had become known as one of the unhealthiest spots on earth. Captain John Byron, who circumnavigated the world in the mid-1760s, recorded that 'I came in here without a man sick in either ship, but as this is one of the most unhealthy places in all the East Indies, the rainy season at hand, and arrack in great plenty, I dreaded the consequences that might attend it, and was resolved to make my stay as short as possible.' He added that 'the Europeans die here like rotten sheep. The heat is excessive and there is no getting a moment's rest for Muscatos [mosquitoes].' These found an excellent breeding ground in the broad and stagnant canals which the Dutch had had built in imitation of those at home and which spread malaria through the population. In the forty-five–year period from 1735 to 1780 there were at least seventeen years in which the number of deaths among Europeans exceeded the figures given for the total European population of that year. This is explained by the high mortality among ships' crews. These deaths were counted but the living crewmen were not unless they were in port at the time the count was made.

This was perhaps a further element in the declining amount of income which came from trade. Increasingly the Batavian government depended on tribute and taxation for its finances, as well as customs dues and tolls on goods coming into Batavia. At nine o'clock each night a boom was lowered across the canal at the entrance to Batavia, and no ship could enter till morning— partly a defence tactic but partly to ensure that dues were safely collected. There were also poll taxes, especially on the Chinese, who had to pay for the privilege of wearing a pigtail. Later in the century, as a tacit recognition of the illegal earnings of many Company servants, some of whom became extremely wealthy, and as an attempt to tap this source of revenue, a tax on these illicit earnings were instituted.

The Dutch were a minority even among the European inhabitants of Batavia. In 1769 Captain James Cook reported that, 'if the Chinese and Indians of different nations who inhabit Batavia and its environs are excluded the inhabitants amount to a small number, not a fifth part of whom are said to be Dutchmen even by descent.' Sir Thomas Raffles, writing in the early nineteenth century, spoke of the ambivalent attitude common among the Dutch in Java. On the one hand there was 'a haughty assumption of superiority' and on the other 'extraordinary timidity' making them suspicious of treachery and danger. During the last twenty years of the V.O.C. Batavia was ruled by a narrow oligarchy, linked together by marriage ties and by mutual connivance at the corruption by which they retained their wealth and status.

Visiting Englishmen noted with indignation that all the inhabitants of Batavia were expected to draw aside when the Governor-General or any members of the advisory council appeared on the road. Two black servants ran ahead of the Governor-General's coach clearing the way. Councillors or members of their family were preceded by one servant. For the

Governor-General, the occupant of the carriage must descend and bow; for a councillor, it was sufficient to remain within one's vehicle, stand and bow. Phillip Carteret, fresh from his unhappy experience of the Dutch at Makasar was highly indignant at such a custom, arguing that, 'they require more homage and it is paid them than any King in Europe'. In 1777 such homage was abolished for Councillors, and later again in the case of the Governor-General. Such customs suggest a certain assimilation to the ways of local rulers, or an attempt by the Governors-General, many of whom had risen from quite humble birth, to compensate for their lack of background by such methods.

The ultimate decline and failure of the V.O.C., was partly due to growth of competition from rival European companies, increased smuggling, and private trade by Company officials. The mounting expense of wars within Java and of administering the additional territory acquired after each new treaty was made also played their part. The immediate cause was the European war 1780-4 between the two trade rivals, England and the Netherlands. The Treaty of Paris gave the final blow to the Dutch policy of monopoly, in the clause allowing free trade in the East. By 1783 the Company's directors were without any ready cash. By 1799 the Company was clearly bankrupt and the Dutch government took it over.

By this time the Company had built up a structure of government in Java no longer entirely based on trade. The Company's bankruptcy did not lead to Dutch withdrawal from Java. Instead, as the nineteenth century dawned, the trading empire was on the verge of becoming a colonial empire under the Dutch crown.

'LIBERALISM' AND REFORM IN JAVA. 1800-30

'We must state that we can hardly imagine in what way a revolution based upon the system of liberty and rights of the people could be introduced into this country without destroying its value for the home country.' So wrote the Batavian authorities in 1796 in reply to their new masters, the Committee for East Indian Affairs, established in the Netherlands under the direct influence of the French Revolutionary ideas of liberty, equality and fraternity. The home government accepted this point of view, for they, along with most of their contemporaries, believed that colonies existed, and should exist, for the benefit of the mother country, the American Declaration of Independence notwithstanding. They would do what they could for the welfare of the indigenous population but when this welfare conflicted, as it so often did, with the successful exploitation of the colony's products, the latter remained their prime concern.

From 1795 to 1810 the Netherlands were under French control and for part of that time direct communication between the Netherlands and Batavia was almost completely severed. The Dutch in Batavia were allowed to sell their products on the open market to neutral traders, and from 1799 to 1807 they benefited from a boom in coffee prices. In the following eight years Batavia was ruled by two men, Herman Willem Daendels and Thomas Stamford Raffles, who, although in many ways strongly opposed to each other, both represented aspects of the new enlightenment in Europe. They both came as outsiders to Batavia and so were well placed to cut themselves free from the existing pattern of government, though not as completely as they had hoped. Each of them was working against time, Daendels under constant threat of a British invasion of Java, Raffles under constant anticipation of the return of the colony by the English to the Dutch. Each was forced by circumstances to carry out policies in contradiction to his own principles because of financial needs. Each had to rely to a certain extent on existing Dutch officials to staff their civil service.

Daendels, Governor-General from 1801 to 1811, was a military man, a supporter and admirer of Napoleon, unconnected with the clique which, for the last twenty years, had run the Company's affairs at Batavia and done very nicely out of it. His willingness to ignore the advice of the old-timers was both his strength and his weakness. He was primarily concerned with the defence of the colony, blockaded by the British. One scheme which he pushed through, a highway from Banten to Pasuruan, cut the journey by road across Java from fourteen to six and a half days, but was built by forced labour, at tremendous cost in human lives.

Daendels reorganized the administration making the Regents salaried officials of the Dutch government. This reduced their power and prestige. He also provided a more adequate salary for Dutch officials but clamped down on the unauthorized additions to salaries which had become so widespread. This aroused considerable hostility. He also aroused bitter, if politely concealed, resentment among the Javanese nobility, not only because of his reduction of the Regents' prestige but also because, in his dealings with the *kraton,* he did not attempt to hide the realities of the power situation by deference, or even by common courtesy, to Javanese royalty. Instead, he appropriated to himself some of the traditional Javanese symbols of rule, such as the use of the golden umbrella of state, even though, as a Napoleonic revolutionary, he was anti-monarchist.

While the government coffers were still full, Daendels bought back many estates sold to private investors, but by the end of his four-year period he was forced to resort again to the sale of government domain land. His biggest sale was a million-dollar deal with a Chinese purchaser who bought the entire regency of Probolinggo in east Java. It was fortunate for the Javanese that his term of office ended before he had alienated too much of the land.

His reforms included a reorganization of the judicial system, providing separate judicial facilities for European, Chinese and Indonesian, thus accelerating the process of separation; and centralization of government control at Batavia. He achieved much by his ruthless, dynamic approach but made many enemies who by 1811 were strong enough to have him recalled. His successor arrived barely in time to hand over to the English who, in 1811, finally added Java to the other Dutch colonial possessions already under their control.

The English governor, Thomas Stamford Raffles, was quite young—only thirty—an ambitious and enthusiastic English East India Company official with a reforming zeal; an outspoken critic of his predecessors, and hence a controversial figure both to his contemporaries and to later historians. Where Daendels had little sympathy with the Javanese, declaring on one occasion that 'protection of the native labourer only encouraged him in his natural laziness, while it discouraged the western planter', Raffles had considerable interest in all aspects of Javanese life and a strong, if rather sentimental and theoretical, concern for the sufferings of the peasant.

Yet, despite the breadth of his sympathy in some fields, he was not particularly sensitive to the atmosphere of the *kraton*. His original commission was 'to leave the possession of these settlements to the occupation of the natives', but when the Sultan of Jogja, in 1812, saw an opportunity of throwing off the foreign yoke, Raffles wrote, 'I have no hesitation in saying that I think it a disgrace to our British nation to allow so barbarous a power to exist in its neighbourhood, if it possess the power to reduce it', whereupon, having defeated the Javanese, he allowed his men to sack the *kraton* 'to cover the expense of the undertaking'.

The arrival of the English was the signal for activity on the part of the Sultan of Palembang also. Raffles had had correspondence with him prior to the conquest of Java, urging him to drive out the Dutch. This he did before the English landed in

Java and so claimed that he had established the independence of his Sultanate. In the changed international atmosphere of 1945, a similar argument by the Indonesians caused the English troops to hesitate in their reinstatement of Dutch authority, but Raffles, despite the terms of his commission, did not hesitate. The Sultan was punished for following the advice given him and was forced to accept British sovereignty. Here Raffles was very much a man of his time.

Where Raffles was ahead of his time was in his realization that the Javanese peasant was not inherently lazy. As evidence he cited the labour involved, and spontaneously undertaken, in the establishment and maintenance of *sawah* cultivation. He recognized that, under the system of forced delivery, there was no incentive for the cultivator to do even the minimum required. He proposed a land rent to be paid in money rather than in kind and to be substituted for all compulsory services, contingencies and forced deliveries. It was to be assessed according to the productivity of the soil, half the yield of the most productive land, a quarter on the least, with an average estimated at about two-fifths. Although dues could be paid in rice rather than money, Raffles hoped that ultimately most payment would be in money, and that the cultivator, given the free disposal of the remainder of his crop, would be encouraged to expand his production.

Such a system really required an initial survey of the land to determine a just assessment of taxation but Raffles, desperately anxious to convince the British authorities that Java should be retained rather than returned to the Dutch, and increasingly short of finance, embarked on this new financial expedient before the survey was completed. Furthermore his financial difficulties meant that he could not, in the interim, afford to dispense with the forced delivery of coffee from the Priangan district, and so had to retain the system of which he was so critical.

Other reforms introduced by Raffles included an attempt to abolish slavery, the introduction of vaccination against smallpox, and the abolition of gaming houses and cockfighting, which, according to one commentator, helped to reduce the unhealthiness of Batavia by reducing the 'infectious and offensive smells of human carcases' drifting up and down the canals. Prior to this reform four or five Indonesians or Chinese a day might be murdered as a result of brawls over gambling debts and then flung into the canal, but since the introduction of the reform in 1812, there had been only one corpse fished up.

One of Raffles' most appealing characteristics was his

enthusiastic interest in the culture, natural history and antiquities of Java. At his instigation an expedition rediscovered Borobudur. During his stay in Batavia he revived the Batavian Society of Arts and Sciences. It was a tragedy for posterity that he lost all his papers, 122 cases of documents, maps, statistical reports, 'the cream and flower' of all his natural history collections, in the shipboard fire which nearly cost him his life, when returning to England from Bengkulu[9].

Raffles' land tax was retained by the Dutch who regained their colonies under the peace treaty of 1815, and from 1818 to 1829 it nearly doubled its returns. The forced delivery of coffee from the Priangan district was also retained. A law of 1820 defined the relationship between the Regent (Indonesian) and the Resident (Dutch) as follows: 'In matters concerning the government of the natives the regents are the confidential advisers of the resident, and he shall treat them as his younger brothers'.

When, just prior to Java's return to the Dutch, Raffles left to become governor of Bengkulu in Sumatra, he still cherished the dream of an English empire in the Indonesian islands, and despite the lack of encouragement from home, he proposed that one be based on the English settlement of Bengkulu. In spite of his urgings, the English, in the treaty of 1824, exchanged their Indonesian settlements for Dutch holdings in India, Malaya and Singapore. The spheres of influence of the two European powers were thus defined. The establishment of Singapore, largely through the energetic activity of Raffles, meant the final end of Dutch monopoly of trade in the area. During the nineteenth century, as the Dutch concentrated more on exploiting Java, the British in Singapore slipped into the role formerly held by the Srividjaya trading empire and its successors, rival to the land-based empire now concentrated in Batavia but increasingly involved in the exploitation of the ancient lands of Madjapahit.

INDONESIAN RESISTANCE TO THE DUTCH. 1816-38

Although the European powers may have settled between themselves to their own satisfaction their spheres of interest, the Indonesians, who had of course not been consulted on the matter,

---

[9] Although some Dutch writers find little to admire in Raffles who was, after all, their implacable opponent (notice, for example, the innuendoes in Vlekke's account, especially pp. 255-7), he seems to have been in many ways a most attractive person. For a further account of his life and career, see N. Epton, *The Golden Sword* (Oldbourne, N. D.). Some of you may also enjoy dipping into the *Memoirs of Sir T. S. Raffles*, particularly some of his letters to the Duchess of Somerset describing life in Indonesia, or Ch. XI, in which there is an account of his exploration of parts of Sumatra;

were unenthusiastic about such arrangements. The Sultan of Palembang, who had protested against the British presence, continued to protest against the Dutch return until 1824 when the area was placed under direct Dutch rule. There were disturbances in Ambon in 1817, in west Kalimantan in 1818 and in Sulawesi sporadic outbursts of hostility occurred at intervals throughout the nineteenth century. The two most prolonged struggles in the early nineteenth century were in west Sumatra and central Java. They demonstrate the nature of the opposition to and support for the Dutch at this time.

(a) *The Paderi War.* 1821-37

The Minangkabau district in the west Sumatran highlands behind the port of Padang was the seat of the ancient kingdom of Pagaruyung, about which little is known, although archaeological evidence suggests that a Hindu-Buddhist kingdom flourished there before Islam arrived some time between 1400-1500. King Adityawarman of Minangkabau spent his youth at the court of Madjapahit. Minangkabau is unusual because its *adat* or customary law is based on matrilineal descent. The inheritance passes not from father to son, but from mother to daughter. The country consists geographically of three districts, in each of which live members of four clans. In each village, where members of all four clans were likely to be represented, the members of a particular clan owed allegiance only to that clan's headman and the village government was in the hands of the four headmen. They and the village elders elected their district chiefs. The real power lay with the council of village chiefs.

When Raffles made his excursion from Padang to Minangkabau in 1818 he recorded, on arrival at the border, that 'as we had now entered the limits of the Tiga belas country [the Thirteen Confederate Towns] our further progress depended upon the goodwill of the chiefs, who are here entirely independent of European authority'. This goodwill, for a consideration, he received. He was impressed by the district's prosperity, describing the area as 'one sheet of cultivation . . . coffee, indigo, maize, sugar-cane and the oil-growing plants'[10] and *sawah* rice cultivation.

In one district he saw bamboo water-wheels used for irrigation and argued that, as neither Europeans nor Chinese had yet penetrated to the area, 'these wheels may be considered of native

hazardous expeditions in which he was accompanied by his wife Sophia (who modestly refers to herself, if need arises, as 'the Editor'). His breadth of sympathy, spirit of enthusiasm and strong sense of the ridiculous are all evident, despite a certain paternalism.

[10] Sophia Raffles, *Memoirs,* Vol. I (James Duncan, London, 1835) , p. 403.

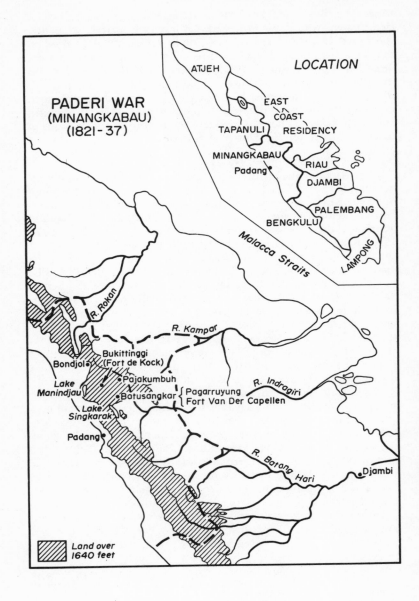

PADERI WAR
(MINANGKABAU)
(1821-37)

LOCATION

ATJEH

EAST
COAST
TAPANULI   RESIDENCY

MINANGKABAU
Padang   RIAU

DJAMBI

PALEMBANG

BENGKULU

LAMPONG

Malacca Straits

R. Rokan

R. Kampar

Bondjol

Bukittinggi
(Fort de Kock)

Pajakumbuh

Lake
Manindjau

Batusangkar

Pagarruyung
Fort Van Der Capellen

R. Indragiri

Lake
Singkarak

Padang

R. Batang Hari

Djambi

Land over
1640 feet

invention . . . I do not recollect to have seen anything of the kind in Java'. On the hillsides unsuited to *sawah* cultivation, sugar was growing and he commented on the 'very neatly constructed mills for expressing the juice, which is afterwards manufactured into a coarse sugar'.[11] These were turned by oxen and again, presumably, were of native invention. In his opinion the Pagaruyung district compared favourably with the plain of Mataram: 'This view equalled anything I ever saw in Java; the scenery is more majestic and grand, population equally dense, cultivation equally rich.'[12]

By the early nineteenth century, although the Pagaruyung royal family remained as titular rulers of Minangkabau, and were revered as such, in practice the council of district chiefs had power to override the authority of the paramount ruler, whose centralizing control was more symbolic than real. The aristocracy, with no real function in government, lived on wealth inherited from landed property, spending much time in cockfighting and gambling at the various villages. Young aristocrats, resplendent in gold-embroidered black, dark red or green velvet loose jacket over trousers; their headgear encrusted with gold; yellow scarf across one shoulder; and woven plaid with gold or silver thread around the waist, moved from village to village, each accompanied by several armed retainers, dressed in black. The latter looked after the fighting cocks and were also available to defend their young master should a brawl arise.

Although Minangkabau had been Moslem for at least two centuries by this time, Islamic teaching had been superimposed upon the old *adat* of the country without conflicting with it. Then, in 1803, three pilgrims returned from Mecca where they had been strongly influenced by the Arabian Wahabi reform movement. This movement sought to purify Islam by reforming society in the light of the original teachings of the Prophet. The three pilgrims, impressed by what they had seen in Arabia, were horrified at the vice, immorality and neglect of Islamic teachings which they saw everywhere in their homeland. They began a revivalist campaign. Moslem preachers moved among the villagers urging a purification of Minangkabau life, and condemning cockfighting, gambling, opium and tobacco smoking, betel chewing, the use of intoxicating drinks such as the popular palm wine, and ostentation in dress. Although condoned by *adat* these were not a necessary part of it. Their followers wore white robes and

[11] *Ibid.*, p. 418-9.
[12] *Ibid.*, p. 426.

turbans similar to those worn in Arabia, and were sometimes known as the White People, or the Paderi (after Pedir, the Islamic centre in Atjeh from which it was believed that Islam first spread to Minangkabau and a place still frequented by many Minangkabau students)[13]. In the name of the Prophet they called people to a new way of life, and found many followers, particularly among the general populace of humbler birth who did not have an inheritance large enough to squander on worldly pleasure.

Soon a group of reformers, known as the Eight Tigers, moved from preaching to more direct action. In some districts, in alliance with local chiefs, reforms were forcibly introduced. Those who indulged in forbidden vices or failed to pray five times a day were severely punished. Gradually the aristocracy began to see the movement as an attack on the *adat* itself. Some aspects of *adat*, particularly concerning the law of inheritance through the female line, were in conflict with Islamic law. Open conflict soon occurred between the rival groups, particularly as it became increasingly clear to the *adat* chiefs that the religious reformers were challenging their traditional political power and endeavouring to set up a form of theocracy, or religious government, in its place.

In 1819 Padang was returned to the Dutch. A few years later some *adat* leaders, having failed to defeat the Paderi, made a treaty with the Dutch, who were prepared, as in Java, to prop up the authority of the feudal nobility against the potentially unifying force of Islam. Raffles had commented that although the Paderi had 'proved themselves most unrelenting and tyrannical', yet 'their rule seems calculated to reform and improve inasmuch as it introduces something like authority, so much wanted over all Sumatra'.[14]

By the time the Dutch entered the scene, the Paderi headquarters were in the fortified city of Bondjol, where their leader, Tuanku Imam Bondjol, was able to hold out against the Dutch for another fifteen years. Dutch intervention drew together some sections of the *adat* in support of the religious leaders. Even after his surrender, guerrilla warfare continued in the mountainous terrain. The reformers had achieved much of what they had set out to do by revivifying Islam and making it an integral part of Minangkabau life, in fruitful tension with the *adat*. In the eyes of many Moslems, the *adat* rulers lost even more of their

[13] The Dutch called them Paderi, as a corruption of the Portuguese name for priest (padre), although Islam has no priesthood.
[14] Sophia Raffles, *op. cit.*, Vol. II, p. 84.

former prestige by allying themselves with the *kafir* (unbeliever) foreign rulers.

(b)   *The Java War.* 1825-30

In some ways the Paderi war was like the earlier Javanese wars which, by inviting Dutch intervention, allowing further Dutch extension of authority, and in one sense the Java War, led by Prince Diponegoro of Jogjakarta, was yet another war of succession of the old style. Yet both were more than this, because in both Islam became the symbol of opposition to the Dutch.

Although the elder son, Diponegoro was passed over for the succession to the throne of Jogjakarta by the Dutch, who gave their support to a younger claimant. Diponegoro came to regard himself not only as the rightful heir to the throne[15], but also as the protector of Islam. To the common people who flocked to his support, he was the *Ratu Adil*, the Just Prince, who would overthrow the foreign infidel. They could also express their resentment of the Chinese toll gatherers and money lenders who oppressed them.

Furthermore, just as Daendels and Raffles had failed to respect the rulers of the Javanese kingdoms, so their successors also infringed their rights. For example the Dutch policy was to reduce the number of private landholders and investors, but these people were able to lease land from the rulers of the native states. In 1821, the Governor-General forbade such leasing. In 1823 he insisted that all leases were null and void and the money paid for them was to be refunded. This was awkward for the regents because, of course, they had long since spent it. Such an enactment undermined the prestige of the rulers. Finally the Dutch built a road from Jogjakarta to Malang over a sacred tomb on land owned by Diponegoro. The purpose of the road was to provide quick access to Dutch troops in times of emergency, and this added further insult to injury. War flared up. The aristocracy of Jogjakarta joined Diponegoro but those of Solo stood aside. (In the long run this did not help them much because the Dutch later penalized them for failing to assist *them*.)

The war was a succession of guerrilla attacks and at first Diponegoro, with the countryside behind him, was victorious. Then the Dutch established a number of strongpoints linked by good roads on which flying columns operated. The expense was considerable but the plan was effective. In 1829 Diponegoro's

---

[15] Initially his claim was not strong because he was the son of a secondary wife.

two lieutenants, Kiyayi Madja and Sentot, surrendered. (One of them, Sentot, then assisted the Dutch to fight the Minangkabau.) In 1830 Diponegoro agreed to negotiate, but refused to give up his title of Sultan, or his claim to be protector of Islam; and so the Dutch closed the negotiations, despite their promise of safe conduct, by arresting Diponegoro and exiling him to Sulawesi.

Although Tuanku Imam Bondjol and Diponegoro were contemporaries fighting a common enemy, the struggle was not, as yet, a common struggle. Indirectly they aided each other by extending the Dutch commitments of arms and men, but this was unplanned. The forces opposing the Dutch were still not unified as is exemplified by Sentot's willingness to support the Dutch in Minangkabau. Yet in each case one potential source of unity was quite clear—the appeal to Islam. Both drew on religious as well as traditional support; both were opposed by fellow members of the aristocracy in alliance with the Dutch.

EXPLOITATION OF INDONESIA BY THE DUTCH GOVERNMENT. 1830-70

The cost of the Java and Paderi wars meant that, despite the increased returns from the land tax, Dutch finances were severely strained. The situation became more desperate when the Netherlands itself, after the loss of Belgium in 1830, faced bankruptcy. Government investment in Java *had* to yield quick returns. The new Governor-General, Johannes van den Bosch, fresh from experiences of the slave labour of the West Indies, was appointed to make the East Indies pay their way. He succeeded by introducing the Culture System.

The name 'Culture System' is not a good translation of the original Dutch, although it has become familiar in English writings. It might more accurately be called a Cultivation System: a System of Government Controlled Agriculture; or as Indonesian historians refer to it, *Tanam Paksa* (Compulsory Planting). These names give a better idea of the nature of the system, and the term 'Cultivation System' will be used in this book. In some ways it seems like a return to the old system of contingencies and forced cultivation, but it was envisaged as an attempt to teach the Javanese to exploit their land more efficiently—for the benefit of the government. The older system made its demands regardless of the ability of the peasant to fulfil them. In theory at least this new system took account of these aspects of cultivation and organized the actual production of the crops.

Instead of land rent, usually assessed at about two-fifths of the value of the crop, the Cultivation System proposed that a percentage of the peasant's land and labour should be at the government's disposal. On this land, set free by remission of land tax, export crops were to be grown under government contractors. According to the original plan, the labour spent on this cultivation should not exceed that required to produce rice from the same area. Where the crop exceeded the value of the land rent due under the old assessment the surplus should be paid to the villagers, but the government would bear the loss of any failure of the crop due to circumstances outside the cultivator's control. The products would be those suited for the European market. In the remainder of his time on the remainder of his land the cultivator could grow rice for his own consumption. So in theory the cultivator was to be free of land rent, and in return was to devote one-fifth of his time and one-fifth of his land to the cultivation of crops suitable for the overseas market.

In practice things did not work in quite that way. For a start most of the original safeguards were quickly dropped if they interfered with profits—as they usually did. The land required was sometimes as much as one-third or even a half of the total land. In some cases the new crops demanded more labour than the maximum allowed for, nor did the government actually bear the losses of bad harvests even when these were demonstrably due to the unsuitability of the land for the particular crops. Several unprofitable crops were cultivated for longer than if the government were bearing the loss instead of the cultivator. Often the Cultivation System was added to the land tax rather than replacing it.

This system was never applied to the whole population. By 1839 it applied to approximately 800,000 families in over half the districts under Dutch control. By 1845 it involved only 5.5 per cent of the total cleared land. Its impact was very uneven. Indigo proved particularly arduous to cultivate and many Javanese from indigo districts migrated to other areas. Sugar cultivation took twice the labour required by the ricefields subject to the old taxes. In some areas there was more than one culture. Furthermore no account was taken of variations in soil fertility when assessing the return expected.

Experiments were made with a variety of crops—tea, tobacco, pepper, cinnamon, cotton, cochineal, silk—but the three main profit-makers were coffee, sugar and indigo. Of these, coffee was grown on land unsuited for rice, but indigo and sugar displaced food crops. Where the market crop failed, the cultivator had no money to buy the rice which he would otherwise have cultivated on his land. (Cultivators received a small cash payment for surplus crops.) In Java in the 1840s there were severe famines in some areas because of the encroachment on ricelands.

When all this has been said about the Cultivation System it must be added that, in terms of the aims of the original planners, the system was extremely successful. They aimed at producing enough profit from Java to make the colony self-sufficient. The profits produced not only achieved this but also saved the Netherlands from bankruptcy and provided the Dutch with railways. That this gain was made by appropriating all available profits and making the cultivators bear all losses was irrelevant to those who still believed that a colony's one function was to benefit the mother country, and that the welfare of the indigenous people should not interfere with this.

The exploitation of the cultivator resembled and was an extension of the demands previously made on the peasants by their rulers, but there were two main differences. In the first place, *adat* provided limits to the exploitation by regents, but under this system the sanctions of *adat* had been replaced by the pressure on the regent as a government servant to ensure the best possible profits. In the second place, under the earlier system, the wealth was not being drained away to a foreign country but was being used in Java.

The Javanese peasant was also liable for various labour services, assisting with public works—fortifications, roads and bridges—and was expected to provide the customary hospitality expected by officials both Indonesian and Dutch, who lived off the country in their own establishments and when journeying.

It has been argued that the only crops which could produce a surplus were those sufficiently well suited to the country and to the overseas market to be productive despite the disadvantages of forced labour. As with the affairs of the V.O.C. there was considerable secrecy about the whole system in the Netherlands East Indies. Much patronage was still involved in appointments to the government service. Promotion depended on good returns, so reports were occasionally adjusted accordingly. Attempts were made to disguise the fact that some areas of Java were famine-stricken. The returns of export and import of rice to the various residencies in Java, where 'export from a Residency means prosperity; import into it means want', when examined and compared, showed 'that rice is so abundant everywhere that all the Residencies combined export more rice than all the Residencies combined import. Here there is no question of export overseas, for which a separate statement is rendered. The conclusion of all this is therefore the absurd thesis that there is more rice in Java than there is. That's prosperity, if you like!'[16] Such secrecy was also designed to prevent other colonial powers from imitating and thus benefiting from Dutch methods, so it was difficult for individuals, even those who felt strongly about the exploitation of indigenous people, to do anything to ameliorate the hardships of the system.

The quotation above comes from a book first published in 1860, and entitled *Max Havelaar or The Coffee Auctions of the Dutch Trading Company,* written under the pen name of Multatuli ('he who has suffered much'). The author, Douwes Dekker, a former Dutch employee in Indonesia, violently attacked the abuses of the system. He wrote:

> If anyone shold ask whether the man who grows the products receives a reward proportionate to the yields, the answer must be in the negative. The Government compels him to grow on *his* land what pleases *it*; it punishes him when he sells the crop so produced to anyone else but *it*; and *it* fixes the price it pays him. The cost of transport to Europe, via a privileged trading company, is high. The money given to the Chiefs to encourage them swells the purchase price further and since after all, the entire business must yield a profit, this profit can be made in no other way than by paying the Javanese just *enough* to keep him from starving, which would decrease the producing power of the nation.[17]

Max Havelaar was as much an attack on the Dutch complacency which made the abuses of the system possible as on the system itself. 'For it is a fact that very few Europeans think it worth their trouble to stoop and observe the emotions of those coffee- and sugar-producing machines we call "natives".' It was not the only criticism being voiced but it was a powerful satire with considerable impact. Ironically enough it was taken up by the advocates of private enterprise who wanted the abolition of the Cultivation System, where Douwes Dekker wanted its retention and reform.[18]

Until 1848 the Netherlands' colonies were under direct crown

[16] Multatuli, *Max Havelaar* (Heinemann and Sijthoff, 1967), pp. 211-4.
[17] *Max Havelaar* besides being powerful propaganda for the Liberals, is also a powerful novel in its own right. For an English translation, see Multatuli, *Max Havelaar* (Heinemann and Sijthoff, London, 1967).
[18] *Ibid*, p. 73.

control but, after the 1848 revolution in the Netherlands, they came under the Dutch States General. In the following ten years, efforts were made to correct the worst abuses of the system, but few people in the Netherlands apart from those directly connected with the colonies knew or cared very much about what went on in them. Enough for them that their railways were provided and paid for and that the country was solvent. The Liberals within Parliament attempted to reform the system, retaining the profits but ameliorating the conditions of those who provided them. The Liberals were also committed to the minimum of government interference in economic enterprises and so were opposed to the system of government-controlled agriculture practised in Indonesia. In the 1860s the Liberals were powerful enough to introduce changes based upon the principles of free trade.

EXPLOITATION OF INDONESIA BY PRIVATE INVESTORS. 1870-1900

The Dutch Liberals had two conflicting aims: to make the Indies safe for the individual capitalist, and to free Indonesians from oppression. It was possible, they believed, to achieve both these aims by abolishing the government monopoly of agriculture. This was done progressively throughout the 1860s, primarily with those crops which were no longer profitable to the government anyway. In 1870 legislation was passed by which sugar cultivation would be relinquished over a twelve year period beginning in 1878, but the most profitable crop, coffee, was retained until 1917. In place of forced cultivation the field was, at the same time, opened to private Dutch enterprise.

In 1870 the Agrarian Law was passed. It prohibited the sale to non-Indonesians of land owned or used by Indonesians. All other land was declared to be government domain which could be leased for up to 75 years. Land could be hired from Indonesian owners for shorter terms of five to twenty years. Dutch investors could thus acquire the use of land, but the rights of Indonesians were protected.

In 1880 the Labour Ordinance regulated foreign employment of local labour, providing labour for the investor while protecting the labourer. There were punishments for either party if the contract system introduced were broken. The labourer could neither desert the job nor be dismissed before his contract expired. Government officials were to register contracts to ensure that the labourer understood his contract's implications, and it was the employer's responsibility to repatriate him at the contract's expiry. In practice these clauses were more valuable to employers than to employees. The labourer could no longer escape by moving when conditions became intolerable. The investors were supplied with labour but many villagers became day labourers on European-owned plantations and on returning to the village at the conclusion of the contract they no longer fitted into the traditional village life. Many were taken from Java to plantations on the east coast of Sumatra, where local labour was lacking, and where the local people were not prepared to work as coolies.

Yet this legislation, while providing private investors with access to land and labour, did limit their activities in the interests of the Indonesians. Despite these limitations Indonesia, during the remainder of the nineteenth century, continued to attract an increasing amount of private capital investment and Dutch immigration to Indonesia increased by about 1,000 per annum from the 1870s onward. New crops were introduced with greater financial success than under the Cultivation System—tea and tobacco, kapok, copra (from the coconut palm), palm oil and cocoa. In 1883 the first rubber trees were planted and by the turn of the century investment was being made in the oilfields of south Sumatra and Kalimantan, reflecting a response to the new industrial demands of the European market.

Netherlands capital investment, and the general prosperity of the colony were increased by the opening of the Suez Canal in 1869. The shorter route lowered transport costs, which in turn increased the market for tropical goods in Europe. The introduction of steamships cut travelling time further and caused increased European interest in the search for coal or iron in Indonesia. Europe's industrial products found a growing market in Indonesia mainly among newly arrived Europeans. From 1870 to 1890 Indonesian exports doubled and imports quadrupled. Railways were built to serve the needs of private investors. This was Europe's golden age of imperialism. In Indonesia exploitation was no longer limited to Java, but plantations were also beginning in the Outer Islands where the soil was suited to the production of raw materials needed by European industry.

Linked with the same movement of expanding European imperialism, missionary activity extended to Indonesia. In Manado, north Sulawesi, by 1890 almost all Manadonese were Christians. In Sumatra the German Rheinish Mission turned the Bataks from cannibals to Christians and gave the Dutch a pretext to extend their protection to the area. Both these areas had previously been animist. Christian missions made little impact upon strongly Moslem areas, or upon Hindu Bali.

INDONESIAN RESISTANCE TO THE DUTCH. 1870-1908

Dutch expansion was not achieved without strong opposition from the inhabitants of the Outer Islands. Dutch expansion in Sumatra brought them into open conflict with Atjeh, while to the east they subdued both Lombok and Bali with difficulty.

(a) *The Atjeh War*. 1873-1908

Atjeh's independence had been guaranteed by the 1824 Treaty of London to which England and the Netherlands were signatories. The same treaty had given the Dutch the task of controlling piracy[19] in the surrounding areas. For about thirty years Atjeh's sovereignty was respected, then in 1858 the Dutch entered into a treaty with the Sultan of Siak, giving them access to Sumatra's east coast. Atjeh regarded this as her territory, so she increased her attacks on Dutch ships in the area and in 1869 the Sultan of Atjeh, who had kept close connections with the Moslem countries of west Asia, sought an alliance with Turkey, who was unable to help. When the Dutch learnt of Atjehnese negotiations in Singapore with the Italian and U.S. Consuls they attempted to reach some agreement with the Sultan themselves. He refused to reveal the details of his other negotiations, which indeed, as a sovereign power, was his right. The Dutch then entered into an alliance with the British, the Treaty of Sumatra (1872), in which they were given freedom to act against Atjeh in return for concessions to the British.

In 1873 the Dutch attacked Atjeh. With the opening of the Suez Canal the Straits of Malacca were the Dutch trade route to south-east Asia instead of the Sunda Straits, which made the control of Atjeh a matter of strategic importance to the Dutch as well as to the British. In their first assault the Dutch captured the Sultan's palace, and shortly after that the Sultan died. The Dutch then offered to his successor a guarantee of autonomy in internal affairs in return for accepting Dutch sovereignty. What they did not realize was that the Sultan was elected by the district rulers (*panglima*), each of whom was sovereign in his own district, while the Sultan was responsible for external relations. To accept these terms would have left him powerless. To the surprise of the Dutch, the capture of the Sultan and his palace did not, as in Java, lead to the end of the struggle. The war

[19] See pp. 103-4, above.

continued, led by local district rulers and by religious leaders, who saw it as a holy war against the infidel.

The Dutch fluctuated between a soft and hard line but guerrilla warfare continued. In 1885 they tried linking up strongpoints by a railway from the east to the west coast encircling the capital, Kutaradja, but this railway proved vulnerable to sabotage. From 1891 to 1893 the Islamic expert, C. Snouck Hurgronje, made a close study of the Atjehnese. He had already visited the Holy City, Mecca, barred to non-believers. He posed as a Moslem convert[20] and discovered considerable communities of Indonesian pilgrims closely in touch with events in Atjeh and anxious for the victory of Islam over the infidel Dutch.

On his advice Dutch policy then aimed at winning over a powerful chief, supplying him with ammunition, and leaving him to win the war for them. The powerful chief whom they won over was Teuku Umar. On his part he realized that the Atjehnese forces were weak because they lacked sophisticated arms and troops. In Dutch pay and provided with arms he conquered several districts and then, in 1896, renounced his temporary alliance with the Dutch to lead the Atjehnese forces again. By 1899, when Teuku Umar was killed in ambush by the Dutch, they had managed, despite the continued guerrilla activity of the entire population, to dominate Atjeh proper, and to drive a wedge between the political and religious leaders, by supporting the former.

In 1898 the Short Declaration was introduced, whereby a ruler recognized his district as part of the Netherlands East Indies, and promised to have no connection with other foreign powers and to follow orders given by the Dutch government. In this way, and with the support of Dutch-led troops from Timor, Ambon, Menado and Java, the Dutch were able to end the Atjeh war. Nevertheless resistance continued until 1903, although till 1918 Atjeh, though part of the Netherlands East Indies, was of necessity ruled by martial law.

From 1877 onward the expense of this war absorbed the surplus profits made by the government in Indonesia. Although the Dutch finally conquered the area by dividing the *adat* chiefs from the Moslem leaders, as in both Java and Minangkabau, the difference this time was that it was a deliberate policy. Only then did the Dutch superior military and technological advantages give them final victory.

[20] Many Moslems resented the deception which had made such a visit possible.

(b) *Lombok and Bali*

To the east of Java the islands of Bali and Lombok had remained independent until the mid-nineteenth century, when the Dutch secured a foothold in north Bali. Although the treaty included a Dutch promise to refrain from interfering in Balinese internal affairs the same pattern of intervention in local struggles was followed as in Java.

In Lombok the Radjas were Hindus from Bali. The Dutch pretext for intervention was the protection of the Moslem majority from its Hindu rulers. Also, the Radja had annoyed the Dutch in 1894 by sending two merchant ships, flying the Lombok flag, to Singapore to trade. These the Dutch had plundered.

The Dutch action against Lombok resulted in the discovery of the manuscript of the *Nagarakertagama*[21] by a Dutch language expert, Brandes, serving with the Dutch army. This and other emblems of sovereignty were plundered and taken to Batavia. At the same time the invasion led to the destruction of a great number of other *lontar*-leaf manuscripts used by Dutch soldiers

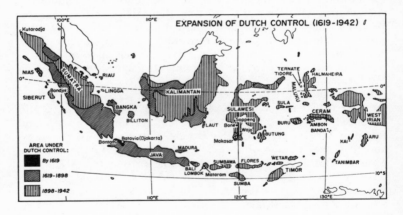

who were not language experts, but who wanted kindling to warm themselves during a tropical downpour. The Moslem majority exchanged Hindu Balinese domination for domination from Batavia.

From Lombok the Dutch moved to Bali. The actual occasion of the Dutch intervention was the same as previously. According to Balinese law a grounded ship became the Radja's property.

[21] See p. 47, above.

Dutch intervention in 1846 occurred because this right had been exercised against a Dutch ship. In 1906 the Radja confiscated a Chinese ship. This the Dutch used as a pretext for intervention. The fighting was fierce, the Balinese ruler and his nobles preferring annihilation to surrender. When the capital, Den Pasar, fell, the local Radja, with his family and followers, dressed in their courtly regalia and each armed with a *kris* advanced to certain death. When the Radja was shot dead, his wives stabbed themselves. The rest of the court, as true Hindu warriors, marched on to inevitable massacre. In 1908 the Radja of Klungkung, the last independent Radja, his family and followers also suffered the same fate. In Bali, still ruled by a Hindu god-king, as in Madjapahit, it was impossible to separate *adat* from religious leaders, although fostering local rivalries served the Dutch as well as it had done in Java.

Although Dutch domination of Java may be said to date from the conclusion of the Java War in 1830, Dutch control of the Outer Islands was not firmly established until the First World War. And this process was accomplished in a very short time. The Paderi War strengthened Dutch power in west Sumatra, the Java War led to the intensification of Dutch administration in Java itself. But for most of the Outer Islands the firm imposition of Dutch control took place after the Agrarian Law of 1870. The massive introduction of Dutch capital went hand in hand with the spread of Dutch territorial control, so that one might almost say that the Netherlands East Indies was created as a single colony between 1870 and 1914. However, by then the forces had already been set in motion which were to undermine and finally overthrow the Dutch colonial empire.

CHAPTER SEVEN

The Ethical Policy
and Twentieth Century
Indonesian Society

'But how glorious is the aim that we pursue! It is: the foundation
out there in the Far East of a social entity which is indebted to
the Netherlands for its prosperity and higher culture and thankfully recognises this fact.' C. T. van Deventer thus expressed the
essence of the new thinking about colonies and colonial relationships becoming current in the early years of the twentieth
century.[1]

When the first Dutch merchants arrived in Indonesia and
established their trading posts, some of the people with whom
they came into contact may have been from less developed
cultures, but many were representatives of cultures as high if not
higher than that of seventeenth century Holland. When, later
in the century, the Dutch came into contact and conflict with the
rulers of Mataram, these rulers and their nobility came from a
much older cultural tradition than did the Dutch, nor were the
Dutch merchants among the highest class of their own society.
Their political ascendancy was won by the superiority of their
weapons and they used this ascendancy, with the assistance of
the traditional structure of government, to exploit the produce
of Java for the benefit of their home country, the Netherlands.

Indonesia's wealth contributed, during the next two centuries,
to the industrialization of the Netherlands, while the Dutch
exploitation of Java arrested any political or economic development which might otherwise have occurred there. Large areas of

---

[1] C. T. van Deventer practised law in the Indies in the late nineteenth
century. He then returned to the Netherlands and in 1905 entered the
States General as a Liberal Democrat. Before then he had established his
reputation as a critic of some aspects of Dutch colonial policy.

Java became one vast plantation whose products, cultivated by Javanese peasants and collected by Chinese middlemen, were sold on the overseas market by European merchants. Initially this was seen as a lifeline which would save the Netherlands after the loss (in 1830) of the more highly industrialized area in the south, modern Belgium, but ultimately the capital derived from the Cultivation System not only saved the financial situation for the Dutch but financed the development of industrialization in the north. During this period, while Javanese economic development remained static and indeed—because of the suppression of the former trade along the north coast ports—even regressed, the Dutch economic system diversified and expanded. The gap between the two increased.

The capital accumulated through industrialization led, as we have seen, to Liberal demands that private capital should participate in the exploitation of the Indies, and by the late nineteenth century this led to closer penetration of the Javanese economy by planters, sugar planters in particular, and the opening up of new areas in the Outer Islands, especially on the east coast of Sumatra. Sumatra and Kalimantan were providing the raw materials needed by the new industries of Europe. Rubber, oil and tin replaced the more exotic exports which used to come from Sumatra.

As the planters opened up these new areas they demanded the extension of Dutch government to protect and support them. For example, the planters wanted Dutch influence to be extended to the Batak lands around the east coast plantations because, while these remained independent villages, they could provide hiding places for absconding contract labourers or fleeing Atjehnese rebels, while if rival Batak tribes were to be allowed to continue fighting among themselves the lowlands tobacco estates might be damaged. German missionary activity also gave grounds for the extension of government.

By the early twentieth century, apart from the introduction of new crops by the Dutch for the Dutch export market, the economic life of the Javanese had advanced very little from that of his forefathers when the first Europeans arrived, except that a tremendous growth of population depressed still further his already borderline standard of living. Dutch economic life and material standards, however, had changed considerably.

It could be argued that the Netherlands was indebted to its colonies in the Far East for Dutch prosperity and higher culture. Van Deventer himself, in a very important article, expressed a similar view when he spoke of a 'debt of honour' owed by the

Netherlands to the Indies. He argued that the 140 million guilders which had been transferred to the Netherlands since 1867 belonged by moral right to the Indies. From 1877 onwards the annual surplus transferred to the Dutch treasury had become a deficit and van Deventer argued that, as the Indies had helped the Netherlands in its time of financial need, the Netherlands should now repay some of this annual surplus to help the Indies, which by the end of the century, was increasingly in debt.

Although it was decided to separate the finances of the Indies and the Netherlands after 1901, a move advantageous to the Netherlands once the Indies had an annual deficit, little attempt was made to repay the 'honour debt'. The Netherlands did cancel the payment of a 40-million-guilder loan to the Indies government. However the 'debt of honour', although not accepted by the government, affected the thinking of those who, like van Deventer, supported the Ethical Policy of the early twentieth century, a small group of influential people, known collectively as the Ethici.

THE ETHICAL POLICY

At the turn of the century considerable and growing interest in colonial affairs was expressed in the Dutch parliament. Two groups had a particular interest in such matters, those who had a humanitarian concern with reports of the decreasing welfare of the Indonesian people, and those who, for financial reasons, were concerned with the need for wider markets for consumer goods and so were interested in raising the purchasing power of the people of Indonesia. The former, the Ethici, outlined the proposals for improved welfare; the latter agreed when such proposals seemed to suit their economic interests. In practice, as often happens, the good intentions of the idealists were only carried out insofar as they did not conflict with the more practical interests of the planters and businessmen in the Indies. We should thus distinguish between the Ethical policy as it was planned and the policy as it was actually put into execution.

Van Deventer, whose article, 'A Debt of Honour' (1899), had contributed to the change of policy, was a liberal of the Multatuli school. He saw the need to protect the rights of the Indonesians and to promote their moral and material welfare. He was supported by van Kol, the leader of the Socialist party. Both were concerned with reports of declining welfare in the Indies. In the 1890s disease had threatened both the sugar and coffee crops. Prices for tropical products had fallen. In 1900-1 there was a crop failure.

In 1901, in her speech from the throne, the Dutch Queen said: 'As a Christian Power the Netherlands is obligated in the East Indian archipelago to . . . imbue the whole conduct of government with the consciousness that the Netherlands has a moral duty to fulfil with respect to the people of these regions. In connection with this the diminished welfare of the population of Java merits special attention. I desire to institute an investigation into the causes of this.' In the same year, Idenberg, Minister for the Colonies and one of the Ethici, outlined his colonial policy: 'Not an increase in our possessions, an increase in our power, an increase in our honour, an increase in our capital is the aim of colonial possession, but the advancement of the Native population . . . the moral mission of a more advanced people towards less advanced nations who are not of a lesser species than the Western peoples, but who constitute with them the single organism of humanity.'

This welfare policy was seen in the context of continuing colonialism. Those who looked far enough ahead to wonder what might happen when welfare had indeed been increased certainly did not envisage an independent Indonesia. Yet, as one of the strange ironies of history, although nationalism might have developed even without the Ethical Policy, it was during this period, and largely as a result of many new forces set in motion by the welfare policies of the Ethici, that Indonesian nationalist aspirations first began to take shape.

The Ethical Policy, then, aimed at improved welfare for the people of Indonesia, approaching this task with a strong sense of mission. It sought to extend to the Indies the prosperity and higher culture of the Netherlands, and expected, as its reward, the thankful gratitude of those to whom these advantages had been extended. Young men were recruited to the Colonial Service with a high sense of purpose. The opening of the new century saw the commencement of an attempt at a vast piece of social engineering in the interests of a people unable to help themselves.

FIELDS OF ACTIVITY

The new policy was to be implemented in several fields. Foremost in van Deventer's thinking were irrigation, emigration and education but there were also plans for improved communications, improved credit facilities for Indonesians, the provision of agricultural advice, the extension of health programmes and proposals for the industrialization and protection of native industry and the decentralization of authority, both by transferring greater autonomy from the Netherlands to the Indies, and, within the Indies, by giving wider powers to local government units.

Some of these policies were more rapidly implemented than others. They were those which had the backing of planters and businessmen less because of their benefit to the indigenous people than because they also added to the welfare of the European population. For example the Ethical policy advocated the extension of irrigation works in order to make more land available for the cultivation of rice to feed the growing population of Java. The sugar planters supported this because, in so doing, it made more land available for the cultivation of sugar, a crop grown on part of the village ricefield leased to the planter.

Emigration, the transmigration from overpopulated Java to the underpopulated Outer Islands, particularly the east coast of Sumatra, was supported by the Deli tobacco planters (from around the city of Medan) as they began to change from the use of contract labour, repatriated at the end of the contract, to free labour. The Ethical policy aimed at reducing population pressure in Java; the tobacco planters supported it because it provided more labour in an area where labour was in short supply and where the local inhabitants were economically well enough off and of sufficiently independent spirit to be unwilling to serve as plantation coolies.

The planters also demanded improved communications which were supplied initially for their benefit, although the local inhabitants benefited too, as the Ethici hoped they would. For example the opening up of roads in the east coast residency of Sumatra, although sited to benefit the tobacco plantations, meant that Batak farmers in the hill country above the tobacco plains could profitably grow vegetables and transport them to market at Medan or even export them to Singapore. Whereas previously they had been limited by the need to use manpower rather than wheeled vehicles to bring their produce to market, now they could transport larger amounts in a shorter time. Yet Furnivall records that 'zealous officers pushed on road building with such energy that the burdens imposed on the people led to serious outbreaks which had to be suppressed by force'.[2]

This is a reminder that, although we talk of the Cultivation System being replaced by the Liberal era, it was a gradual process. Government sugar cultivation continued until 1890 and government coffee cultivation continued until 1917, just as the exploitation of resources by private planters, and increasingly by large

[2] J. S. Furnivall, *Netherlands India* (Cambridge University Press, London, 1967), p. 330.

monopolistic concerns, continued to the end of the colonial period—and beyond. Forced labour on the roads also continued; and then we perhaps find ourselves asking whose welfare is to be considered more important—that of the roadbuilders or that of the prospective road users?

Extended health facilities clearly had a humanitarian side, but also had a practical appeal to planters, especially those on the east coast of Sumatra and other Outer Island areas where labour was in short supply. A supporter of Dutch colonialism commented that the planters of the east coast proved 'that proper medical care of the workers was neither altruism nor luxury' but 'that only healthy people are capable of efficient work'. Planters therefore encouraged the extension of health facilities and of medical education to Indonesians. Indonesian doctors could be paid a lower salary than any European doctor would accept. Preventive medicine, particularly when aimed at such scourges as smallpox, cholera and bubonic plague, benefited the Indonesians but also reduced the danger of such diseases spreading to Europeans.

One method of preventing plague was to use tiles rather than palm matting as roofing material, because plague-carrying rats used to nest in the palm-thatched roofs. This illustrates another aspect of the welfare policy. It requires a certain level of sophistication to realize that disease is spread by infection and that rats are carriers of bubonic plague. Tiled roofs were more expensive. The peasant had to be encouraged by 'gentle pressure' to change from an inexpensive and traditional form of roofing to a more expensive one. To him it was just one more demand made on him by the government. He felt little gratitude for what was being forced upon him.

The intensified exploitation of the soil by private planters caused an extension of the use of money as a medium of exchange. This process had began under Raffles with the institution of the land rent; although, under the Cultivation System and even later, it was still by no means universal. Through it the Chinese middleman was able to extend his power, by acting as moneylender. Advocates of the Ethical Policy saw the need to reduce the power of the Chinese over the Indonesian villager, by providing credit on better terms than did the Chinese. A People's Credit System was established.

At the village level this consisted of the encouragement of village grain sheds, an indigenous development, where credit was given in kind to tide a cultivator over from one harvest to the next. This helped stabilize rice prices. Village banks, with capital borrowed from a district bank, provided small loans at the local level, while district or regency banks were designed to

lend money to Indonesian associations, thus aiding the development of an indigenous middle class. Like the rice bank or village
grain shed, the village bank developed from an already existing
institution to which the government gave its backing. The district bank, which did not, had little success in its immediate aim.
Such banks were mainly important in providing openings for the
newly educated class of Indonesians who staffed them.

Another extension of credit facilities was the government
monopoly of the pawnshops previously operated by the Chinese,
often along with the sale of opium, for which they had a monopoly. Both pawnshops and opium sales were taken over by the
government, the latter to control and ultimately reduce its use,
the former to overcome Chinese exploitation. The pawnshops
were again important in providing occupations for Indonesians
with some western education. As credit institutions they had two
drawbacks. Firstly, only 500 were established for the whole of
Indonesia. For many peasants, the nearest pawnship was too far
away to be of use. Secondly their interest rates were often little
lower than those of the Chinese, so peasants sought loans through
the old, familiar channels of finance rather than the new,
unfamiliar, bureaucratic government channels. Initially introduced as a welfare measure, they were increasingly seen as a
potential source of revenue, so that interest charged on goods
was not reduced. They were used by Indonesians in cities more
than by peasants.

As instructive as the reforms implemented are those advocated
by the Ethici but not implemented. One was industrialization.
It was never seriously envisaged that Indonesia would compete
with European industrial development, nor were the Netherlands' industrialists anxious to see any industrial development
in the Indies, which they wanted to retain as a market for their
own mass-produced goods. They argued that industrialization
would not use enough labour, and that if Indonesia became
self-sufficient in industrial products this might affect her export
of primary products, because she would import less overseas
goods. Overseas markets might therefore retaliate by buying less
of her produce. The most the Ethici could achieve was some
stimulation of handicrafts and cottage industry.

Decentralization of government, the delegation of power by
the Netherlands to government in the Indies, and by the Indies
government at Batavia to the regions was also advocated.
Although in 1918 a *Volksraad* (People's Council) partly elected,
partly nominated, was established in the Indies, it was given no

real power except that of criticism. Nor did the plan for decentralization within Indonesia proceed very far. Instead, the government officials centred at Batavia penetrated further and further into village life. The various health campaigns, the extension of communications, the establishment, in 1905, of an Agricultural Advice Bureau, all involved greater contact between villager and government officials. These officials usually preferred efficiency to co-operation where both were not possible. One of the most common criticisms made by overseas visitors was that the Dutch welfare policy was too paternalistic and too interfering.

The Dutch regarded the villagers as children whom they sought to help. They gave them what they felt that they ought to want, whether they wanted it or not. They believed that they had the right to impose their will on their village subjects thinking not of the liberty of the individual, but only of his welfare. 'Let me help you, let me show you how to do it, *let me do it for you*'[3] is one writer's graphic description of their attitude. This excessive interference turned the villager against Dutch rule which, in previous years, had not impinged so directly upon him.

The Agricultural Information Service established in 1905 did little good until the Dutch realized that, before offering information and advice, they needed to study the agricultural methods actually used to find out what improvements were practicable under existing conditions. This problem arose in other specialist services when men were appointed on the basis of their professional knowledge alone, without being required to study the society in which they would be working.

The Ethici and the Spread of Western Education

We have not yet considered the third of van Deventer's trio—education. It deserves separate consideration because its results were the least predictable and the most far-reaching of any of the Ethici proposals. Along with most Liberals and Socialists of the time they saw education as an instrument of modernization and social advancement, and advocated its extension to disseminate their 'higher culture', particularly among the aristocracy through whom their rule was exercised. By 'education' they meant 'western education'.

By the late nineteenth century there were quite good elementary educational facilities available for Dutch children living in the Indies, but it was still exceptional for any Indonesian children, except a handful from the very highest class or some Indo-

[3] Furnivall, *op. cit.*, p. 389.

nesian Christians, to be admitted to Dutch schools. Traditional
culture was transmitted not through formal schooling but, for
the aristocracy, by participation in the life of the *kraton* or
through the regent's family life. Through *wayang* performances,
traditional literature and ethical concepts were passed on to the
younger generation. Arts such as *kris*-making, wood carving or
silver-work were passed from father to son; *batik*-making, weaving and household management from mother to daughter. In the
village the traditional culture, reflecting that of the aristocracy,
but yet distinct from it, was also passed down without formal
schooling. The same was true of *adat*, folk tales and legends in
other parts of Indonesia.

Islamic schools, found particularly although not exclusively in
Sumatra, taught Islamic doctrine and sufficient Arabic for students to recite the Koran. The humblest schools seldom took
their pupils far enough to understand what they recited, but the
bigger schools gave an extensive theological training. Some Indonesians who made the pilgrimage to Mecca stayed on to study
advanced Theology and Arabic. There, as had the *Paderi* a
century earlier, they came into contact with Islamic reform, now
stressing the modernizing of Islam to enable Islamic nations to
come to terms with the modern world. On their return they
revived the Sumatran Islamic school system, introducing reformed methods of study. They were opposed to the other-
worldly emphasis of older Islamic teaching, its belief 'that this
world was meant to be the infidel's paradise, and that the faithful would only attain their heaven in the after life'; but they
were also opposed to Western teaching divorced from an Islamic
religious context. In 1912 the Reformist society, *Muhammadiyah*,
was formed in Java where it concentrated on social and educational work.

Snouck Hurgronje, the Islamic expert, head of the Department
of Native Affairs from 1889 to 1906, was one of the earliest
advocates of extended Western education as an instrument of
modernization and a counter to the influence of Islam. He himself sponsored, among others, the education of two sons of the
aristocratic family of Djajadiningrat from Banten. At least one
of the boys, in order to be admitted to a Dutch school, had to
be passed off as Eurasian, taking the name Willem van Banten.

Hurgronje hoped that in central and east Java, where the
aristocratic class from whom the regents were drawn, the *priyayi*,
were more strongly influenced by the traditional Javanese *adat*
than by Islam, the introduction of Western education might
influence them to lead in modernizing society along Western

lines. This was an extension of the policy he had advocated as a means of concluding the Atjeh war, dividing the *adat* leaders, themselves Moslem, from the Moslem religious leaders, and allying them instead with the Dutch government.

WESTERN EDUCATION AND THE JAVANESE ELITE: RADEN ADJENG[4] KARTINI

Initially many regents were suspicious of the Western education offered to them. Many Javanese regents preferred to act as if the Dutch did not exist, ignoring the distasteful fact that their authority depended on Dutch rule rather than on the power of the Sultan or Sunan. Others were more forward-looking. One of the earliest to unlatch his door to Western civilization was the Regent of Demak, who, during the 1860s, employed a Dutch tutor for his sons. (Later this tutor became editor of *De Loco-motief,* a Dutch newspaper published in Java and a strong advocate of the Ethical Policy.)

The sons of the Regent of Demak, in their turn, provided western education for their own children, and at least one of them, the Regent of Djapara, went even further by allowing his daughters as well as his sons to attend the Dutch elementary school in Djapara, just across the road from his residence. Some of the more conservative regents saw this as a great crime against the customs of the land. An unmarried girl of the aristocratic class should remain at home until a marriage was arranged for her by her parents and she left as the bride of a man unknown to her. The Regent of Djapara was only prepared to deviate from custom until the girls turned twelve, after which they were to be kept at home in the customary fashion. In any case the nearest secondary school was at Semarang, many miles away.

The second daughter, Kartini, within those six years of school-ing, found that her Western education had undermined the hold of custom. She regarded her years at home as 'imprisonment', she resolved never, never to marry an unwelcome and unknown bridegroom, and she survived the time 'in the box' only by the voracious reading of as many books as she could lay her hands upon and by corresponding with Dutch friends. To one of them she commented, with considerable insight, that 'Father could not foresee that the same bringing up which he gave to all of his children would have had such an effect upon one of them. Many other regents had given to their families the same advantages that we have had, and it has never resulted in anything but in

---

[4] Raden Adjeng is a title for an unmarried aristocratic Javanese woman.

native young ladies with European manners, who speak Dutch.'[5]

The effect upon Kartini was to make her query the 'burden of Javanese etiquette' which she found both 'silly and terrible', and to oppose the polygamy permitted under Islamic law, but a heavy burden upon women whose husbands took more than one wife. She criticized very frankly to her Dutch friends the type of behaviour among Europeans in a colonial society which caused bitterness and resentment among its subject members. 'I love the Hollanders very, very much,' she wrote, 'and I am grateful for everything that we have gained through them. Many of them are among our best friends, but there are also others who dislike us, for no other reason than we are bold enough to emulate them in education and culture.'[6] Such criticism, in the past, was unlikely to be openly expressed.

Her letters, which have been collected and published, reveal much about life in Java in the early twentieth century. Here, for the first time, we meet an Indonesian, young, sensitive and intelligent, who had caught, above all, the sense of mission which inspired the Ethici and wished to contribute to the uplifting of her fellow Javanese and to the bridging of the gap between the European and the Javanese worlds.[7]

Kartini was born in 1879 and her period of 'imprisonment' lasted until her sixteenth year, when the pleading of Dutch friends, combined with her own, persuaded her father to allow her, although still unmarried, to visit Batavia in the company of the Abendanons. J. H. Abendanon, a leader of the Ethici, and Director of Education in the Indies from 1900 to 1904, encouraged her plans to open a school for the daughters of regents, while her Dutch penfriend, Stella, encouraged her plans to study in Holland. Through Stella she came to the notice of the Socialist leader, H. H. van Kol, who attempted through the Dutch Parliament to obtain a government grant to enable her to study in Holland. Instead, having finally won her father's most reluctant consent, she decided to heed the warning of

[5] Kartini, *Letters of a Javanese Princess*, p. 41.
[6] Kartini, p. 61.
[7] The English edition of her letters, entitled *Letters of a Javanese Princess*, is available in a Norton Library paperback (1964). You may already have read Kartini's description of her sister's wedding in L. Mitchell, *Pacific Picture*. Many of you would enjoy the other letters with their descriptions of life in a Javanese regent's household, and their outline of plans for Kartini's own future as a pioneer, 'to clear the way which leads to freedom and independence for the native woman'. At the same time you can learn a lot about life in Indonesia in the early years of this century. Professor A. H. Johns has called her 'perhaps the first real Indonesian intellectual in the modern sense of the word' and 'the first modern Indonesian writer'.

friends, including the Abendanons, who said that her stay in Holland might alienate her from the very people whose children she wished to teach.

Her parents arranged a marriage with the Regent of Rembang, himself a supporter of progressive social policies. She now realized that she would have far greater influence within Javanese society if she followed Javanese convention. She opened a school for the daughters of regents in her new home at Rembang. She and her husband planned to encourage the revival of woodcarving and other traditional crafts among the villagers, and to collect traditional Javanese legends for publication. These plans were destined to remain unfulfilled also. In 1904, four days after the birth of her son, Kartini died. She was only twenty-five.

Her influence continued after her death due at first to the work of her sponsor and friend, J. H. Abendanon, who collected and published her letters in the original Dutch, under the title, *Through Darkness to Light*. They appeared first in 1911 and by 1923, when the first English edition appeared, the book had been through four editions. For the Ethici it vindicated their hopes and plans for co-operation between Indonesians of high birth and status, and the Europeans who sought to guide their welfare. 'Oh I am so proud of my people, they are capable of so much,' Kartini had written, 'but you Hollanders must lead us . . . We are like children, and you are our protectors, who must guide and help us to be grown men and women.'[8] This was exactly the reaction for which the Ethici hoped.

Yet her writing also appeals to Indonesian nationalists. Her birthday, 21st April, is celebrated in Indonesian communities throughout the world as a national day, and it is easy to see why. In her first letter to Stella she says: 'But it was not the voices alone which reached me from that distant, that bright, that newborn Europe, which made me long for a change in existing conditions. Even in my childhood, the word "emancipation" enchanted my ears . . . and awakened in me an ever growing longing for freedom and independence—a longing to stand alone. Conditions both in my own surroundings and in those of others around me broke my heart, and made me long with a nameless sorrow for the awakening of my country.'[9] Furnivall comments that her letters show that 'nationalism was already present in the social order as a saturated solution, ready to crystallise at the first shock'.

[8] Kartini, pp. 173-4.
[9] Kartini, pp. 31-2.

THE EFFECTS OF EXTENDED EDUCATION

There was support for some Western education by those who were not themselves firm believers in the Ethical policy, although their aims and specific educational requirements were different from those of the Ethici. The increasing scope and range of government activities under the Ethical policy and the diversification of economic activity, the growth of banks and business houses, meant a growing need for Indonesians with some elementary Western education, so there was support for the establishment of schools which could provide sufficient Indonesians with these skills.

Later those involved in Western industrial enterprise attempted to establish schools giving sufficient technical and vocational training to equip Indonesians for subsidiary roles in industry. Such reasons toward the end of the nineteenth century led to the extension of national education to the European working classes where formerly it had been an upper and middle class prerogative. In both cases the problem was how to give just enough education to just enough people without making them critical of the society in which they lived or a challenge to the classes holding the traditional monopoly of formal education. In neither case could the problem be solved to the satisfaction of those who wished to preserve the exclusive character of education. The extension of education is a process more easily started than stopped.

Even those who in theory supported the Ethical policy were not always quite as enthusiastic about its educational aspects when their own interests seemed likely to be threatened. Proposals to extend medical education to more Indonesians was opposed by non-Indonesian doctors, but supported by planters in Sumatra wanting a cheaper medical service to keep their coolies healthy. The proposal to open a law school for Indonesians was opposed by many lawyers. This has a parallel in Western society where the extension of higher education to women was strenuously resisted by those men who saw the entry of women into the professions as a challenge to their own positions.

In spite of such protests the Dokter-Djawa School, which first trained medical orderlies, between 1900 and 1902 became a six-year School for the Training of Native Doctors (STOVIA), accommodating 200 students. By 1914, it had produced only 135 graduates, although perhaps this is not surprising when we realize that a six-year course would be a considerable financial burden even upon a regent, the most highly paid Indonesian government official, whose salary had not only to support the dignity of his office but a large family, often including many distant relatives. Even after completing only part of the STOVIA course a non-graduate was better qualified than the majority of his fellows. In 1910 there were only fifty Indonesians attending five-year secondary schools, and in 1919 when government general secondary schools were established, there were only twenty-two Indonesians attending.[10] Both graduates and ex-students of STOVIA were among the earliest supporters of the early 20th century nationalist movements because, as so often happens, the things which they learnt were rather different from the things which their teachers believed themselves to be teaching. They did not always thankfully recognize their indebtedness to the Netherlands for their prosperity and higher culture but became increasingly aware and resentful of the restrictions placed on their economic and cultural life by European society in the Indies.

The Dutch educational policy in the early twentieth century reinforced the general Dutch colonial policy of 'divide and rule'. Eastern-oriented village schools (second-class schools) taught the rural Indonesian population in the vernacular. Dutch-language schools in the provincial capitals designed primarily for the European population admitted some of the nobility. Even when admitted to such schools Indonesians were made to feel 'inferior'. Kartini said: 'What have I not suffered as a child at school through the ill will of the teachers and of many of my fellow pupils? Not all of the teachers and pupils hated us. Many loved us quite as much as the other children. But it was hard for the teachers to give a native the highest mark, never mind how well it might have been deserved.'[11]

By 1908 Chinese pressure on the government caused them to open Dutch Chinese schools, with Dutch as the medium of instruction. There were seventeen of these by 1910 and fifty-two by 1920 attended almost exclusively by Chinese. In 1910, of 2,740 pupils at such schools only 7 were Dutch and 36 Indonesian. Later provision was made for Dutch Indonesian schools, of which 132 had been established by 1920 and 192 by 1930. These provided primary education in Dutch with Dutch teachers.

There was a big gulf between these six-year primary schools and the three-year village or vernacular schools where the lan-

[10] You should consider these figures in connection with the general population figures, see below, p. 163.
[11] Kartini, p. 58.

guage of instruction was the local language, Javanese, Sundanese or Madurese in Java for example, and where the teachers were Indonesians with only seven years of schooling. According to de Kat Angelino, exponent of Dutch colonialism, the use of either Malay (i.e. Indonesian) or Dutch as the medium of instruction would have been simpler, particularly for teacher training, but 'in view of the pedagogical principle . . . the difficulty of multiplicity has been cheerfully faced in the Dutch East Indies'. This principle was the desirability of making the school fit into the local indigenous society. Kartini said of them that, 'in the schools of the second class the children learn only Javanese, reading, writing, and a little reckoning. No Malay is taught as formerly— why it is not made clear. The Government believes to my thinking, that if the people were educated they would no longer be willing to work the land.'[12] Perhaps, from rather different viewpoints, each was expressing the same idea.

The village schools proved too expensive for the available government finance. It was argued that the villagers ought to feel a greater sense of involvement if they helped to provide their own school; and it would help the financial situation. So schools were to be built by the villagers and financed to the extent of 90 guilders a year, while parents were to pay a small fee. The villagers were reluctant both in financing the schools and in sending their children to them. They regarded them rightly enough, as instruments of the central government, and saw little relevance in the formalized education given. Many text books used for teaching reading were based on books used in Holland, translated into the local language and memorized by the pupils. It was hardly surprising that the teaching *seemed* irrelevant. It *was*. Even de Kat Angelino admitted that 'a certain amount of mild compulsion on the side of the authorities' had to be exerted to 'encourage' attendance and reduce 'a sometimes frightening absence figure'.

In 1928 the Dutch Native Educational Commission estimated that, at the current rate of progress, it would take 167 years, or the expenditure of a billion florins for a quarter of a century, to wipe out illiteracy. As a minimum of four years of primary schooling was needed to prevent a lapse back into illiteracy, the three-year village schools did not fulfil the expectations of their founders.

Three main aims lay behind the extension of Western educational facilities in Indonesia. The first was that foremost with the Ethici, the desire to spread enlightenment, to repay the 'debt of

[12] Kartini, p. 56.

honour' by providing access to the higher culture of the Netherlands for the natural leaders of Indonesian society, who, in
alliance with their teachers, would then help found a new social
entity in the Far East. They also hoped by spreading elementary
education at the village level, to raise the level of welfare while
keeping these village communities intact from too much Western
influence. The extension of Western education did spread
enlightenment, but this undermined the foundations on which
the colonial system rested. At the village level it failed to achieve
its aims.

The second aim was the attempt to counter Pan-Islam, the
revival of reformist teaching, and the Islamic educational system,
by offering government-sponsored Western education and by
encouraging missionary activity and better facilities for education
in areas with large Christian communities. In practice this stimulated the Islamic revival even further.

The third aim, the provision of a pool of Western-educated
Indonesians by whom the lower clerical and administrative positions in government and business could be relatively inexpen-
sively staffed, was achieved, but too well. The new, westernized
group, because of discriminatory employment policies in both
government and private business, were not fully absorbed into
the employment market, but the desire for western education,
stimulated by even a limited provision of facilities, grew rapidly.
Minor clerical posts, although poorly paid by European standards, offered higher salaries than were available to most Indonesians, so Western education was an avenue of advancement.
Parents undertook incredible sacrifices to send their children to
school. Sometimes in the Outer Islands, a family or village pooled
resources to give a bright child the opportunity to study, which
often involved a prolonged stay in Java, or even Holland, to
attend the nearest available school. Often when these children
had completed their education they proved a bitter disappoint-
ment to the parents who had sacrificed so much, sometimes more
than half their income, for when they returned to the village, if
indeed they did return, they found themselves estranged from the
old community life and from parents and family.

At the same time a growing number of Western-educated Indonesians was either unemployed or underemployed in terms of
their qualifications. Many began to query the inequality upon
which the colonial system was based; many turned to teaching
in private schools which sprang up in response to the growing
Indonesian demand for more Western education.

This was the bitterest blow of all to the Ethici's high hopes.

The new Western-educated generation, the young men and women whom they had encouraged, did not thankfully recognize their indebtedness to the Netherlands but began to envisage a new social entity out there in the Far East, one in which the Dutch themselves would be superfluous and in which, as in previous centuries, Indonesians would have some say in deciding their own destiny. (Ironically enough this awareness of their own past was fostered by European scholarship, the work of archaeologists, linguists and historians—for example, the discovery of the *Nagarakertagama* manuscript in Lombok.) The Ethici had set themselves an impossible task, and the higher their hopes, the deeper their ultimate disillusionment.

THE ETHICAL POLICY: AN ASSESSMENT[13]

As the *laissez-faire* Liberalism of the late nineteenth century was replaced by a concern for the welfare of the indigenous people of Indonesia, the State attempted increasingly to control and direct the course of change in the colony.

One problem for the social engineers was the lack of unanimity about the ultimate goal of such change. What kind of society did the advocates of controlled social change really want? Many had no clear picture of the future except as a continuation of their present relationship, but with its harsher aspects smoothed away. Others envisaged a gradual unification, with legal and legislative systems united under one code based on European law and one system for all inhabitants, in the civil service, education, and the field of taxation. Discrimination based on race or social status would gradually be abolished. Some saw unification coming about by gradual assimilation of non-European cultures into a wider East Indian society with a culture predominantly based on that of the Netherlands. Others saw it as being based on association, respecting the value of indigenous cultures and preserving them side by side with the Dutch culture. De Kat Angelino talked about synthesis under Dutch leadership. It was more a difference about means than about ends, for there was fairly common agreement that the Dutch would continue, certainly in the foreseeable future, to act as leaders, as guides, as guardians— which only serves to remind us that the future is rarely foreseeable, whatever we may think at the time.

[13] Notice that this is *an* assessment, not the only assessment, so that you need to compare it with other assessments and with what you can learn about the Ethical Policy both from what has already been said here and from other sources. Then you can make your own assessment in the light of all the evidence available to you. Where you differ from other assessments is it because you differ about what actually happened or because you differ in your evaluation of what happened?

The Ethici neither achieved nor attempted any thoroughgoing technological change. Their solution to the problem of diminishing welfare in Java was the extension of agriculture to intensify crop production and the encouragement of emigration to reduce population pressure on the existing food supplies. A tentative beginning of smallholder sugar cultivation in Java was ruined by the 1930 depression when Dutch sugar interests received priority. There were no sharp divisions within Javanese village society between 'haves' and 'have-nots', only a graduation from 'just enoughs' to 'not quite enoughs', a shared poverty or disguised unemployment which was reinforced by the communal nature of village life. Welfare programmes simply reinforced the rigidity of the traditional village structure.

Both the welfare policies and the intensification of traditional agricultural methods barely kept pace with the tremendous population growth of the century, itself stimulated by Dutch intrusion. Internal peace imposed by the *Pax Neerlandica* reduced the death toll from warfare and from its aftermath of destroyed crops, famine and disease. Improved health facilities had the same effect, while improved communications reduced the likelihood of starvation from local crop failure, as supplies could be brought from outside. In 1815, on the eve of the Dutch return to Java, the Javanese population was estimated at about 4.5 million. By 1870 it had risen to 16.2 million; by 1900 to 28.4 million and within the next 20 years to 34.4 million. It has also been estimated that, in the period from 1913 to 1923, after a temporary improvement in the colonial economy with the price rise at the beginning of the century, there was a decrease in real income per head of population, and a further decrease from 1926 to 1932, while the taxation levied on the Indonesian section of the population was gradually increasing, partly to cover the increased cost of welfare programmes. Despite all the efforts made in the intervening period, the diminishing welfare noted in 1901 was still diminishing thirty years later, even before the catastrophic effects of the 1930 depression.

There were several basic contradictions in the whole concept of an Ethical Policy in a colonial environment. The first was between the idea of improved welfare for the subject race and imperialism, which was always self-interested and in which the interests of the colonies were inevitably subordinated to those of the home country, although where previously it was assumed that colonies existed for the benefit of the 'mother country', now many people argued simply that colonies should not be a burden on the 'mother country'. (Very few took the idea of a 'debt of honour' literally, even though it inspired some.) If the colony could afford a welfare programme, this could be introduced, although in any conflict between welfare and Dutch capital the latter received first consideration.

It became clear during the depression that this was also true of conflicts between Dutch and Indonesian economic interests. Although Indonesian smallholders in Sumatra had been producing 300,000 tons of rubber per annum as against 220,000 tons produced by Western-owned estates, when the government, under the international rubber control regulation of 1934 had to cut back the amount produced, the Indonesian growers were cut back to less than half their former quota (145,000 tons) while European growers were given a quota of 200,000 tons, only a slight cut back on their former production figure.

There was also a basic conflict between welfare programmes imposed from above in the interests of efficiency and the development of the spirit of co-operation necessary to ensure that the reforms were understood and accepted by those in the village for whose benefit they were intended. Dutch emphasis was on efficiency rather than on co-operation, and here the execution of the Ethical Policy was in the hands of the Dutch Civil Service officials, not all of whom shared the humanitarian spirit of the policy as originally conceived. Nor did the enthusiasm of new arrivals always survive in face of the discouragements on the job. When a Dutch controleur accused the Madurese of obstinacy in failing to co-operate, an Indonesian regent replied: 'The Madurese is "obstinate" because he wishes to retain his feeling of independence.' And although the regent was prepared to accept the idea that the villagers must be instructed as though they were children, he added that the official should treat them 'as his own children, not as abandoned waifs'. The 'gentle compulsion' through which the officials carried out their village welfare programmes gave villagers no opportunity to distinguish between legal or illegal orders. J. S. Furnivall, comparing British with Dutch colonialism, commented that whereas the British spoke of 'law and order' the Dutch used the phrase 'peace and order'.

There was another sphere of basic contradiction. The Dutch themselves, as a nation, remembered proudly their struggle against the power of Spain to retain their national integrity as united provinces against external efforts to enslave them. Western-educated Indonesians, with a knowledge of Dutch history, saw them playing the same role toward Indonesia as the Spanish had played toward the Netherlands. In terms of their own national identity, this was an essentially demoralizing position for those with sufficient perception to admit the validity of the comparison.

As it became increasingly apparent that the Ethical Policy was not achieving its aims, opposition to it in the colony grew, particularly among the increasing number of newly arrived Europeans whose main interest was the exploitation of colonial wealth. They resented the restrictions placed upon them in the interest of native welfare. They also became increasingly fearful of growing nationalism which, rightly or wrongly, they blamed upon the 'soft' policies of the Ethici. Increasingly the attitude commented on a century earlier by Raffles began to predominate. European arrogance increased, and so did fear and suspicion of 'the native'.

The Ethical Policy did not conclude at any particular date. Some say its impulse was spent by 1913, on the eve of the First World War; others claim that it continued, in theory at least, until 1942, for few dared openly repudiate its nobler aspects even if they no longer acted on them. Clearly, by the 1920s, although many warm friendships still existed between Indonesians and Dutch, the general attitude was less optimistic. The opposition to the colonial system was twofold—from those who felt that the government went too far in what it did for 'natives' and from those who believed that it did not, and perhaps could not, ever go far enough.

THE PLURAL SOCIETY

Although the Ethical Policy aimed at drawing together the different social groups, colonial life was becoming increasingly divided. While the Ethici worked for greater harmony, modernization was emphasizing and widening the divisions within society. The three main divisions, used for all governmental statistical, administrative and legal purposes were European, Foreign Oriental, and Native, although each group was further divided. The three groups represented three levels of privilege and status.

Although using these classifications, we shall not use exactly the same terms for them, for both 'Foreign Oriental' and 'Native' were used in a derogatory fashion resented by those so classified. The classification 'Indonesian' is an anachronism, for the Dutch forbade its use up to 1942, and yet the Dutch classification 'Native' is a title which is still offensive to Indonesians, a reminder of the indignities which many of them suffered when so classified.

(a) *Europeans*

The European group was the smallest and most highly privileged in East Indies society. Socially speaking, the full-blooded Europeans born in Europe predominated, particularly those from the Netherlands. The classification 'European', though made on a racial basis, was not in practice entirely racial. By far the greatest number were the Eurasians, those of mixed descent, outnumbering those of unmixed European descent by four to one at the beginning of the century. Some Eurasians were absorbed into the general Indonesian population but about fifty thousand of them in 1900 regarded themselves as Dutch, and legally, if not socially, were accepted as such. So were some Indonesian Christians. In addition, from 1899, the Japanese had won the right to be classified as Europeans and, although they were only a small group, there was a significant increase in the flow of Japanese businessmen and capital to Indonesia before 1942.

The small group of *totok* or newly arrived Europeans held almost the entire monopoly of big business in the towns, as well as financing and managing the plantations established by private capital from the 1870s onward. Within this group there was a relative increase in the numbers of newcomers from countries other than Holland. On the whole the non-Dutch group was more interested in a quick return on their capital while a growing amount of Dutch capital was invested in fields more closely connected with the permanent welfare of the Indies, irrigation works, communications and the like, promising a steady return and implying a belief in the continuing Dutch presence in the colony. This division reflects the division between those who regarded Europe as home and those who came to regard the Indies as home.

With the growth of big combines, and city-centred banking and finance companies during the century, wealthier European city dwellers had less and less contact with Indonesians except with their personal and household servants or those employed in other menial tasks. Improved communications made the European community more distinctively European, for they had radio contact with European life and culture, while the shorter, quicker sea route through Suez and the introduction of a weekly air connection with Europe also kept them more closely in touch with their homeland. The arrival of more European women to live in the colony had a similar effect. Most of the women led a restricted life, with little to do except to entertain, to complain about the servants and to gossip about the private affairs of others in the small European enclave.

Kartini was just seventeen when she first found herself in a European society crowd, celebrating the coronation of Queen Wilhelmina. She took silent note of the petty bickering and deceits of the small class-conscious society of Batavia, which, along with the general noise and racket, made her cold to the heart. Some years later, when commenting on the widely expressed European opinion that Javanese were deceptive, she wrote, 'We only smile when we read or hear such pleasantries, we think to ourselves of European society life which often gives glaring proof of the truth and sincerity of those who sit in high places and look with scorn upon the lying, untrustworthy Javanese'. She then recalled her first experience of 'the comedy play of the European world behind the scenes' where she had witnessed with growing distaste, ' "gentlemen" who spread the horrible breath of alcohol around them when they spoke', ladies who kissed affectionately and talked most intimately only to make spiteful remarks about each other when they went their separate ways. 'And it was not the despised Eurasians who did this, but white people of unmixed blood; educated, and brought up with every advantage.'[14]

Europeans wanted greater autonomy from Holland for themselves, but were not anxious to extend political autonomy to other groups in society. It was perhaps fortunate for the non-Europeans in the country that the Dutch Parliament was unprepared to grant this, for it would have added political power to the already considerable economic and social power which the Europeans held.

Newcomers were soon absorbed into the European enclave where their scorn of other groups in society was only equalled by their ignorance of them and their fear of the unknown. The talk of the clubs, and the sense of solidarity, made it very hard for those Europeans in the colony with sympathy towards the Ethical Policy's welfare programmes to speak out against the general attitudes, particularly as representatives of the old school argued that the 'natives' were an ungrateful lot, and that encouraging them simply led to trouble, and the danger of a challenge to the whole basis of European superiority. To stand out against this group solidarity was regarded as a betrayal of one's birthright as a European.[15]

In dealing with Indonesians many Europeans did not distinguish between the different groups within Indonesian society, and

[14] Kartini, pp. 201-2.
[15] This sense of social solidarity and suspicion of those who made friendships across these racial barrier lines was not peculiar to Dutch colonies but was a general colonial phenomenon. George Orwell, *Burmese Days*, and E. M. Forster, *A Passage to India*, both portray it vividly.

even made a point of humiliating Dutch-educated Indonesians to 'put them in their place'. Kartini commented on the many Europeans who spoke broken Malay to Indonesians who they knew understood Dutch and added, 'It would be a matter of indifference to me in what language they addressed us, if the tone were only polite'.

The Eurasians formed by far the greater part of the European community. Usually the father was European and the mother Indonesian, mostly from the lower classes. Those whose fathers were prepared to acknowledge them and to assist with their education were able to obtain government clerical and technical positions or to find other positions in the middle ranks of society. Those whose fathers ignored them, and who often had the additional stigma of illegitimacy, led an unhappy existence between two worlds, unable to obtain acceptance in the European world and yet feeling themselves superior to those with no claim to European status. Most Eurasians were taught to look down upon the Indonesian side of their inheritance and so to have a sense of shame rather than a sense of pride in their double inheritance. They were threatened from above as European society became more exclusively European, and threatened from below, with the expansion of Dutch language education and the increasing numbers of both Chinese and Indonesians seeking employment in areas previously almost exclusively theirs. During the twentieth century some attempts were made by humanitarian members of European society to assist these people, but their position remained difficult, and their need to assert their own status made them, on the whole, strong supporters of the European group.

Christianity was regarded as the religion of the Europeans, and although the government was officially committed to a policy of religious neutrality, there was growing pressure in the early twentieth century for some government support to missionary activities, springing from much the same motivation as inspired the Ethici. The profession of Christianity by Indonesians who would otherwise have been classed as 'Natives' gave them the same sort of precarious legal equality as was afforded to the Eurasians. According to de Kat Angelino this indicated that the three-fold division was not racial but a question of legal needs which just happened, on the whole, to coincide with racial groups. Non-Christian Indonesians were unimpressed by this argument. To them it demonstrated the government's hypocrisy in claiming religious neutrality. The privileged position of Indonesian Christians under the colonial regime has been a stigma which the Indonesian Church has had to live down in the post-colonial period.

(b) *Chinese and Arabs*

Predominant in the group classified for legal purposes as Foreign Orientals were the Chinese, the largest foreign ethnic group in Indonesia. The largest concentration of Chinese settlement was found in an arc around Singapore, from north Sumatra to Kalimantan. There were sizeable Chinese communities in most Javanese towns, the more conspicuous because, as had always been the case, they lived in the Chinese quarters. Although to the outsider they appeared homogeneous, there were also divisions within their community. Chinese immigrants came from different parts of China and different groups spoke different dialects. There was also a wide occupational range from coolies imported under contract to work the estate land around Medan (Sumatra), to Chinese of such wealth that they were as rich as all but a handful of Europeans. They were excluded by government legislation from direct participation in agriculture although they had some indirect control, at least at the beginning of the century, as moneylenders and pawnbrokers, controlling the crops on which they paid advances.

In times of stress, such as the economic recession at the turn of the century, the Chinese were often used as scapegoats by the Europeans, while some Ethical Policy welfare programmes were intended to reduce the hold of the Chinese on many rural areas. In practice this diverted Chinese capital previously invested in such areas to other fields, which meant that up to 1930 many of them moved from a parasitic role in the economy, drawing off money through moneylending and opium sales, to investment in more constructive enterprises. By 1911 they conflicted with the small newly-emerging class of Indonesian entrepreneurs and, although the Indonesians held their own in the cigarette manufacturing industries, they faced severe competition in the *batik* industry (for batik was no longer the exclusive preserve of the *kraton*), and were ousted from the kapok industry.

As with the European community, there was a division between newcomers, full-blooded Chinese (*totok*), and the *peranakan*, descendants of mixed marriages. Some writers, incorrectly, use this term to denote those of full Chinese descent born in the country, an error which perhaps arose because, as with the Dutch, a high proportion of the Chinese community was of mixed descent. Usually such a marriage occurred between a Chinese man and an Indonesian woman, partly because, as in any immigrant group, the men tended to outnumber the women. In such a marriage the woman was assimilated into the Chinese community. Over against both *totok* and *peranakan* was the small group of unmixed Chinese descent who had lived in the country for several generations.

The Chinese community, particularly the wealthier members, even though third or fourth generation, still kept close links with their country of origin. During the early twentieth century such links were strengthening, for in the nineteenth century they had tended to be alienated from the Manchu government, regarded by the majority of Chinese as foreign. The growth of a republican movement in China meant that the overseas Chinese, including those in Indonesia, again became closely concerned with the politics of their home country. The overthrow of the Manchu in 1911 was largely financed by overseas Chinese, and the establishment of the Chinese Nationalist government strengthened further the links between China and those of Chinese descent in south-east Asia. They were still regarded by China as Chinese citizens by right of ethnic origin. The Nationalist government established a Ministry of Overseas Chinese and opened a consulate in Indonesia.

The Chinese in Indonesia soon began to demand improved status. They resented the classification of Japanese as European, while they were still subject to various kinds of restrictive legislation, for example the control of their movement within the country by the issue of passes. Some was repealed during the early twentieth century. They also demanded increased privileges, such as Dutch-Chinese schools, while there was extended Chinese-oriented education and a growing identification with Chinese culture. In some of their schools they even taught English rather than Dutch as having more value in the commercial world. Just as the European community was becoming more consciously European so the Chinese community was becoming more consciously Chinese, attempting to encroach on the privileges of the European community, but presenting a solid barrier to Indonesian progress.

The other sizeable group included under the classification 'Foreign Oriental' was the Arab community. As with the Chinese there had been Arab settlers in Indonesia for centuries, although because they were Moslems, they had been more easily assimilated into Indonesian society. In the second half of the nineteenth century there had been an increase in their numbers from about 7 to over 20 thousand, small in comparison with the estimated

280 thousand Chinese in Indonesia in 1900 but yet a considerable increase. The Dutch restricted their movements outside the urban areas, fearing, not without justification, their influence in encouraging rural Islam, but in any case most Arabs were by occupation urban, either small businessmen, merchants or money-lenders.

(c) *Indonesians*

There were also different groups within the population classed together as 'native' for the administrative convenience of the Dutch, and in the early years of the twentieth century they too showed growing awareness of their distinctive characteristics. Here too the trend of events emphasized the plural nature of society, while also emphasizing similarities between the members of each different group. It is impossible to separate this process from the development of Indonesian nationalism, considered more fully in the following chapter.

Mention has already been made of the tremendous population increase in Java during the nineteenth century. Unless we keep this in mind we may fail to realize the relative sizes of these three legal divisions. The Chinese formed about 2% of the total population of Indonesia while the European population was only about a quarter the size of the Chinese. And within the group classified as European only 25% were Europeans of the *totok* group. We may perhaps wonder how so small a handful of people could control so vast an empire for so long. We should not be surprised at the 'general feeling of uneasiness' at any potential challenge to this minority rule.

The Indonesian population in 1905 was estimated at about 37 million, of whom almost 30 million lived on Java and the other 7 million in the Outer Islands. By 1930 the total figure was over 59 million, of whom almost 41 million lived in Java and over 18 million in the Outer Islands. The typical Javanese was the villager cultivating his *sawah,* the typical Outer Island Indonesian (excluding pockets of *sawah* cultivation found in the island of Bali, or Minangkabau and Toba in Sumatra) was the swidden cultivator, whose slash-and-burn farming maintained a delicate balance between the normal cycle of plant growth in the tropical forest and the area annually cleared for food crops. In Java there was overpopulation and a growing land shortage, while in the Outer Islands there was abundance of land but a labour shortage. Of the total Indonesian population, 90% were villagers. Politically speaking, the 'little man' was completely unimportant outside his immediate village setting. The people who had any

political importance, and that of a very limited extent, were the
2% of the Indonesian population making up the elite, the
nobility of the different ethnic groups. Of potential political
importance were the remaining 8% who were becoming part of
the urbanized population of the developing towns, although the
majority of these were newly urbanized peasants who retained
a good deal of their peasant outlook on life and lived in urbanized rural slums on the outskirts of the cities.

Clifford Geertz, speaking of Java, differentiates between three
separate, but interrelated cultural groups. The first he identifies
as the *prijayi* or aristocracy, the group associated with Javanese
adat and the old *kraton* traditions. This was the group, in east
and central Java from which the Indonesian Civil Service was
largely staffed. The second he calls the *santri,* those whose moti-
vating force is Islam rather than *adat,* often, relatively speaking,
newcomers from the coastal towns, who supplied the bulk of the
merchant trading class. The third and largest division he calls
the *abangan,* who draw to some extent on both the other traditions, but are distinguishable from either, and include the
bulk of the peasantry, the villagers.[16] This is a useful division if
we do not draw the lines between the three too sharply and if
we remember that it applies *only to the ethnic Javanese,* that is
the Javanese who live in central and east Java, but not to other
areas of Indonesia, even Sunda (western Java) or Madura.

Within the 98% of ordinary Indonesians, some general distinctions can be drawn between those Indonesians who were still part
of the village tradition of the area in which they lived, and two
groups of ex-villagers, the plantation workers, and the urbanized
peasants in the *kampong* areas of the growing cities.

Nevertheless the most important division remains that between
the 98% of Indonesians who formed the broad base of the pyramid of Indonesian society, and the 2% of Indonesian elite whose
contact with Western ideas and culture served to make a significant number of them critical of the whole structure of Indonesian society. A number of factors was working to make this
group, despite its diversity, a more closely-knit national elite.

COLONIALISM: AN ASSESSMENT[17]

This is perhaps a convenient point at which to attempt an
assessment of the whole colonial era. By 1928 the Dutch possessions in the archipelago extended, in the words of de Kat
Angelino, 'from Sabang to Merauke, from Banten to the Talaud

---

[16] C. Geertz, *The Religion of Java,* pp. 5-6. See also the glossary.
[17] This again is *an* assessment, not the only assessment possible.

Moslem public prayer where all participants pray simultaneously rather than individually. Here they are performing the *sudjud*, acknowledging their complete submission before Allah

Noon prayer in the fields. The man to the left is performing his preliminary ablutions, the two men in the foreground are at different stages of prayer while behind them a woman is praying in the all-enveloping white robes she keeps exclusively for wear during prayer and worship
(see pp. 55-6)

In this Minangkabau village, the village mosque (with the dome) is in the foreground and beside it is the traditional *adat* house with roof curving up as do the horns of the buffalo. It symbolizes the fusion of Islam and *adat* typical of the district (see p. 126)

This stilt-type Riauw fishing village house with palm thatch is similar to those described in early accounts of Malacca and Atjeh (see pp. 66, 82)

Archipelago'. Not only had the empire reached its farthest geographic extent, but also the Dutch now saw themselves as having a mission, an historic task to govern in the best interests and for the greater welfare of the colony itself.

They argued that Dutch capital, Dutch management and Dutch enterprise had developed the country, extending the area under cultivation, introducing new crops such as coffee, tea, quinine, tobacco and rubber, and increasing the production of indigenous crops such as sugar. Dutch capital had also financed the exploitation of tin and oil resources. Without this stimulus the potential wealth of the Indies may have remained untapped. As against this the critics of colonialism pointed out that these new crops were introduced by the Dutch for the benefit of the Dutch and that they were grown on Indonesian land by Indonesian labour to benefit the Dutch economy, the Dutch merchant and the Dutch financier. The wealth of the Indies was not simply being tapped but drained away for the benefit of the Dutch economy. The Indonesians reaped few direct benefits, some indirect benefits and in the process lost a great deal. It had been wrongly assumed from the time of Raffles onward that land not directly occupied was 'waste' land which had thereupon been appropriated by the government for disposal as it saw fit, but in so doing the government had in fact appropriated land, which, in former times, would have been available for natural expansion. Furthermore the clearing of natural forest to make room for coffee plantations often caused soil erosion which affected potential food-growing land, while the exploitation of sugar made inroads into the *sawah* lands of Java.

The Dutch also pointed to modernization under their rule, particularly improved communications and, during the nineteenth and twentieth centuries, the introduction of new forms of communication: miles of roads and railways, telephone, telegraph, post and wireless communications, inter-island shipping and air transport. The critics of colonialism acknowledge this as true, but suggest that such improvements were made primarily for the benefit of the colonizers, though indirect benefits may have come to the colonized. The first main road in Java, that built by command of Daendels, was to defend the Dutch against the Javanese, and was exclusively for European use. Dirt tracks alongside were provided for the 'natives'! The first railway in Atjeh was built as part of the Dutch offensive in the Atjeh war. Roads and railways of a later period were built according to European demand, to serve European financial interests. And, add the Indonesians, they were built by forced labour quite as

harshly treated as that which was used by the Japanese during
the Second World War to build the Burma Road. Nor were most
Indonesians able to make use of these new facilities. Although
rail fares were cheap, one cent per kilometre, with a flat rate
of four guilders for four hundred kilometres or further, the
average income per person in Java was about 20.3 guilders *per
annum*.

The Dutch had also established the *Pax Neerlandica*, pacify-
ing the countryside and terminating the intertribal and dynastic
warfare common prior to their extension of political power. This
was one of the main factors contributing to the population increase in the area, one of the greatest problems facing the present
Indonesian government. The pacification of the country did lead
to stable and peaceful development and a growth of population,
and in the early stages, the Dutch intervened reluctantly in local
quarrels, but they became less reluctant as time wore on, and in
some cases were even instrumental in fomenting the initial
quarrel. Whoever started the quarrel, the final victors were
always the Dutch, who quite often gained as much power at the
expense of their allies as they did over the vanquished. Dutch
charges of treachery and oppression as pretexts for conquest, particularly during the forward movement at the end of the nineteenth century are met with counter-charges of treachery and
oppression in their establishment of the *Pax Neerlandica*, for
example their exiling of Diponegoro and their failure to recog-
nise Atjeh's sovereignty. This also applied to its maintenance in
the face of nationalist challenges. It remained an uneasy peace
depending on continuing force to maintain it.

The Dutch can claim, with some validity, that they were the
creators of a united Indonesia, through centralization of colonial
government at Batavia. The unity of coinage, the gradual unification of weights and measures, the unifying effects of the Dutch
and Indonesian (Malay) languages, the establishment of the
Volksraad, the centralized administrative service, all brought the
diverse elements in Indonesia into closer contact than in the past,
even under the Madjapahit or Srividjaya Empires, for now such
contact was facilitated by modern transport. Their critics claim
that they may have facilitated the expression of such unity, but
that they did not create it. Furthermore their method of government fostered disunity, seeking to divide and rule their subjects
by stressing differences, by reducing the power of the natural
leaders of Indonesian society and substituting for it Dutch
authority and power, by devising different legal, educational and
administrative services, based on racial divisions within society.

PART IV

Nationalism and Independence

CHAPTER EIGHT

Rise of the Nationalist Movement

'A change will come in our whole native world—the turning point is fore-ordained; it is coming. But when will it be? That is the great question.'

Kartini to Stella Zeehandelaar, 6 November 1899.

The rise of nationalism in Indonesia was part of a worldwide development of national consciousness. In Europe by the close of the nineteenth century a unified Germany and Italy had joined the other nation-states in the race for colonies, while in colonial countries throughout the world nationalism developed in the late nineteenth and early twentieth centuries as a response to the imperialist expansion through which the European nations expressed their national greatness.

The elements in the Indies' plural society were becoming increasingly separate, and part of this separateness was an increased awareness of national identity, the Europeans associating themselves more closely with life in Europe, the Chinese influenced by Chinese nationalism, and the Indonesians reacting to the intensified awareness of the other groups by a growing awareness of the similarities which underlay their regional differences and the burdens placed upon them by foreigners.

The changes planned by the Ethici had unplanned results, especially in the field of education, and as the Dutch colonial empire reached its fullest extent and its greatest degree of penetration into the lives of its subjects, the seeds of its own destruction were already being sown. This was not because Dutch colonialism was harsher than that of other colonizing powers. It sought, as far as possible, to promote the welfare of its subjects, and it was regarded by students of colonialism as a model worth imitating in this respect. The Dutch empire was lost as much

because of the virtues of the Dutch colonial ruler as because of
the vices.[1]

Although Dutch control had extended from Java throughout
the entire archipelago, it had done so in the face of considerable
opposition. Even during the early twentieth century, from 1911
to 1917, there were at least nine uprisings in east Indonesia (five
in Sulawesi, and others in Ambon, Bali, Lombok and Ternate),
another nine in Sumatra, and five in Kalimantan. Yet neither
these, nor the earlier uprising of Diponegoro in Java, nor the
long struggle in Atjeh, could really be called nationalist. They
were localized struggles for independence, similar to the struggle
of the Sultan of Palembang, or Sultan Hasanuddin of Gowa. Yet
they were an inspiration to those participating in the nationalist
movement.

As Dutch administration welded Indonesia into one centrally
governed administrative unit, the people of Indonesia, particularly the small group of educated upper class Indonesians,
became more aware of their basic similarities. Among the
educated, Dutch was sometimes used as a common language. The
Dutch use of Malay, the basis of modern Indonesian, as the
language of government, spread it further throughout the archipelago. By the 1920s it was a symbol of national unity, 'one
country, one people, one language'.

Another common link between the majority of Indonesians as
against either their Dutch overlords or the Chinese was their
common adherence to Islam. This was one element in many
earlier struggles against the Dutch, and the more the Dutch
sought to ally themselves with *adat* leaders against Islamic
leaders, the stronger became the symbolic value of Islam as a
common bond against them.

With the extension of education and the growing interest of
Dutch scholars in the history and antiquities of Indonesia,
educated Indonesians had a growing awareness of their own past.
The restoration of Borobudur reminded Indonesians that, when
it was built in the eighth century, the tribes of the Netherlands
were still at an early stage of development. The deciphering of
Nagarakertagama, with its account of the glory of the Madjapahit
empire, which, it was then believed, stretched at least as far as
the area under the *Pax Neerlandica*, reminded Indonesians of a
glorious age before invading foreigners established their
dominion. The history of the Netherlands itself reinforced their
desire to struggle against foreign oppression. The Eighty Year

[1] J. D. Legge, *Indonesia*, p. 114.

War (of the Netherlands against Spain) was often quoted by nationalists. Common suffering and common oppression under both Dutch and Chinese linked Indonesians together.

In 1900, when Kartini was dreaming of studying in Holland, only five Indonesian students were studying there. By 1908 there were twenty-three, who formed an Indies society, including both Indonesian and Eurasian students. By 1922 student numbers had increased considerably, and its name was changed to *Perhimpunan Indonesia* (Indonesian Association), exclusively for those of Indonesian descent. The Indonesian name, replacing the earlier Dutch one, and the use of 'Indonesian' rather than 'Indies' in the title, both emphasized a growing sense of nationalism among the students, many of whom, on their return to Indonesia, became leaders of the nationalist movement there.

In Holland students were better treated by the Dutch, and more readily accepted as equals than in the colonial society of the Indies. They also met students from other Asian countries, and came into direct contact with various strands of European thought which were underrepresented in colonial society. The post-war period in Europe was one in which national revival was in the air. Many were influenced by events in post-revolutionary Russia, especially by the liberation of the Baltic states. Other Indonesian students, also members of the Indonesian Association, attended the universities of Cairo and Mecca, where they made common cause with other Moslem students, many also suffering direct or indirect Western domination.

Russia's defeat by Japan in 1905 encouraged many Asians, who saw it as the first sign of European vulnerability to Asian attack. The Chinese revolution of 1911 had a twofold influence. Sukarno, in his speech, 'The Birth of Pantjasila', has acknowledged that Sun Yat Sen's Three Principles, 'Nationalism, Democracy, Socialism', influenced his thinking when he read of them as a seventeen-year-old student, and the influence of revolution in making the overseas Chinese more aware of their Chinese identity, and more arrogant toward non-Chinese, in turn made many Indonesians more resentful of the privileged position held by the Chinese in the economy and in society in general. The Modernist movement and Islamic reforms in Egypt and Turkey were partly in reaction against the encroachments of Western powers. Indian nationalism also had its influence in Indonesia; the passive resistance advocated by Gandhi and the *swadeshi* movement, the domestic manufacture of previously imported goods, both made an impact on Indonesian thinking.

As more Indonesians received Western education, they became

more aware of discrimination against them in various fields. Many were either unemployed or employed in jobs where they could not use their Western education. Not only was it more difficult for them to obtain employment in the first place, but when they did so they were paid a lower salary than was paid to a Chinese, Eurasian or Dutch employee with exactly the same qualifications, doing exactly the same work. Although there were six Indonesians employed in the Civil Service for every one Dutchman, yet 92% of the top positions were held by Europeans. Non-Indonesians attempted to monopolize the professions. Objections were raised to the establishment of medical, legal and engineering faculties in Indonesia and the STOVIA School for Training Native Doctors did not enable a graduate to continue at a Dutch medical school, although it was considered 'good enough' to train Indonesian doctors for Indonesians. Despite the increased provision of educational facilities the Indonesians, proportionate to their percentage in the total population, were still most inadequately provided for by the authorities in comparison with facilities for Chinese and Dutch students.

Alarmed by the effects of even this small provision of Western education, the government was reluctant to increase such facilities, and was concerned by the growing number of private schools, staffed largely by unemployed Indonesians with Western education. They suspected, often quite rightly, that such schools were spreading nationalist sentiments. Attempts to control these 'wild' schools by a licence system were countered by a successful campaign of passive resistance.

The Dutch authorities consistently underestimated the strength and extent of national sentiment. They believed that the nationalists were simply a small, disaffected minority who could be dealt with, as they had dealt with past challenges to their power, by armed force, by arrests and by banishing the leaders. After the First World War, the Dutch believed that nationalism was subversive and fostered from outside either by the USA, the USSR or Japan. Conscious of their own efficiency and their policy of welfare, believing that they 'understood the native mind', they could not recognize that paternalism bred resentment rather than gratitude. In addition, the Dutch empire was essential to the national prestige and economic welfare of the Netherlands. Almost one in three of the inhabitants of the Netherlands had some direct or indirect financial link with the colony.

With the changing nature of world opinion, as expressed by the establishment of the League of Nations after World War I, and the enunciation of the principle of national self-determination by the Paris peace treaty, the Dutch could not use force against the nationalists without justifying this at the world forum. Even so, there were many cases where suspected nationalists were held prisoner or exiled 'at the governor's pleasure'. Sutan Sjahrir's letters in *Out of Exile* open with this entry: 'March 29, 1934. I have now been behind bars for a whole month but I still haven't the least idea why I have actually been placed here.'[2] The more the Dutch used force against the nationalist leaders, the more this was seen as further evidence of Dutch injustice by both leaders and followers, and the more closely the bonds of common suffering drew them together.

Despite this growing unity, considerable divisions remained within Indonesian society, affecting the development of nationalism, just as they continue to affect events in present-day independent Indonesia.

The first was Java's predominance. At the beginning of the century Java held two-thirds of the total population of Indonesia, but only one-fourteenth of the total land area. It was the seat of the central government, and the area in which Dutch contact had been longest and Dutch penetration deepest. All the tertiary and all but one of the secondary government educational institutions were on Java. Yet Java and the Outer Islands stood in contrast to each other in various ways. Indonesian nationalism developed by seeking the unity in such diversity.

The feudal nobility, the allies and instruments of Dutch rule, resented colonialism, which robbed them of much of their former prestige, but they feared nationalism, which threatened not only Dutch power but with it their own. Once again Kartini had already noted this, commenting in 1900 that:

> The aristocracy sees with sad eyes how sons of the people are educated and often even elevated to their ranks by the government because of knowledge, ability and industry. Sons of the people go to European schools and compare favourably in every respect, with the high and honorable sons of the nobles. The nobles wish to have rights for themselves alone; they alone wish to have authority and to make western civilisation and enlightenment their own. And the Government helps and supports them in this; for it is to its own advantage to do so.

Eurasians tended to support the colonial regime, because they needed the continued link with the Netherlands to justify maintaining their privileged position within society. Most regarded themselves as members, even if fringe members, of

[2] Sjahrir, *Out of Exile*, p. 1. See below p. 200.

European society in the colonies. Yet in the early years of the twentieth century there were some of them, in alliance with Western-educated Indonesians, who proposed working for independence for all Indies-born, regardless of race. The increasing separateness of the different groups within the plural society doomed such a project from the outset.

The Indonesian middle class was small, and predominantly urban—government officials and clerical workers in private business concerns. Many were dependent for their livelihood upon the goodwill of European superiors and employers, and hesitated to join the more outspoken nationalist leaders. There were, after all, more applicants for such jobs than jobs available. Leadership of the nationalist movement came from the left wing of the middle classes: those who, as a matter of principle, chose not to work for the government. Support came from the masses, the peasants who formed over 80% of the Indonesian population, who had no idea of the world movements from which their leaders drew their inspiration, but who resented the Chinese middleman and moneylender, the European employer, and the interference of government officials. The peasant grievances were real enough. They only needed leadership in expressing them.

CULTURAL NATIONALISM. 1908-42

(a) *Budi Utomo (Glorious Endeavour)*. 1908-35

While it can be claimed that Kartini's letters contain the first articulate expression of nationalism, she spoke as an individual, expressing the longings and aspirations of other individual nationalists. Indonesians date the awakening of national consciousness from the founding of *Budi Utomo* (Glorious Endeavour), the first organization based on Western lines of association, where individuals joined as individuals, to share in a conscious united effort toward common goals, the extension of both traditional and Western education among the peoples of Java and Madura, and the advancement of agriculture, industry and commerce. At first it was nationalist in only a limited sense, extending beyond the ethnic Javanese of east and central Java to include the other Javanese ethnic groups, the Madurese and Sundanese. National Awakening Day is celebrated each year in Indonesia on 20 May, to commemorate the foundation of *Budi Utomo*. It is a recognition that nationalism involves, in the words of Renan, 'the will to unite', a sense of belonging to a national group.

Significantly, the movement's original impetus came from a retired Javanese doctor, Wahidin Sudiro Husodo. He found a response among the STOVIA students, particularly those from the Jogjakarta princely house of Paku Alam. Most *Budi Utomo* members were from the *priyayi* class, and by 1909 there were almost 10,000. Initially it was largely controlled and led by the older, more conservative *priyayi*, who naturally took this role and were accepted in it because of the traditional respect of the younger for the older person. By 1913 it had lost many members because some of the more conservative withdrew to form the Regents' Union, while many younger, more radical members were drawn into membership of newer and more overtly political associations; but it continued to be a small yet significant group within the nationalist movement, drawing its membership mainly from the Javanese aristocracy, government officials and Indonesian intellectuals.

Primarily it remained a cultural and educational association. After 1918 as it was represented in the *Volksraad* it came to have a political role too.

Although after 1931 its membership was opened to non-Javanese and it encouraged the use of the Indonesian rather than the Javanese language, it continued to be primarily a Javanese party up to 1935 when its identity was merged with the Greater Indonesia Party (*Parindra*). Some writers dismiss *Budi Utomo* as fairly conservative and of minor significance after its initial impact, yet it had links with several other nationalist groups up to 1935 and it did provide for many Indonesians, both Javanese and non-Javanese, either directly or indirectly, a national awakening.

Take, for example, one of *Budi Utomo's* co-founders, Dr. Sutomo, from a lesser *priyayi* family. He graduated from STOVIA in 1911, three years after *Budi Utomo* was founded. He was one of the younger members of the association who remained a member after the group shed many conservatives and radicals. After seven years as a government doctor he went to Europe for further study, and, as one of the older students there, was adviser and guide of the student organization *Perhimpunan Indonesia* (Indonesian Association) at the critical period when it was changing its name and nature to become more consciously part of the nationalist movement.

After his return to Java he established in 1924 the first Indonesian Study Club at Surabaya. Its primary function was to give members an awareness of social responsibilities, and to prepare Indonesians socially and economically for future independence. Many were also members of *Budi Utomo*, as of course was Dr. Sutomo himself. Along with the club's study programme, practical expression was given to a sense of social responsibility by the establishment of schools, a national bank, health clinics and foundling homes. Study clubs were established in other cities on this model. Then in 1926 in Bandung a *General Study Club*, similar in form but rather different in nature, was founded by a young engineer named Sukarno, later to become first President of the Republic of Indonesia.

In the late 1920s and the 1930s, when Sukarno and his more politically oriented no-co-operating contemporaries were in and out of prison and exile, the older, more moderate leaders, including Dr. Sutomo, continued their less spectacular preparation for independence within the limits of the colonial environment. In 1931, on Dr. Sutomo's initiative, a federation of moderate study clubs was formed, with membership limited to Indonesians, called the Union of the Indonesian People (*Persatuan Bangsa Indonesia*). In 1935, *Budi Utomo* and this new union, under Dr. Sutomo's chairmanship, formed the moderate political party *Parindra* (Greater Indonesia Party), the most influential Indonesian group in the *Volksraad*. Although Dr. Sutomo worked mainly through *Budi Utomo* and kindred associations, he was also one of a small group of Western educated Indonesians active in both Javanese cultural and Islamic reformist societies. He was a member of the *Muhammadiyah* (Followers of Mohammad) social welfare organization's executive.

(b) *Muhammadiyah (Followers of Mohammad)*. 1912-42

Budi Utomo arose from the Javanese *priyayi* cultural tradition as seen by the Western-educated *priyayi*. It represented one nationalist stream of thought. Another, which is still of great importance, owed its inspiration to religious sources, and its cultural expression was the *Muhammadiyah* movement.

Islam was one source of inspiration for earlier opponents of Dutch rule. During the nineteenth and twentieth centuries the pilgrimage to Mecca provided one of the few direct contacts between Indonesians and the outside world. Initially the Dutch authorities, fearing the results of such contact, made the pilgrimage as expensive and as difficult to undertake as possible. With a change to Snouck Hurgronje's policy in the early twentieth century these difficulties were largely removed. It was still easier for Sumatrans to make the pilgrimage than for most Javanese. They were closer to Mecca; they were also relatively wealthier than most Javanese. Consequently a higher percentage of pilgrims per head of the population came from Sumatra than from Java, both a cause and a consequence of the different impact which

Islam had made on Java and on Sumatra. Yet it was in Jogjakarta, home town of Diponegoro, that the first Islamic cultural
movement originated in 1912.

Initially increased Christian mission activity, particularly in
central Java itself, was one impulse behind the formation of
Muhammadiyah. (Missionary activity had been forbidden in
some of the more strongly Islamic areas such as Banten and parts
of Sumatra.) From the 1920s on *Muhammadiyah* was the largest
and most strongly organized movement in colonial Indonesia.
It was Modernist in inspiration, the Indonesian expression of the
Modernist reform in Mecca and Egypt in the early twentieth
century, an attempt to reform Islam so that it could come to terms
with the twentieth century world in which Moslems lived. Such
ideas had been brought back to Indonesia by returning pilgrims,
particularly those who had spent some time as students in Mecca
or Cairo. The Modernists criticized some traditional Islamic
beliefs in the light of reason, rather than accepting them unques-
tioningly, distinguishing between those matters essential to
religion and those which were not.

They were more individualistic in their approach than the
older traditionalists and drew more members from the newly
developing urban society than from the traditional rural society.
They met the challenge of Christian missionary activity by using
the same organization and methods in the interests of Islam.
They established schools using Western methods, and taught
Western subjects (including Dutch), and also religion. They set
up orphanages, hospitals and other social service activities.

From its founding in Jogjakarta in 1912, *Muhammadiyah*
grew rapidly, and by 1923 there were already 12 branches in
Java. By 1937 there were 913 branches, although more than half
were in the Outer Islands, with 370 branches in Sumatra.
Because it was careful to remain non-political, the movement did
not alienate the Dutch, even though they were suspicious of
Moslem activity. This particular form of activity, modelled on
Western patterns in social non-political fields, seemed harmless
enough and, by the end of the colonial era, some of the *Muhammadiyah* schools were even qualifying for and accepting subsidies
from the colonial government, for which they were criticized by
other nationalist organizations that preferred not to accept such
support.

For the Moslem a government of non-believers was necessarily
both evil and illegal, while the Moslem religion, in teaching the
equality of all men, was a challenge to the inequalities of a
colonial society, particularly those practised against Moslems.

Taxation raised from Moslem Indonesians was used dispropor-
tionately to subsidize Christian missionary activity. As late as
1940, where only 115 private Moslem native language primary
schools received subsidies, 2,470 Christian schools received them.
For Western-style education 7 Moslem and 61 Christian schools
were subsidized. And while subsidies to religious worship in 1938
amounted to just under 700,000 guilders for Protestants and just
under 300,000 for Roman Catholics, Moslems received only 7,500.
In the following year both the Protestant and the Roman Catholic subsidies were increased by over 100,000 guilders, while the
Moslem increase was a mere 100 guilders.

(c) *The Youth Movements*

Budi Utomo established the first of the many youth move-
ments which sprang up during and shortly after the First World
War, when, in 1915, it founded *Tri Koro Dharmo* (Three Noble
Goals). In 1917, *Young Sumatra* was founded, and in 1918 *Tri
Koro Dharmo* became *Young Java,* including all ethnic groups
within Java. By 1920 both the Madurese and the Sundanese had
formed their own youth groups. *Young Ambon* and *Young
Minahassa* represented areas with large Christian communities.
These youth groups seemed to be moving from a wider to a
more localized nationalism. The non-Javanese groups were
formed first in Java by students from other areas studying there.
When these students returned to their home district they established youth groups there.

The influence of the students studying overseas was important.
Study in Java often made students more aware of differences
between them and the Javanese; overseas study either in Holland, Mecca or Egypt, but particularly the first, made them more
aware of their similarities.

In 1925 a Moslem youth organization, the *Young Islamic
League,* was founded by Hadji Agus Salim[3] to develop and
express 'a conscious orientation towards . . . the peculiar characteristics of our own people . . . their defence against everything
alien' under the banner of Islam. This was significant because
it was ideological rather than regional and so cut across regional
loyalties. It also emphasized divisions between Moslem and non-
Moslem.

In 1926 the first Conference of Indonesian Youth (*Pemuda
Indonesia*) was held, a union of the secular nationalist youth
movements in an association representing a wider nationalism.

[3] See below, p. 197. 'Hadji' is a title bestowed on a Moslem who has completed the pilgrimage to Mecca.

As with the student organization in Holland, the change from a Dutch to an Indonesian name expressed growing national feeling. The conference adopted the slogan 'One country, one people, one language', and took as their flag the Red and White.

The nationalist movement was led and supported by the young people, the new generation whose Western education cut them off from their traditional place in society and made them question the whole framework of traditional and colonial society. Because it was mainly a youth movement, the Dutch, allied with the older *adat* leaders, wrote it off as insignificant, and believed that 'gentle pressure' in the form of exile or imprisonment would soon provide a corrective. Instead the exile of various nationalist leaders to different parts of Indonesia simply spread nationalism further in these areas. Sukarno was exiled first at Flores and later at Bengkulu, while the large numbers of prisoners in the Upper Digul detention camp in West Irian helped to draw this most recent Dutch acquisition into the nationalist stream.

(d) *'Wild' Schools*[4]

The spread of Western education was one of the most powerful forces in the promotion and extension of nationalist sentiment. The cultural nationalist movements, both secular and Moslem, were active in extending it to the growing number of Indonesians who desired it but could not obtain a place in any government-sponsored schools, because of the expense, the distance to the nearest, or lack of places. Many private schools were started by unemployed Western-educated Indonesians, some primarily as a means of livelihood for the teacher concerned rather than as centres of nationalist teaching. Even so, whether deliberately or not, some of the dissatisfaction which such people felt with the colonial situation must have been communicated to their pupils, who themselves, in many cases, were attending these schools as their second choice.

Schools were also established with a particular educational aim. Earliest of these were the *Muhammadiyah* schools which attracted not only students unable to enter a government school, but also those whose parents hesitated to send them to a secular government school where their faith might be undermined, but wanted for them a more Western education than the local *pesantren* or religious school provided.

[4] The very use of such a term to describe the privately run schools was itself offensive to Indonesians attending such schools and gave them a feeling of being discriminated against even without discriminatory legislation, later introduced to control such schools.

A third group of schools were of the *Taman Siswa* ('Garden of Pupils') cultural movement, founded by Suwardi Surjaningrat, one of the STOVIA students who joined *Budi Utomo* in 1908. He was descended from the Jogja royal house of Paku Alam, and was later to marry a descendant of Diponegoro. Like Dr. Sutomo, he was a moderate nationalist in the early '30s at the height of repression, and like him too he had links with different nationalist groups. Suwardi Surjaningrat is more commonly known by the name he adopted at forty, Ki Hadjar Dewantoro, signifying a renunciation of his claim to privilege as a member of the Javanese nobility (*ningrat* signifies noble birth), and his deliberate choice of the role of teacher. The new name signifies 'Teacher of all the Gods'. We shall refer to him as Ki Hadjar even for the period before his change of name.

Ki Hadjar had to leave STOVIA before graduation to earn a living. He was one of the more radical *Budi Utomo* members, and in 1912 with a fellow member, Tjipto Mangunkusumo, and an Eurasian nationalist, Douwes Dekker (a distant relative of Multatuli), he became co-founder of the *Indies Party*, which immediately came into conflict with the authorities because their aim was 'to pave the road toward their life as an independent people'. In the same year, Ki Hadjar was also chairman of the Bandung branch of the *Sarekat Islam* (Islamic Union)[5] and was contributing articles to the nationalist press, including 'If I were a Dutchman . . .'. Because of this article he was sentenced to exile, but as a member of the royal house of Jogjakarta he was given a choice of place and so went to Holland. Here he became active in the *Indies Union*[6], and continued his journalism while studying for a Dutch teaching certificate. In 1913 the Indian poet and teacher, Rabindranath Tagore, won the Nobel Prize. Ki Hadjar was influenced by Tagore's ideas on national development and on education, including his criticism of the stunting effect on the child of an education in a foreign tongue, unrelated to the child's own environment.

Ki Hadjar's release was obtained through European friends in 1917. He stressed the fact that he had regained his freedom without making any commitment or statement which in whatever remote way could have had any bearing on this success. Within a year of his return to Indonesia he was again on trial for 'seditious writings'. By 1922, convinced that national education for independence was an essential prerequisite to political independence, he devoted himself to cultural activities with the founding of the

[5] See below, p. 185 ff.
[6] See below, p. 196.

Prince Diponegoro (*c.* 1785-1855) (pp. 127-8)

Tuanku Imam Bondjol (*c.* 1772-1864) (p. 126)

Raden Adjeng Kartini (1879-1904) (pp. 147-9)

Dr Wahidin Sudiro Husodo (*Budi Utomo*) (p. 174)

Ki Hadjar Dewantoro (Suwardi Surjaningrat) (1889-1959) (p. 180)

President Sukarno (1945-1968)

President Suharto (1968-   )

Vice-President Mohammad Hatta
(1945-1956)

Sutan Sjahrir (d. 1966)

Sultan Hamengku Buwono IX, of
Jogjakarta

General Abdul Haris Nasution

Taman Siswa parent school in Jogja in 1922. Foreign culture was incorporated only in so far as it could become a national possession, harmonized with the natural growth of a child in his natural environment. The school was an extension of the home and the teachers were to be as parents toward the children, a contrast to the formal authoritarian teaching common in government schools. Some government inspectors condemned the use of low tables, at which the children sat crosslegged on mats as they would at home in place of the Western school desk. Because of Ki Hadjar's past political record the authorities kept an anxious eye on the spread of the movement from Jogja, to Tjeribon in the following year, to Batavia in 1924, and as far afield as Medan by the end of the decade.

In Java the schools taught Javanese dancing, music and literature, but in other parts of Indonesia they incorporated the local dances and traditions of each area, seeking always to enrich indigenous culture by nationalizing foreign cultural values. Most schools were in east and central Java although they spread as far as Sulawesi and Medan (Sumatra). They were all linked to the Central Council at Jogja. By 1932 a total of 10,639 students attended *Taman Siswa* schools ranging from primary to teacher training level, slightly less than half of the total number of Indonesian students who attended government post-primary schools and government Dutch-language primary schools. Some *Taman Siswa* pupils attended because they had failed to gain entrance to government schools, and through pressure from them, Dutch was taught and 'rescue work' undertaken to help them proceed to higher education. Perhaps only a minority attended because their parents believed in the cultural movement itself, yet a surprising number of future nationalist leaders either attended or taught at *Taman Siswa* schools in their younger days. Unlike *Muhammadiyah*, *Taman Siswa* refused any government subsidy on principle, and continues to do so.

In 1923, a year after *Taman Siswa* was founded, legislation was introduced to control teaching in private schools because of Dutch concern at the spread of nationalism. Schools had to be registered and teachers could be suspended for any breach of public order—as defined by the government—but nationalism continued to spread through private schools. In the early 1930s in Medan at the private Dutch-language school of about 1000 students established by the Sultan of Deli, with a mixed staff including liberal-minded Dutchmen and Indonesians, fifty to a hundred students organized and participated in the annual celebration of Kartini Day. They dressed in national dress and, despite the ban against it, sang *Indonesia Raya,* the national anthem.

In 1932 a new regulation demanded that private teachers should obtain permission to teach from the Provincial Governor of the district. This was strongly opposed. In Minangkabau the protest was led by Hadji Abdul Karim Amrullah of *Muham-madiyah* (who was later to defy the Japanese authorities on behalf of Islam[7]). In Java, Ki Hadjar led the protest, strongly supported by *Budi Utomo* and other nationalist groups. He sent a cable to the government warning of a passive resistance campaign. So seriously was this opposition regarded that the Government's Commissioner for General Affairs with the *Volksraad,* where the passage of the legislation had been strongly opposed by Indonesian members, was sent to contact Ki Hadjar to explain (or explain away) the government intentions. Ki Hadjar told him that 'to ask for a licence is a restriction of the freedom of our conscience, because it is an assault on the freedom of education', adding that such an ordinance delivered the private schools into the hands of officials and that 'we do not distrust the Government but we do mistrust many of her officials . . . from experience we know that they will try by not granting us a licence to hinder our activities . . . I do not want to say that all of them aim at offending or ill-treating us, but there are nevertheless only a few who treat us as equals, who extend to us the normal courtesies and who do not want to pretend that they consider us a band of revolutionary and dangerous people, whom they cannot trust.'

The campaign was successful. In 1933 the objectionable legislation was replaced by the provision that teachers should give notice of their intention to teach without having to obtain a permit, although the government could still forbid a teacher to teach, under previous regulations. In a period when Dutch policy was increasingly repressive this was one small gain for the nationalists. For the first time the government had been forced, by combined Indonesian pressure, to repeal repressive legislation.

(e) *The Indonesian Language*

For Indonesia one of the most important cultural aspects of nationalism has been the development of the national language, Indonesian, from the *lingua franca,* Malay, used throughout the area from at least the time of Srividjaya. In India and Ceylon there have been language riots, and in Malaysia, tension over the introduction of Malay as the national language. In Indonesia the

7 See below, p. 213.

national language is a symbol of nationalism, and through its present use as the medium of instruction in all schools from grade three of primary school onwards, it has helped unify a country where about a hundred different languages and dialects are spoken.

This was encouraged by Dutch reluctance to extend the knowledge of Dutch. Many believed that 'natives ought not to know Dutch', and spoke in broken Malay even when they knew that the Indonesians to whom they were speaking understood Dutch. On one occasion a Javanese noblewoman was moved to say, 'Sir, excuse me, but may I make a friendly request, please, speak to me in your own language. I understand and speak Malay very well, but alas, only high Malay. I do not understand this *pasar* Malay.'[8] Very many Dutchmen spoke this simplified, ungrammatical version of literary Malay, and although the Dutch desired 'to base their superiority on native ignorance', their broken Malay demonstrated to those who spoke no Dutch that, however superior the Dutch might be in other ways, many were ignorant and childish in their use of the local language.

The Ethici encouraged the spread of Dutch as part of the extension of Western education to bring Indonesians and Dutch into closer association. The widespread desire to learn Dutch was partly because the policy of limitation made it a status symbol, and partly because it was essential for entry to higher learning other than Islamic.

Malay, spoken on the east coast of Sumatra and in the Malay Peninsula, was a traditional, pre-Dutch *lingua franca* and comparatively simple to learn at the *pasar* Malay level of competence. While nationalism was limited to the elite, Dutch could be used for communication between different language groups; but the leaders soon realized that it would never be a suitable language of communication for the mass of the people. In addition, as Dutch itself was a minority language, not a world language like English or French, it was easier to relinquish it in favour of a national language than it was for British or French colonies to relinquish the colonizing language.

The Javanese, as well as others, realized that the language of the largest single ethnic group, Javanese, was unsuitable as a national language because it was feudal in origin, using different levels of vocabulary depending on whether the speaker was of

---

[8] This was a polite Javanese way of saying that the Dutchman's Malay was so bad that she could not understand it while she, on the other hand, spoke Dutch. There is not the same gap between *pasar* Malay and high Malay that there is between high and low Javanese. Kartini, p. 61.

higher or lower status than the person addressed. *Budi Utomo,*
basically a Javanese movement, started encouraging Malay. Ki
Hadjar, while in Holland as a participant in the First Congress
on Colonial Education, held at The Hague in 1916, proposed the
teaching of Malay at all schools, which *Taman Siswa* did from
the outset. In the *Volksraad* a victory was recorded, as early as
1918, for those who wished Malay, with Dutch, to be a recognized
language of debate, although the majority of Indonesians
appointed or elected to the *Volksraad* were probably more fluent
in Dutch than in Malay.

In 1928, at the Second Congress of Indonesian Youth, Malay
was adopted as the national language and its name changed to
Indonesian. From then on determined efforts were made to
extend its use, as a tangible symbol of unity. In 1933 a new
journal, *Pudjangga Baru* (New Writers), began publication to
encourage the development of a national literature. Much was
written during the thirties, predominantly by Sumatrans, partly
because, for the Javanese, Indonesian was still a second language,
although they too began using it in general writing. In 1938 the
Indonesian nationalist members of the *Volksraad* deliberately
began speaking Indonesian in debates, which, as they had
expected and intended, aroused strong protest from the Dutch
press and government.

By 1942, just before the Japanese invasion, the use of Indonesian
was already spreading. Dutch opposition simply encouraged this.
The existence of a relatively simple *lingua franca* of the same
family as most other languages spoken in the archipelago; the
relative difficulty and feudal character of Javanese, the language
of the largest single ethnic group; the Dutch retention of their
language, a minority one in the world at large, as a status symbol,
have made the Indonesian national language a unifying rather
than a divisive force.

NATIONALISM AND MASS MOVEMENTS. 1911-27

So far we have considered nationalism as it affected the upper-
and middle-class Indonesian minority whose contact with Western
culture had made them more conscious of their own cultural
traditions and critical of the injustice of colonial society. From
1911 to 1927 mass movements of protest also developed, drawing
support from the peasants and from the small but growing newly
urbanized proletariat. Some writers have called these movements
pre-nationalist because they drew inspiration less from national
sentiment than from world ideologies, while at the grassroots
level their main support came from those with a general sense of

grievance and the hope that these new leaders could improve the lot of the ordinary man.

The two world ideologies which contributed to the development of mass movements from 1911 to 1927 were pan-Islam and international Communism. Fundamentally they were in conflict over basic issues, yet had enough in common to work in harmony initially, particularly as the colonial government was a common opponent. These ideologies contributed more to the thought and activities of the leaders than they did to the support of the masses.

(a) *Sarekat Islam (The Islamic Union).* 1911-16

In 1910 a depression in the central Javanese *batik* industry affected Indonesian *batik* manufacturers already facing strong competition from Chinese manufacturers. In 1911 a group of *batik* manufacturers in Solo formed the *Sarekat Dagang Islam* (Islamic Trading Union) as a co-operative to strengthen them against Chinese competition. The Javanese merchants were supported by fellow-Moslems, both Minangkabau and Arab. In 1912 anti-Chinese riots occurred in both Solo and Surabaya. In that same year the association changed its name to *Sarekat Islam* and extended its membership beyond the original trading association. Umar Said Tjokroaminoto, a man of aristocratic origin, a forceful speaker, became organizer. His oratorical appeal to the villagers enabled the movement to win tremendous popular support. By 1916 its membership was estimated at 360,000, although many of these were perhaps only nominal members. Still the leaders could claim to have mass support.

We must distinguish between the leaders and their mass following. The change from Islamic Trading Union to Islamic Union marked a decline in the influence of the original group of traders, and leadership was increasingly in the hands of Indonesians who, although not those with the highest education, had received more Western education than most Indonesians, and who had also had above average contact with Europeans, especially among the Ethici. They were generally from the middle income group and most of the Javanese leaders were from the lesser *priyayi* class. Although some merchants remained among the leaders, none were from the active *santri* Islamic group in Javanese society. There were three overlapping leadership groups —the original commercial group, the Western-educated intelligentsia dissatisfied with the colonial government structure, and the religious leaders mainly important at the local level.

Sarekat Islam's aims were fourfold: the advancement of the commercial spirit among Moslems, mutual assistance to members, the advancement of spiritual development and general welfare, and opposition to misunderstandings about Islam. The order shows the Reformist Islamic influence, the concern with leading Moslems into the modern world.

The mass following among the villagers was mainly interested in the organization as one which could protest against the changes made by modernization and the extension of government activity in village life. During the late nineteenth and into the twentieth century Islam had been growing in strength among the Javanese villagers. The closer association of local *adat* leaders with the Dutch alienated them from the villagers. The official Moslem leaders, appointed by and responsible to the regent, were seen as part of the government machinery, and leadership came increasingly from the independent Moslem scholars, many of them returned pilgrims, who ran the village religious schools or led the mystical *Sufi* brotherhoods still important in Javanese Islamic thought. Itinerant Arab leaders, too, even if they had no close connection with the Prophet himself, were respected because they came from the Holy Land. Even though, after the Java War, there were no further large-scale risings in Java, spasmodic peasant outbursts against Western penetration continued, and were undertaken in the name of Islam.

The appeal of *Sarekat Islam* to the religious bond between fellow Indonesians struck a chord in the hearts of the villagers. Usually a *Sarekat Islam* branch would start in a particular district through the influence of an independent Moslem teacher, and often the large membership would be partly due to his authority in the eyes of the villagers. Once the foundations had been laid, a central leader would come to speak to the villagers. Tjokroaminoto was especially at home in such a role, and because his name, Tjokro, was one name of the *Ratu Adil,* the Just Ruler, his mystical power in their eyes was further enhanced. They flocked to pay their ten to fifty cent membership fee and the more who joined the stronger was the social pressure on those who had not yet done so. There was a sense of belonging, security from baffling and bewildering changes in the familiar pattern of life. People would unburden themselves to the *Sarekat Islam* leaders, and much early activity was simply the channeling of these grievances back to the colonial government.

Dutch reactions to the growth of *Sarekat Islam* were varied. To the Ethical-minded it was a favourable sign of the awakening of the East and of growing self-reliance among the peasantry. Yet Governor-General Idenburg, though one of this group, was sufficiently paternalistic to withhold recognition of *Sarekat Islam* Central Committee, fearing that it could not control the branches. By withholding such recognition until his departure in 1916 he helped bring about what he feared. By that time the branches had developed independently and were reluctant to bow to the Central Committee's ruling.

The average European, uninfluenced by Ethical policies and isolated in his exclusive European club, was apprehensive. General uneasiness was strengthened by the rumour, in 1915, that armed uprisings were being planned. The government sent a young Indonesian secret police investigator to the headquarters of *Sarekat Islam* to check on this. He found the rumour untrue, and was so impressed by Tjokroaminoto's aims and sincerity that he resigned from the government to join *Sarekat Islam*. His name was Hadji Agus Salim; later one of its best-known leaders. Even in 1915, at twenty-one, he was one of the most highly educated of those so far attracted to the movement. He came from an upper-class Minangkabau family, and after graduating from a Dutch secondary school had been employed at the Dutch Consulate in Jeddah, port of arrival for pilgrims to Mecca. Here he was influenced by Islamic Modernism, of which he was one of the first Indonesian proponents. With Abdul Muis, also from Minangkabau, he provided organizational skill, guiding the movement toward Islamic Modernism. Abdul Muis, one of J. H. Abendanon's protégés, was yet another ex-STOVIA student to become a nationalist leader. After J. H. Abendanon returned to the Netherlands, Abdul Muis was demoted within the government service and moved to freelance journalism. In 1912, with Ki Hadjar, he helped establish the Bandung branch of *Sarekat Islam*.

The First National Congress of *Sarekat Islam* met in June 1916 after recognition of the central organization. Speakers urged co-operation, and welfare under government protection, looking forward to self-administration within the next ten years. All, except perhaps the time limit, was in line with Ethical thinking; but already external influences were coming to bear on the situation, leading to the development of more radical thought within *Sarekat Islam*. The effects of the First World War (1914-18) were beginning to be felt in Indonesia. Although not directly involved, the Indies government was cut off from the mother country, leading to a slowing down of the Ethical policy, inevitable in a wartime atmosphere. The interruption of trade with the Netherlands led to increased trade with the United States and Japan, and to an increase in prices and taxation, which fell most heavily on the Indonesian population. The war itself shook Indonesian respect for Europeans, while the repercussions of the Russian Revolution of 1917 began to be felt in other parts of the world.

(b) *The Rise of Indonesian Communism.* 1914-21

Indirectly the growth of *Sarekat Islam* owed much to the influence of the Ethici, as reflected in the ideas and activities of the Western educated; but its phenomenal growth seems to have been connected with its indigenous leadership, and the resentment of many of its leaders toward colonial society, and their disillusionment with the employment available to them in the government civil service. By contrast the first Marxist organizations in Indonesia were among Dutch Socialists with leadership in Dutch hands. While Marxism resembled Islam as a world movement stretching across national frontiers and yet contributing to the development of Indonesian nationalist sentiment, and while, as an ideology it was likely to spread in a colonial environment, yet it was alien and Western in origin and patterns of thought.

In 1914 Hendrik Sneevliet, a young Dutch labour leader working in the Indies, founded the Indies Social Democratic Association (ISDV), which by 1915 had between 85 and 100 members and by the following year 132, mainly Dutch. They were more closely linked with the Netherlands movement than with the Indonesian situation. Although critical of the Indies' plural society they were divided from any potential mass following by the language barrier. When the Socialist uprising in Holland failed shortly after World War I, reaction set in both in Holland and in the Indies. The Dutch Indies Social Democratic Association (ISDV) leaders were gradually expelled by the authorities and Indonesian leadership and membership grew. Efforts were made to attract more members, whether they understood Marxist goals and ideology or not, and to work within *Sarekat Islam,* the one large mass organization. To do this, individual Communists became members of *Sarekat Islam.* They emphasized similarities between Communism and Islam and played down Communism's anti-religious elements. By 1918, at the third *Sarekat Islam* National Congress, the Semarang branch, under Marxist leadership, strengthened radical demands by threatening withdrawal from the movement.

Semarang, a port on the north coast of central Java, was the centre of left-wing activity. With Batavia, Bandung and Surabaya, it was one of the most rapidly growing Javanese towns in the early twentieth century, and a centre of political activity among the newly urbanized proletariat. A Semarang housing survey in 1909 showed that, while seven in every hundred Javanese families lived with other unrelated families, and while in the *kampong* areas not a single habitable house (even if it barely qualified as such) was left empty, in the European area villas were set in spacious grounds right near the heart of the town. Where in the village the difference was one between the just-enoughs and the not-enoughs, and the contrast between the average Javanese standards of living and the foreign communities was less visible because Chinese and Europeans lived elsewhere, this obvious contrast in living standards contributed, as in other urban areas, to growing discontent among the have-nots.

Semaun and Darsono, both of Semarang, were the two chief advocates of a more revolutionary approach by *Sarekat Islam*, and so came into conflict with Hadji Agus Salim and Abdul Muis, radical in outlook, strongly Islamic but not revolutionary, prepared to denounce 'domination by sinful capitalism', that is by foreign capital, but not to place the class struggle above the national one by denouncing all capital, nor to consider it except in an Islamic context.

In 1919 Tjokroaminoto, concerned with preserving unity at all costs, was even prepared to declare himself Communist in principle, although strongly attacked by the Marxist leader, Darsono, as a fair-weather Communist, the bourgeois owner of a motor car. *Sarekat Islam* was further criticized for its parlous financial situation despite the large membership claimed—2,500,000 by 1919, the height of its expansion. Many were peasant members who may simply have paid their initial membership fee. This figure probably shows that this number of people had, at some stage, joined the movement, without indicating what the current active membership was. In particular *Sarekat Islam* was criticized for accepting financial assistance through advertising by Chinese businessmen in its journal, leading to a dropping of the original anti-Chinese emphasis. This, with the growing radicalism of the association, lost it many merchant and trading supporters, those best able to provide financial assistance.

By 1919 two strong groups were thus represented in *Sarekat Islam*: Modernist Moslems led by Hadji Agus Salim and Abdul Muis, drawing their strongest support from the Outer Islands and West Javanese *Sarekat Islam* branches; and the Marxists, led by Semaun and Darsono, drawing their strongest support from Semarang and other growing urban centres. Tjokroaminoto, with typical Javanese love of harmony, sought to preserve the unity of the movement, and to retain the services of both groups within the Central Council. These two rival groups were also increasingly active in the development of Trade Unions into a Union of Labour Movements. The chairman of this new organization was Semaun, a member of ISDV, and the secretary, Agus Salim.

The economic decline of the immediate post-war period favoured the more radical elements. Rural unrest in Java, and an uprising in Sulawesi shortly after Abdul Muis had toured the area, were both blamed on *Sarekat Islam* by the authorities, who claimed to have uncovered a secret section within *Sarekat Islam*, not known to the regular members. They held this 'Section B' responsible for an uprising in Garut, in west Java. This government investigation frightened away the more moderate members, some of whom joined *Budi Utomo* instead.

In 1920 the Indies Social Democratic Association (ISDV), from its inception an uneasy union of moderate Socialists with more revolutionary Marxists, split through the withdrawal of the more moderate elements. In May of that year (1920), the remaining revolutionaries changed their name from the former Dutch one to *Perserikatan Komunis Indonesia* (United Indonesian Communists—PKI). They became linked with international Communism through the Comintern, while, at the same time, the use of 'Indonesia' in their name emphasized their awareness of national identity, even though the Indonesian national state was simply one aspect of a wider strategy. By 1920 their membership included 250 Indonesians, and 15 Europeans, whereas in 1915 the Indies Social Democratic Association had numbered only 3 Indonesians and about 100 Europeans.

At the Fifth *Sarekat Islam* National Congress, held in March 1921, there was uneasy compromise between the two groups. Agus Salim stressed true Islam's democractic and socialistic nature while, for the sake of unity, Semaun accepted a statement favouring Islam. At the Sixth National Congress, in October of the same year, with Tjokroaminoto, chief advocate of unity, in custody under suspicion of implication in the Garut uprising, Abdul Muis and Agus Salim deliberately raised the issue of party discipline, putting to the vote the question whether a member of *Sarekat Islam* could also be a member of another political group. Semaun argued that religion alone could not provide the basis for an Indonesian popular movement as not all Indonesians were Moslem, and as religion could serve capitalism as well as socialism. He was supported by Tan Malaka, a Minangkabau, European-educated school teacher, whose personal experience of life in the Netherlands compared with colonial life had driven him toward Socialism. Tan Malaka urged the exception of the Communists (PKI) from the party discipline clause as Communism and Islam were natural allies against imperialism.

Hadji Agus Salim, supported by Abdul Muis, won the day, arguing that everything contained in Karl Marx's writings, even dialectical materialism, had already been anticipated centuries ago in the Koran.

Even before the Communists were expelled from the central council, *Sarekat Islam* was in decline. Although it claimed to have 196 branches, only 36 sent delegates to the October Congress; only one from outside Java. The five central Javanese branches opposing the party discipline vote then left, reducing the active membership to 31 branches. Indeed, the introduction of such a clause tacitly admitted that *Sarekat Islam* was no longer a mass movement, but one party among others. (By 1929 this process was completed when, under Hadji Agus Salim, it became *Partei Sarekat Islam Indonesia*—Indonesian Islamic Union Party —PSII.)

The split revealed that, within the mass organization based on Islam opposed to foreign encroachment, there were seeds of more secular political movements. *Sarekat Islam* was also the first example of a movement attempting to bridge the gap between the villager and the new Western educated elite.

DISINTEGRATION OF THE MASS MOVEMENT. 1922-27

The split in the leadership of *Sarekat Islam,* led to a struggle between rival groups for control of the various branches. Here the weakness of the central body, because of the government's delay in granting it recognition, worked against the moderates. Control of the central body did not necessarily give them control of the branches. In many districts rival *Sarekat Islam Merah* (Red Islamic Union) Communist groups were established alongside the original ones, confusing the villager, particularly as the Communists were not expelled because of opposition to their socialist principles as such but because these were divorced from the Koran's teaching.

Both groups, during the next five years, emphasized the international aspects of their ideologies. From 1922 onward the *Sarekat Islam* leaders were involved in promoting annual All-Indies Islamic Conferences in co-operation with *Muhammadiyah,* and planning a proposed World Pan-Islamic Conference, until it became clear, in 1926, that this could not be held.

At the 1926 All-Indies Islamic Conference it became clear that Islam purged of Communism was still not united. A split developed between the urban-centred, often Western-educated, Reformists and the rural-centred traditionalists. The latter, those who provided the original village leadership in the establishment of *Sarekat Islam,* formed a new organization, *Nahdatul Ulama* (The Awakening of Islamic Theologians). Significantly they chose an Islamic title representing their more traditional, less intellectual interpretation of the faith and their less critical attitude to local *adat* where its customs opposed Islamic teaching.

Meanwhile the United Indonesian Communists (PKI) were increasingly out of step with Comintern edicts. International Communist strategy was based, they believed, on the Chinese rather than the Indonesian situation. The Comintern was poorly informed about Indonesian events. The self-appointed delegate representing Indonesia was Sneevliet, who had been expelled by the Indies government shortly after the 1914-18 War, and who knew little about events there since. When the Indonesian Communists were working with *Sarekat Islam,* the Comintern was advocating a coalition with bourgeois nationalism, whose only Indonesian representative was *Insulinde,* descendant of the former *Indies Party,* which was increasingly Eurasian, hoping to obtain independence from the Netherlands and to transfer Dutch control to Eurasian hands. The Comintern also urged a struggle against pan-Islam, so its programme made very little sense in the Indonesian situation.

When the Communists were being expelled from *Sarekat Islam* the Comintern was advocating the capture of nationalist mass movements from inside, 'the bloc within'; and when a considerable section of the Indonesian Communist movement was using increasingly revolutionary language, the Comintern was attempting to play down Communism's revolutionary aspects. Comintern strategy was not designed with the situation in a colonial dependency in mind.

In the period following the *Sarekat Islam* split, both *Sarekat Islam* and United Indonesian Communist (PKI) leaders were rivals for the control of the growing trade union movement. Apart from the transport workers' unions, the majority were white collar ones, such as that formed by the employees of government pawnshops. There were several abortive strikes, and as a result of the one by the government pawnshop officials the union leader, Abdul Muis, was arrested and sent back to his own district, Minangkabau. He took no further part in political activity but instead turned to literature. His themes were the disruptive effects of Western education and the dangers inherent in mixed marriage.

By 1924, the Communist popular following, fed by the hope of revolution is claimed to have been the greatest of any single group, estimated at about 1,000, although it should be remembered that at the 1924 Special All-Islam Conference there were 1,000 present. It is impossible to tell how far, if at all, the peasants distinguished between Islamic and Communist doctrines and leadership or recognized the difference between *Sarekat Islam* and *Sarekat Rakjat* (People's Union, successor to the Red Islamic Union) except in personal and local terms.

Late in 1925 the Dutch government, alarmed at the spread of Communism and yet reluctant to admit, by outlawing the party, that its Ethical policy had failed completely, imposed restrictions which, without actually making the Indonesian Communist Union (PKI) itself illegal, nevertheless made most of its activities subject to legal restrictions. For example, it became increasingly difficult to hold public meetings, while Dutch secret police and spies made communication between the different branches increasingly difficult, and the Comintern programme of seeking alliance with other interests and widening the basis of the movement beyond the proletariat became virtually impossible, particularly as government servants were first forbidden to join the Indonesian Communist Union (PKI) and later forbidden to buy its journal.

These restrictions made the Indonesian Communists increasingly impatient with the undue caution of the Comintern, although it turned out to be a more realistic assessment of the revolutionary potential of the Indonesian masses than the optimistic one of the Indonesian Communist leaders themselves. Increasingly, as the Dutch on various pretexts imprisoned or banished the top Communist leaders, the movement's leadership was assumed by younger, less experienced, more impatient people. Central control of the movement within Indonesia was weakening just as the utopian hopes of the masses were being strengthened and encouraged by local Communist groups. These included the hope, with no evidence to support it, that outside aid might come either from Kemal Ataturk of Turkey, or from Russia and China.

The Central Executive urged the delay of widespread revolution, but a series of small, mainly unsuccessful strikes occurred in Java in mid-1925 and others, equally unsuccessful, in the urban centres of Batavia, Medan and Surabaya later that year. When these failed and the employers took tough retaliatory measures, fingerprinting and then blacklisting suspect workers, discriminating against the literate in such blacklisting, the only choice seemed to be surrender or open rebellion. A secret meeting of eleven top party members held at Prambanan[9] at Christmas, 1925, made concrete plans for an uprising, setting its tentative date for mid-1926; but by then the Indonesian Communist Union was hopelessly divided on whether the time was ripe for revolt. Tan Malaka, who was observing events from Singapore, urged restraint; the Bandung executive urged united action or none at all; while those already committed to revolution attempted to widen their mass support in the face of opposition within the party itself.

In most of Java the revolts either did not start or were crushed at the outset. For example, at Tegal, in north Java, where the regional authorities, four years behind in their collection of taxes, were beginning to demand the arrears (which had of course been spent), there was considerable unrest but, as the rebels gathered on one night to await the signal for revolt, and the person responsible for giving it did so the *following* night, by which time his confederates had dispersed, the revolt failed. In Batavia, although armed bands roamed the streets and one even managed to hold the Telephone Exchange for several hours, the whole affair was over in two days. Only in Banten (west Java), and Minangkabau (central Sumatra) did any uprising take place and then not simultaneously, as planned. The Banten revolt was crushed by late 1926 but the Minangkabau one did not start until early 1927, and was completely finished by 12 January.

Neither Banten nor Minangkabau was typical of general Indonesian conditions. Both were relatively wealthy, with some private Indonesian business developing and with a relatively high percentage of pilgrims. Both were strongly Islamic areas, closed to Christian missionary activity, with strong *Sarekat Islam* groups. Both were thinly populated in comparison with east and central Java and free from Western estates. Minangkabau young men were encouraged to travel before settling down and a high percentage had some Western education. Banten was known for its individualism, and unwilling co-operation with European authorities, who reciprocated by seeking a transfer to less independent, more courteous districts as soon as possible. Consequently the government secret service had been less well informed of the situation in Banten, while in Java the secret police had been as well informed about the date of the uprising as many of the would-be participants. In Minangkabau the Dutch policy of sending troublemakers back to their area of origin meant that many Communist agitators and other disaffected people were

⁹ See above, p. 40.

recalled to the area, yet in both places there are grounds for wondering whether the main impulse was the new Communist doctrine or whether this was predominantly another old-style uprising mainly Islamic in inspiration.

The failure of the revolts marked the effective end of Communist activity in colonial Indonesia. The Dutch authorities arrested a total of 13,000 people, sentencing 4,500 of them to prison after trial, and over 1,000 who could not be convicted under existing laws to exile at the governor's pleasure in the horror camp of Upper Digul (West Irian). If, as has been estimated, not more than 3,000 people at the most belonged to the Communist Union as distinct from the *Sarekat Rakjat* mass movement (estimated at about 30,000), and not more than 5,000 were actively involved in the armed uprising, the large number of people arrested may justify the claim of the Dutch Communist Party that the rebellion was provoked by the government to give it a pretext to crush the revolutionary movement. While it was largely a Communist-inspired movement, it seems to have taken place as much in spite of as because of the Communist leaders, who could no longer control the forces they had set in motion.

In Minangkabau more serious disturbances had occurred between 1908 and 1909, in protest against the new taxes introduced to replace the proceeds from compulsory coffee cultivation and delivery, abolished only in that year. Economic grievances were reinforced by Moslem leadership of the protests and several clashes occurred, with about a hundred casualties on the Minangkabau side and, among losses on the Dutch side, the assassination of one district Controller. In 1927, after less than a fortnight of rather badly co-ordinated activity, there were barely half a dozen casualties and only a few inconsequential skirmishes, used as a pretext to clamp down on Communist activity.

The underlying cause of the revolts was the sense of grievance against the existing order, linked with expectations for the future aroused in part at least by Communist propaganda, and often bearing little relation to reality. These included messianic hopes of foreign intervention. In Banten particularly there were overtones of a holy war against the infidels. Yet what marked these revolts off from the earlier ones was their close connection with Communism in the rest of Java, and their timing in relation to the plans made at the Prambanan conference. It was not, as the Communists had hoped, a rebellion of the whole people but an abortive and easily crushed *putsch*. Nor could it be called nationalist, though it extended beyond Java.

Not only was the Indonesian Communist Union (PKI) effectively destroyed for the remainder of the colonial period, with its leaders either self-exiled to avoid arrest or detained by the Dutch and exiled or imprisoned within Indonesia, but it was also split between followers of Tan Malaka and those who regarded Tan Malaka as chiefly responsible for the failure. As the government had behind it the coercive power both of the military and of the police force, a more widespread revolt could hardly have been more successful. Musso, Alimin and their followers believed otherwise and labelled Tan Malaka a Trotskyist, which is abusive language in Communist circles. Meanwhile Tan Malaka, in Bangkok in 1927, established his *Pari (Partei Republik Indonesia*—Indonesian Republic Party) aimed at training Indonesian underground workers, to build up underground cadres in Indonesia. During the 1930s an Indonesian popular novel, an Indonesian version of *The Scarlet Pimpernel* appeared, based, though it did not say so, on the life of Tan Malaka. Everyone knew to whom it referred, which helped to establish him as a folk hero among some Indonesians.

Along with the destruction of the Communist movement went the final tacit abandonment of the Ethical Policy. Many Dutch opponents saw it as responsible for the unrest, by advocating excessive kindness to 'natives'. Many belonged to the school which argued in the European press that one should 'treat a dog like a dog. If a coolie understands kindness, be kind to him; but since he understands the language of the whip, take the whip to him', doubly insulting sentiments to Moslems for whom, strictly speaking, dogs, like pigs, are unclean animals. The harsh treatment meted out to the rebels was the beginning of a much tougher policy on the part of the Dutch toward all opposition of whatever nature. Many Ethici were themselves deeply disappointed at the path taken by some of their protégés, for they saw this in personal terms as evidence of ingratitude and of opportunities misapplied. As attitudes hardened it became more difficult for those on either side of the gulf to establish friendships.

POLITICAL NATIONALISM. 1912-41

The first nationalist political party, the Indies Party,[10] founded in 1912, lasted barely a year before its founders were dispersed through government action. It aimed at establishing an organization drawing support both from Eurasians and from Indonesians and seeking ultimate self-government for those to whom the Indies were home. When Douwes Dekker, its Eurasian leader,

[10] See above, p. 180.

reconstituted the party, this time named *Insulinde*, it was absorbed into the Eurasian fringe of Dutch Society.

(a) *The Volksraad (People's Council).* 1918-42

The *Volksraad* or People's Council was introduced in reply to pressure from various groups within colonial society seeking greater autonomy and from 1916, when it was established by legislation, to 1918, when it first met, many hoped that this legitimate forum for criticism might affect the development of the colony's political life. Although in line with Ethical thinking, it was a case of too little too late. Even at the first *Volksraad* meeting there was opposition. When the Governor-General, in his opening remarks, foreshadowed a greater degree of autonomy for the Indies, the Chairman, himself a government appointee, replied, 'We are grateful but not satisfied.' The Council then rejected a proposal that a loyal cable should be sent to the Queen, and insisted that Malay, along with Dutch, should be an official language of debate, although the majority even of the Indonesian members spoke Dutch more fluently than they did Malay, and some may have spoken no Malay at all.

In 1921, when Hadji Agus Salim [11] became *Sarekat Islam* representative in the *Volksraad*, he was the first person to use Malay in debate. This was clearly a nationalist gesture, for he also spoke fluent French, German and English in addition to Dutch, Arabic and his own local dialect, Minangkabau.

Many Dutch were surprised by the extent and vehemence of opposition in the *Volksraad*. So revolutionary were the speeches at the second session that the Governor-General sent a message to the *Volksraad* promising further reform. It was doubtful, though, whether any reform acceptable to Dutch interests would have satisfied the nationalists. As late as 1939 when Indonesian representation was thirty members, and non-Indonesian also thirty (twenty-five Dutch and five other Asians), of which two-thirds were elected and the remainder appointed, only 10% of the Indonesian population had any vote for the *Volksraad*. Even so the Indonesian representation was at the rate of one candidate to every seventy-seven voters, while the Dutch was one to every fifty-five. Because an increasing number of nationalist groups favoured non-co-operation, the Indonesian representation reflected only the more conservative groups within the community. In the early years, on the initiative of a Dutch socialist member, his group, along with *Sarekat Islam, Insulinde,*

[11] See above, p. 178.

Budi Utomo and the Indies Social Democratic Association, formed the Radical Concentration, a reminder that the terms 'left' and 'right' in politics are very relative. Within the *Volksraad* this was the left wing; outside, the component parts ranged across to the right of the nationalist movement.

The *Volksraad* gave political experience to a small handful of Indonesian leaders. It drew together leaders from different parts of the country, enabled them to work together and to realize their common grievances and aspirations. It provided a forum for criticism of the government and for contact between government and governed, but had no real share in governing, as both its criticisms and suggestions could be overridden. It also divided the nationalist movement as the central issue between co-operators and non-co-operators.

By the mid-1920s *Sarekat Islam* withdrew from the *Volksraad* under growing radical pressure, while the Communists refused from the outset to co-operate, believing that the *Volksraad* would fail and hoping to profit when this happened. In 1932 the *Volksraad* Indonesian members protested strongly but in vain against the proposed Wild School legislation. Organized pressure from outside the *Volksraad* was more influential than that exercised by the representative body. In 1936 a *Volksraad* member, Sutardjo, presented a petition favouring evolutionary development toward self-government in a ten-year period within the existing limits of the Dutch Constitution. Three years later an evasive and disappointing reply was finally given. By then it was clear that the most vigorous political activity was finding expression outside rather than within the *Volksraad*. The reaction to the Sutardjo Petition dashed the hopes of those working for evolutionary development toward greater independence.

(b) *Secular Nationalism*

Secular nationalist parties arose after the mass parties disintegrated. By 1921 Islam and Communism had divided the mass movement; by 1926 Islam itself was divided into Modernists and Traditional Theologians and after 1927 the remnant of the Communist movement was also divided—although politically it counted for little in Indonesia as several leaders were overseas, and the rest, along with the bulk of the members, were in exile, effectively silencing any remaining sympathisers.

The first secular nationalist movement was the Union of Indonesian Nationalists (*Perserikatan Nasional Indonesia*) founded in 1927. By 1928 it had taken the name *Partei Nasional Indo-*

nesia (Indonesian Nationalist Party—PNI)[12] and advocated as its ultimate objective 'Independent Indonesia' *(Indonesia Merdeka)*. It arose from the Bandung Study Group formed by Sukarno, and included among its original members many former members of the Indonesian Association *(Perhimpunan Indonesia)*, the student organization. It sought a mass following which its leader, Sukarno, quickly won by his oratorical skill and awareness of the 'little man's' thinking.

Sukarno, although one of a small handful of graduates of tertiary institutions, had not been overseas to study, as had many of his fellow leaders in the nationalist movement. He was the son of a Javanese schoolteacher from a lesser *prijayi* family, and a Balinese mother, both of whom encouraged him to 'be a man who is significant, a man who is useful, a man who is fit to greet the rising of the sun, a man with ideals'. When young, he was strongly influenced by the *wayang* performances of the Javanese world in which he lived and its portrayal of Indonesia's former greatness. He attended a Dutch high school at Surabaya (1915-21), living with Tjokroaminoto's family, and reading widely in many languages, in a variety of fields. His extracurricular activity in such a household, including contact with leaders in both the Islamic and Socialist wings of *Sarekat Islam,* helped to mould his future career, for in many ways, as orator, as spellbinder and as seeker of unity, he resembled his benefactor.

From Surabaya he went to the Bandung Technological Institute to study engineering and architecture, although, when Tjokroaminoto was in custody during 1921, Sukarno interrupted his studies to help the family during their resulting financial difficulty. In Bandung, in 1926, he established the General Study Club. In 1927 the Study Club members, with Sukarno as secretary, established the new Indonesian Nationalist Party which by 1929 boasted a membership of 10,000 and so alarmed the Dutch authorities that the party was dissolved and Sukarno and three other leaders imprisoned.

During this period, as Dutch attitudes hardened, the fragmentation of the nationalist movement continued. In 1931, Sartono, a former member of the Indonesian Nationalist Party, formed *Partindo (Partai Indonesia*—Indonesian Party) similar to the PNI in general objectives but with its methods of procedure modified in the interests of survival. Sukarno, released at the end of 1931, joined *Partindo* in 1932 and was elected chairman. It

[12] The post-war PNI had no direct link with this earlier party of the same name.

aimed at becoming a mass movement and by mid-1933 had 50 branches and a total of 20,000 members. After its inevitable dispersion by the Dutch and Sukarno's exile first to Flores and later to Bengkulu, where he was kept until the Japanese arrived, a new party, *Gerindo (Gerakan Rakjat Indonesia*—Indonesian People's Movement), replaced it, becoming the powerful left wing of the Nationalists. Though militantly nationalist it was prepared, in face of the threat of Fascist attack, to co-operate with the Dutch.

Meanwhile other members of the Indonesian Association *(Perhimpunan Indonesia)* had returned to become active in the nationalist movement. Two of them, Mohammed Hatta and Sjahrir, preferred a small educated elite, extending nationalism gradually, rather than a large unco-ordinated mass following. Both were from Minangkabau, Hatta from a merchant family in Minangkabau itself, Sjahrir from the quite significant group of Minangkabau resident in Medan, a thriving cosmopolitan city across the strait from Singapore. (Sjahrir sometimes had something of the attitude of the city man for his country cousin in his comments about Hatta.)[13] They established the Indonesian National Education Club *(Club Pendidikan Nasional Indonesia)*, with a total of about a thousand members, deliberately choosing to use this group rather than joining *Partindo,* successor to the Indonesian Nationalist Party. Mass movements with only a few leaders were vulnerable to government attack. With the leaders gaoled, the movement would collapse. They hoped instead to train a wider number of more self-reliant, well-informed leaders, less dependent on a few key figures; but even this activity was no longer acceptable to the Dutch. Seeing the threat it involved to their regime, they arrested both Hatta and Sjahrir.

The Nationalist parties were also divided on the question of co-operation against non-co-operation. Many younger generation Nationalists saw non-co-operation as a matter of principle; many of the older generation, and the more realistic among the younger, saw it simply as a matter of tactics, appropriate in some situations, less appropriate in others. In practice, the hardening attitude of the Dutch authorities made non-co-operation less and less appropriate.

Finally, attempts were made during the 1930s to achieve a wider unity between different nationalist groups. *Parindra* (Great Indonesia Party—*Partai Indonesia Raja)* in 1935 had been one such party, and became one of the most powerful groups within

¹³ Sjahrir, *Out of Exile,* pp. 41, 86-7, 104-5, 121, 181.

the *Volksraad*.[14] In 1939 *Gapi* (*Gabungan Politiek Indonesia*—Federation of Indonesian Political Parties) united eight of the most important nationalist organizations and sponsored a *Kongress Rakjat Indonesia* (Indonesian People's Congress) with representatives of *ninety* different nationalist organizations, an indication of the extent to which the nationalist movement was fragmented. At this meeting the Indonesian language (*bahasa Indonesia*), the Indonesian flag (the Red and White) and the national anthem, *Indonesia Raja,* were officially adopted.[15] The anthem had been composed for a youth congress held in 1929 and since that time had been sung on national occasions, although preferably out of earshot of Dutch authorities, in many parts of Indonesia.[16]

(c) *Dutch Reaction—A Police State*

The final years of Dutch rule in the Indies coincided with world-wide depression, when the Dutch salvaged their own financial interests at the expense of the Indonesian sector, and later with impending war as the Second World War broke out in Europe and seemed increasingly likely to spread to Asia. The Dutch in the colony were by then involved in an all-out effort to supply the Allies with the raw materials needed for the war effort, and felt impatient with Indonesian nationalist political demands, while most Indonesians waited with growing optimism for the expected arrival of the Japanese who, as long ago as 1905, had showed themselves a match for a European power. Indeed, 'the people derived a vicarious satisfaction from the misfortunes of their rulers'.

After Hatta and Sjahrir had been arrested, untried for about three months, they were finally charged with spreading hate and endangering public tranquillity and order through their educational efforts. Exiled to Upper Digul in West Irian, they were moved a year later to almost as isolated a spot, Bandanaira, a small island in the Banda Sea south-east of Ambon where they were free to undertake a limited amount of teaching, and to live freely as long as they stayed on the island. They were evacuated just ahead of the first Japanese raids there in 1942.[17] Both of them, newly returned from the more liberal atmosphere of student life in Holland, found their arrest and exile a severe

[14] See above, p. 197.
[15] See above, p. 184.
[16] See above, p. 181.
[17] Sjahrir, *Out of Exile,* pp. 224-30.

shock. Their opposition to the Dutch had intentionally and consciously been within what they understood to be legal limits. They had still believed in the government's reason and respectability. Their arrest and subsequent exile without adequate trial showed them that the colony was actually a police state.

Sjahrir's letters to his Dutch wife, published under the title *Out of Exile,* make an interesting comparison with Kartini's *Letters,* written scarcely thirty-five years earlier. Like Kartini, Sjahrir is aware of his intellectual debt to Holland, writing that 'for our spiritual needs we are in general dependent on the West, not only scientifically but culturally. We intellectuals here are much closer to Europe or America than we are to the Borobudur or Mahabharata or to the primitive Islamic culture of Java and Sumatra', but he regards this less as a matter for gratitude than as part of his birthright as an intellectual. He is also aware that his education has cut him off from the peasantry, who are closer to Borobudur or primitive Islam. This had brought him back to Indonesia in the first place, while the injustice of his sentence made him feel 'more firmly and indissolubly bound to my people than ever before'.

He gives a vivid picture of life in the Upper Digul concentration camp, established originally for the exiles implicated in the 1926 and 1927 uprisings, but later used for any political prisoners sufficiently displeasing to the authorities. On the crocodile-infested Digul river banks a camp of about 400 exiles was established with a guard camp separated from it by a ditch. The exiles had to build their own houses, finding the timber for themselves from the forest, and using as roofing material government zinc, which turned the little huts into hotboxes during the tropical afternoons when temperatures soared to 100° F. It was a malarial area and the prisoners, on insufficient rations, fell easy victims to malaria. They could become voluntary workers, but as Sjahrir commented, the 40 cents a day for coolie work from 7 to 12 in the mornings was 'just too little to make us hesitate', as they also had to cook, care for their hut and their clothes, fish to supplement the monthly rations of rice, dried fish, dried green peas, salt, tea, cooking oil and brown sugar or else try to grow vegetables on the poor soil around the camp. For those classed as non-extremist, those not advocating the forceful overthrow of the existing social order, a gratuity of 7.50 guilders a month replaced the 2.60 guilders worth of food supplied to those not working for the government.

Sjahrir himself was barely 27 at the time of his exile. Others were even younger,[18] and many from the original 'Communist' group, who had already spent eight years in exile, were broken in spirit and in health. Of them Sjahrir wrote: 'There are not many European Communists who could recognize anything of their communism in this Indonesian variety', which he described as 'a mystical Hinduistic-Javanese, Islamic-Minangkabau, or Islamic-Banten sort of Communism, with definite animistic tendencies'.

Meanwhile the gulf between the Dutch and the Indonesian intellectuals was widening. Public talk of *Indonesia Merdeka* (Independent Indonesia) had been declared by the Dutch to be an 'act of treason and disloyal to the lawful sovereign', and in a police state (for the whole system of Dutch colonial government by the 1930s depended upon police informers), it was folly to be accused of treason or disloyalty. Such talk ceased, and the Dutch wrongly assumed that no thought of it continued.

As early as 1929 the European community responded to growing nationalist feeling by forming the *Vaderlandsche Club* (Union of Patriots), an ultra-conservative party. Civil liberties were increasingly eroded during the 1930s and 1940s. Douwes Dekker[19], who had by the late 1920s withdrawn from political activity to become principal of the Ksatria Institute, a private school in Bandung, in 1936 published a history of the world, and was prosecuted for having publicly manifested 'hostility, dislike or contempt of one or more of the population groups of the Indies' because he had been critical of colonizing activity in the past. His defence, that the statements were derived from Dutch scientific studies, that official Dutch scholarly works were more critical of the government than he had been, that the work was historical, and that he had in fact consulted Dutch authorities before publication and understood that he had official consent to do so, did not prevent his being sentenced to three months' imprisonment. In appealing, he quoted instances from the European press, and there were plenty, of 'hostility, dislike or contempt' expressed against Indonesians. The judge admitted the substance of the defence but he only reduced the sentence to a heavy fine, thus applying a form of censorship to historical writings, although no corresponding censorship was placed on the derogatory writings of the European press.

[18] In Ivan Southall, *Indonesia Face to Face*, pp. 38-42, there is an account of the experiences of Bondan, one of the young exiles sent to Upper Digul at the same time as Hatta and Sjahrir. He stayed there until the remainder of the group was evacuated to Australia, allegedly as prisoners of war, in 1943.
[19] See above, p. 180.

In the prevailing atmosphere of the colony, even high-ranking persons who disagreed with the judgement dared not protest. People were anxious to avoid involvement with anyone caught up in the legal processes of the government. Sjahrir compared this with the situation he had known in Holland, but commented that 'under the Napoleonic regime or under Phillip II (of Spain) the same feeling of fear and timidity prevailed in Holland as one now finds among us in Indonesia, as well as among the Indians in British India'. The Dutch attitude had changed very little from that described by Raffles a hundred years before. There was still 'a haughty assumption of superiority' mixed with 'extra-ordinary timidity' among the Dutch themselves toward their subjects. Yet Governor-General de Jonge, whose term of office during the depression was the first period of harshly repressive measures against nationalism, was confident that the Dutch would still be ruling the Indies in another 300 years. He was, of course, wrong.

CHAPTER NINE

War and Occupation

Indonesia, my native country, land which bore and nurtured me,
Here I stand now, prepared and eager, pledging you my fealty.
Indonesia, my nation, country, you my mother, I your son!
Let us shout with voice united: "Indonesia shall be one!"
Come to life, nation mine! Come to life, native land!
O my country, my people arise!
Let our spirit awake, let our bodies awake
To create Indonesia the Great.
Indonesia Raja, independent and free,
Native land, country mine which I cherish,
Indonesia Raja, independent and free,
Come to life Indonesia Raja.

W. Supratman, 1928.

Under the Dutch this song, *Indonesia Raja* (Great Indonesia),
later to be the Indonesian national anthem, was banned; nor was
the flying of the Indonesian flag, the Red and White, permitted.
Even the use of the terms 'Indonesia' and 'Indonesian' were
forbidden. It was becoming increasingly difficult in the later
1930s to offer any criticism of Dutch colonialism, past or present,
without facing the prospect of imprisonment or exile. Nor were
many Indonesians particularly impressed by the vague promise
made by Queen Wilhelmina in 1941. She said that, after liberation, she intended 'to create the occasion for a joint consultation
about the structure of the Kingdom and its parts in order to
adapt it to the changed circumstances'. Many nationalists
believed a stalemate had been reached and that Indonesia 'independent and free' was as far off as ever. Yet so rapidly did the
circumstances change within the following nine years that Indonesia not only proclaimed her independence but defended it
successfully in the face of Dutch attempts to restore the old
regime.

Looking at the Second World War (1939-45), which brought
about these changed circumstances, from the point of view of the
people of South-east Asia it was a conflict between the old

205

colonial powers—England, the Netherlands, Belgium and France —and the more recent arrivals—Germany and Italy—fought partly in Europe itself and partly in the colonial areas under dispute. At least one point at issue, although not the only one, was that of spheres of influence in colonial areas and the right of the newer nation states to 'a place in the sun'. In 1940, with the signing of the Triple Alliance between Germany, Italy and Japan, the third new arrival in the colonial field announced her community of interest with the other two. In particular Japan was anxious to participate in the exploitation of the oil and minerals which made Indonesia of such strategic importance in the era of the diesel engine and the aeroplane. As she could not achieve this through peaceful negotiation she turned instead to military activity. Japan succeeded in destroying the old colonial system in Indonesia; the Allies succeeded in destroying the new colonial empire of Japan, and when the World War, a fight between two foreign powers on Indonesian soil, ended, the real struggle began for the people of Indonesia as they sought to free themselves from colonialism once and for all. This struggle ended with the establishment of one united, independent and free Indonesian nation.

THE RISE OF MODERN JAPAN. 1868-1941

For over two hundred years (1638-1854) Japan had turned its back on the outside world, having no further contact with it than was provided by an annual Dutch trading ship which called at Nagasaki. Finally, in the mid-nineteenth century, she was forced by foreign pressure to reopen trade with foreigners and even to grant extra-territorial rights to foreign powers in certain Japanese ports. The year of the Meiji Restoration, 1868, is taken as the date from which the modernization of Japan commenced. The new oligarchy which ruled through the authority of the Divine Emperor realized that, for the expulsion of the Western barbarian, Japan needed first to be on equal terms with the European powers. For this it was necessary to crowd into the life span of one individual the changes which Europe had taken at least three centuries to achieve.

By the end of the century, barely thirty years later, feudalism had been abolished (1871), the Emperor had granted a constitution on the Prussian model (1889), a programme of industrialization had been undertaken, and, as a result of Japan's attack on China (1894-5), Formosa had been ceded to her and Korea declared a fully independent Empire. Japan was launched on her career as a colonial power. In 1899 the extra-territorial system, by which foreign powers in Japan were subject neither to Japanese law nor to the tariffs she imposed on imports and exports, was abolished. In the same year the Netherlands Indies government recognized the Japanese as 'European' within the plural society of the Indies.

By the end of the First World War (1914-18), Japan had consolidated her position as a world power. Her allies were beginning to wonder whether they did not need some safeguards themselves in the face of Japanese expansion. As a colonial power in Taiwan (Formosa) and Korea, Japan efficiently developed the economy of the colonial territory in the interest of the home country, through the medium of private Japanese capital investment. Japanese economic interests were paramount and she used education as an instrument of assimilation, to draw the local population into an empire owing its higher culture to Japan.

After World War I Japan extended her Indies trade and her influence among the local population. In 1929 she provided 11% of Indonesia's total imports, by 1935 30%, although she took only 5% of Indonesia's exports. The Dutch were concerned about this unequal trade balance. Japan expressed willingness to buy considerable quantities of oil, coal and other mineral products while the Dutch made it plain that they were primarily concerned about the sale of sugar, coffee, tea or tobacco. Since her acquisition of Taiwan, Japan was self-sufficient in sugar and other foodstuffs but dependent on foreign countries for the oil and minerals needed for her industrial expansion.

During the 1930s, the Dutch limited Japanese activities in the colony through legislation requiring import licences, regulating foreign labour, fixing immigration quotas for certain foreigners, controlling fishing in territorial waters. The Japanese resented the immigration quotas because they undermined their equality of status. By 1939 Japan was openly advocating a Greater East Asian Co-Prosperity Sphere in which she would play the leading role, similar to that played by Great Britain in the British Empire.

The influx of cheap Japanese goods directly benefited the ordinary Indonesians with limited monetary earnings especially during the depression. Most Chinese, the traditional middlemen, boycotted Japanese goods, while the Japanese aimed at competing with the Chinese by selling Japanese goods imported by Japanese merchants in Japanese ships and sold in Japanese stores or by Japanese middlemen. These shops were staffed by courteous Japanese whose 'usual facial expression was something like a smile', as Sjahrir put it. Ordinary Indonesians saw them as men of refinement, especially when their behaviour was compared to the coarse behaviour of either the Dutch or the Chinese.[1]

There is a certain irony about the Dutch criticism of Japanese exclusiveness. According to van Mook they looked upon their economic pursuits in foreign countries 'as integrated parts of the economy of the Japanese empire' and they desired to 'recruit nothing from the local population but labour', a complaint that comes rather quaintly from a Dutchman whose own country had pursued similar policies for several centuries. Nevertheless it was clear that, during the 1930s, the Japanese were engaged in an organized penetration of the economy of the Indies.

In the 1920s Japan 'discovered' Islam and began to be interested in Islamic affairs. Several big mosques were built, and Japanese were sent overseas to become Islamic experts. In 1939 the Japanese Islamic Association organized the First Islamic World Conference to which an Indonesian delegation was invited. In Japan the guests were also taken on excursions to government offices, factories and military training centres. Even if they reserved their judgement about the piety of their hosts, they were impressed by the signs of material advancement in a self-governing Asian country. As early as 1937 Sjahrir commented: 'As far as I can make out, the whole Islamic population of our country is now pro-Japanese . . .'

In the undeclared Sino-Japanese war which broke out in 1937, most Indonesians sympathized with the Japanese rather than with their traditional oppressors, the Chinese.

THE SECOND WORLD WAR. 1939-45

When war was declared in Europe in September 1939, it seemed at first as if the Netherlands Indies, as in the First World War, might be only indirectly affected. In 1940 Germany invaded the Netherlands and the Dutch government moved to London. In that year the Japanese sent a trade mission to Batavia. It was particularly interested in access to oil concessions in the archipelago. The Dutch were unco-operative, and when that year Japan became a signatory to the Triple Alliance with the Axis Powers, Germany and Italy, Dutch attitudes hardened further, opposing the Greater East Asia Co-Prosperity Sphere openly advocated by the Japanese.

A second trade mission in 1941 was equally unsuccessful and

---

[1] This was particularly important in Java where the distinction between refined (*halus*) and coarse (*kasar*) behaviour was the most important one made in social behaviour.

in July the Netherlands followed the example of the United States, Great Britain and the British Dominions by freezing Japanese assets, suspending also the recently drawn-up Dutch-Japanese financial agreement. In December 1941, the Japanese, who saw their economic expansion being strangled by concerted Allied opposition, launched a surprise attack on the American fleet at Pearl Harbor. The following day the Netherlands, although almost entirely unequipped to defend the Indies, declared war upon Japan.

The first Japanese landed in Indonesia in January 1942, hoping to capture intact the oil installations at Tarakan (north-west Kalimantan), Balikpapan (west-central Kalimantan) and Palembang (south Sumatra) and to restore the oil refineries to working order so they could take by force what they had not obtained by negotiation.

Three months after the declaration of war and eight days after the first Japanese landing in Java the Dutch Commander-in-Chief surrendered in the name of all Allied forces in Java, thus preventing the 8,000 British and American troops in Java from any further hostility. The Indonesians, who saw only the land fighting, knew nothing of the courageous record of the Dutch sea and air forces, and were further convinced of Japanese power and of Dutch impotence in face of it. Sjahrir commented that, 'for the average Indonesian the war . . . was simply a struggle in which the Dutch colonial rulers finally would be punished by Providence for the evil, the arrogance and the oppression they had brought to Indonesia'. The revival of the prophecy attributed to Djoyoboyo[2] led many Javanese villagers to believe that the invasion would be brief and that the Dutch had gone for ever.

Many Indonesians, particularly those who were aware of the nature of Japanese totalitarianism, felt betrayed. They had pleaded in vain with the Dutch for the right to defend their own homeland but had been entrusted with neither arms nor freedom. The Netherlands East Indies forces were Dutch-led, with professional soldiers drawn mainly from the Christian areas of Indonesia, especially from Ambon. They were used to small-scale fighting against fellow-Indonesians, usually inadequately armed and quite untrained. They were no match for the well-armed, well-trained Japanese troops, seasoned by almost five years of fighting in China, and preceded by rumours of their invincibility.

In many parts of Indonesia the Japanese were first welcomed as liberators. In Atjeh, for example, uprisings preceded their arrival. In Medan, north Sumatra, Hamka describes the

[2] See p. 21, above.

thousands who gathered in front of the Great Mosque to welcome the invaders with shouts of 'Banzai' (Long life). The
Japanese had landed on the coast and made their way to Medan
on bicycles commandeered along the route. At least one nineteen-
year-old, who shouted 'Banzai' along with the rest, revised his
views of the Japanese almost immediately when his bicycle was
taken from him by a Japanese soldier as he joined the welcoming
crowd. For others the awakening was slower, although it was soon
apparent that the Japanese as colonizers differed from their predecessors mainly in the ruthlessness with which they applied
themselves to their task. Closer contact with Japanese appointed
as supervisors in administrative and technical positions also convinced many Indonesians that they themselves knew more than
their supervisors. 'If these barbarians had been able to replace
the colonial authority, why had that authority been necessary at
all?' they asked. The three and a half years of Japanese occupation was a time when, in the words of Sjahrir, 'everything
spiritually as well as materially, was shaken loose from its old
moorings'.[3]

THE JAPANESE OCCUPATION. 1942-5

Under the Japanese, Indonesian territory was divided between
three separate authorities. Java and Madura, with headquarters
on Java, were under the 17th Army; Sumatra, administered
from Singapore, was under the 7th Army; and east Indonesia was
under navy administration. East Indonesia, just as in earlier
times, was dependent on Java for supplies of food and clothing,
and Rear-Admiral Maeda acted as liaison officer for the navy,
with headquarters in Java. An important background to events
in Java, which are better documented than events in other parts
of Indonesia, was the traditional rivalry between the Japanese
army and navy. The latter was the elite service and many of its
members had a more cosmopolitan outlook on life than did the
average army man. Maeda, prior to the war, had been Naval
Attaché at The Hague and his interest in Indonesian nationalism
may have included a genuine sympathy for some of its aims and
aspirations.

(a) *Effects on the Plural Society*

The first major change to follow the arrival of the Japanese,
although it took at least a year before the process was complete,
was the gradual internment of all the Dutch except those few
who could successfully disguise their Dutch background. For

[3] Sjahrir, *Out of Exile*, p. 248.

most of them the issue of collaboration did not arise. Apart from the handful retained to train their replacements, they had no option in the matter. Dutch schools were closed, use of the Dutch language forbidden, and all privileges formerly given to the Dutch abolished. Many internment camps were overcrowded and insanitary. As the war continued food rations dropped to starvation level, and every opportunity was taken to humiliate the former colonial rulers in the eyes of their former subjects. Their standard of living and general conditions were probably no worse than those of the average villager, subject both to conscription of labour and forced delivery of crops, but the contrast with their former affluence perhaps made conditions harder for them than for the peasants who had never known affluence.

Many Eurasians, previously anxious to deny their Indonesian descent, now became anxious to proclaim it in order to avoid internment. The occupation marked the end of the privileged position of Eurasians and Chinese in society. Japanese policies favoured the Indonesian middle class rather than the Chinese, who to them were enemy aliens. Yet both groups, if they survived the first violence of the invasion, could do rather better than the average Indonesian either by selling personal possessions accumulated during their years of privilege, or by taking positions for which their Western education had equipped them. Others survived through black market and other illegal trading, stimulated by the Japanese policy of attempting to establish self-sufficient regencies, and by limiting trading between different areas within Java as well as outside.

(b) *The Japanese and the Nationalists*

The Japanese took over from the Europeans many top positions and the comfortable accommodation which went with these, but were largely dependent on the co-operation both of the Western-educated Indonesians and of the traditional leaders through whom the Dutch had worked.

In 1942 the Japanese launched the Triple A Movement, to rally Indonesian support for the Japanese war effort by propaganda extolling 'Japan, the Leader of Asia; Japan, the Protector of Asia; Japan, the Light of Asia'. This was a failure, and the Japanese realized that they must work through the established nationalist leaders, rather than through new ones; which meant in turn that the nationalist leaders had an opportunity to work through the Japanese. Believing that the anti-Dutch sentiments of the Indonesians would make them willing collaborators, the Japanese were prepared, for example with Hatta, to overlook any anti-Japanese sentiments expressed earlier. The rapid collapse of the Dutch gave the nationalists little time for elaborate planning but it was decided that Sukarno and Hatta, best known among the nationalist leaders, should work openly through the Japanese while Sjahrir should lead one of several underground movements.

Later the Dutch were very bitter about this collaboration, failing to realize that to the Indonesians both Dutch and Japanese were alien rulers. If in retrospect and by comparison Dutch rule may have appeared less harsh than that of Japan, the Indonesians still did not want Dutch rule restored. Their aim remained an Indonesia 'independent and free'. Although collaboration may have involved some compromise, they could also win concessions from the Japanese and protect their colleagues in the underground. Many Indonesians found themselves in positions of authority to which they previously could not have hoped to aspire. This increased their self-confidence and their determination not to lose what had already been gained.

To mark the first anniversary of 'liberation' in Java and Madura, the Japanese 'allowed' the establishment, in March 1943, of *Putera (Pusat Tenaga Rakjat*—Centre of People's Power), an all-inclusive nationalist organization headed by the Four-Leaved Clover (*Empat Serangkai*), the leading nationalists Sukarno, Mohammad Hatta, Ki Hadjar Dewantoro, and—representing Moslem thought—Kiayi H. M. Mansur. *Putera* was widely believed to be a genuinely nationalist organization leading to the self-government promised by Premier Tojo of Japan when he visited Indonesia in July 1943. To the Japanese its main purpose was the rallying of Indonesian support behind the war effort; to the nationalists it was a medium for spreading nationalist ideas among the masses. The abolition of *Putera* in late 1943 suggests that it was more successful from the nationalist than from the Japanese point of view. Most important of its auxiliary organizations was *Peta (Sukarela Tentara Pembela Tanah Air*—Volunteer Army of Defenders of the Homeland), a Japanese-trained military organization with Indonesian officers. Both *Putera* and *Peta* were limited to the Java-Madura command only, but already many nationalist leaders active during the war in Java came from different ethnic groups throughout the archipelago. The nationalism represented in Java was no longer Javanese but Indonesian.

In March 1944 *Putera* was replaced by *Djawa Hokokai* (People's Loyalty Organization), significantly known by its Japanese rather than its Indonesian name. Japanese control was more direct than in *Putera,* although Sukarno was nominal chairman. It had branches in every village called Neighbourhood Organizations, but it was maintained through Japanese compulsion. It was important, though, in creating channels of communication down to village level for the nationalists as well as for the Japanese.

(c) *The Japanese and Islam*

The Japanese also sought the co-operation of the Moslems. Japanese Moslems arrived with the first invasion forces. The Japanese recognized the importance of Islam as a connecting link with the villagers. By March 1942 they had established a Religious Affairs Office, and they paid special attention to Moslem leaders, re-establishing the Great Islamic Council of Indonesia (M.I.A.I.) six months before the creation of *Putera,* and inviting groups of Moslem leaders to conferences, or training courses where they were entertained by the Commander-in-Chief at the Palace. Some leaders had never even visited the city before and such invitations were unknown under the Dutch. The Japanese thus encouraged division among the elite leadership.

However, although the Moslems had good reason to be both anti-Dutch and anti-European there were points at which they were also bound to come into headlong collision with Japanese policy and when they did so they were sustained by religious fervour in their opposition. Emperor worship was in direct conflict with Islamic teaching. The Japanese insistence that all public occasions should open with the *saikerei,* or deep ceremonial bow toward Tokyo and the Emperor, was particularly resented by Moslems because it was to them indistinguishable from the bow, directed toward Mecca and showing reverence to Allah, which formed part of the ritual of Moslem prayer. Early in 1943, a leading Moslem, Dr. Amrullah, father of the writer Hamka, was co-chairman of a meeting of fifty-nine religious leaders from all over Java. It met in Bandung, and he was the only Indonesian seated on the platform along with the Japanese officials. As the meeting rose to perform the *saikerei* he was also the only person to remain seated, an open challenge to the Japanese (and a reproach to his fellow Moslems). The Japanese had to overlook this defiance to prevent undoing the work already done through Moslem leaders. Ultimately Moslems won the right to dispense with the *saikerei* before religious meetings.

Another point at issue was the teaching of Arabic in Moslem schools. The Japanese permitted the teaching of Arabic only if Moslem schools accepted the standard non-religious curriculum which the Japanese had already imposed upon the government schools, including Japanese language as a compulsory subject. Once again the Japanese were forced to make concessions in order to use Islam for their own purpose.

(d) *The Japanese and Indonesian Youth*

The Japanese directed much propaganda at the young people, whom they also sought to influence through the school system. They reserved to the government all educational facilities, except purely vocational training, above primary level. Yet Japanese disciplinary methods aroused resentment among students. The standard form of punishment was a sharp blow on the head, unpleasant enough in itself but doubly unpleasant and humiliating to Indonesians, who regarded the touching of the head as a grave insult. The Japanese succeeded in inculcating authoritarian attitudes and in strengthening anti-Western sentiments among some student groups and among uneducated Indonesian youth groups, which were given political indoctrination and some military training by the Japanese propaganda service, although they were not supplied with arms.

The Indonesian underground movements, largely recruited from among the educated youth, attempted to penetrate such mass organizations and to influence them in a nationalist rather than a pro-Japanese direction. This was dangerous work, for the Japanese also had their spies in such organizations. (Many of those who had worked for the Dutch secret police under colonialism were available for similar work under the Japanese.) Then in mid-1944 the Japanese, in an attempt to control the hostile elements among the educated youth, established *Angkatan Muda* (Young Generation), a youth organization under their close control. Those suspected of underground work were forced to take prominent positions in the new organization where they would be kept in the open and more easily supervised.

As ultimate defeat came closer the Japanese depended more upon the support of the people themselves, and so granted concessions to these groups. Even then support was not always forthcoming. At one Japanese-sponsored meeting of about four thousand students in Surabaya in June 1944, the opening speaker presented the official view that Indonesian independence must be won by fighting with Japan against the Allies. An *Angkatan Muda* (Young Generation) member broke in to say that, although Indonesian independence must be won by fighting, this would *not* be against the *Allies*. He was greeted by such a tremendous ovation that the Japanese hastily dispersed the meeting by switching on the air raid sirens.

In organizing and unleashing the forces of mass youth groups the Japanese were channelling an energy which they themselves found difficult to control. Later, on several occasions, this force threatened to sweep the older nationalist leaders along with it into recklessness which they themselves did not condone. Yet this was one of the strongest nationalist weapons. The Dutch regarded all nationalists opposing them as 'extremists'. These young men included the real extremists whose revolutionary fervour was often unhampered by any realistic weighing up of the issues involved. They were hard to control; they proved impossible to defeat.

(e) *The Economic Effects of the Occupation*

Under the Japanese occupation Indonesian economic life was seriously disrupted. The Allies were increasingly successful in a blockade which hampered communications between Japan and Indonesia, making it impossible for the Japanese to import machinery for the establishment of industries, reducing the Indonesian export market, and causing a serious shortage of previously imported goods, particularly clothing. Inter-island shipping and the fishing industry, an important source of food for many parts of Indonesia, were interrupted.

There was also internal disruption of the economy. The Japanese destroyed the former economic structure, but did not establish a viable one in its place. Priority was given to wartime needs, the restoration of oil installations, the switching of such factories as existed to wartime production. Estate production declined sharply, largely because of the collapse of the export market and the need to extend the area available for food cultivation. Rubber production fell by 80%. Tea, coffee and palm oil also declined sharply. Despite pressure to increase food crops their output also declined, although not quite so sharply. Rice output fell by 25%, affected by a shortage of labour and by a resulting neglect of irrigation works, coupled with drought conditions.

Communications within Java were also disrupted. The Japanese made deliberate attempts to make each regency self-sufficient and to prevent trading between the different regencies. The shortage of foodstuffs and of consumer goods, especially textiles, encouraged a large black market and extensive smuggling both within Java and Sumatra and between Sumatra and Singapore. Yet people survived and many lived with some semblance of normality, although this period rather than any other saw the most serious inroads upon traditional morality and the values by which the older generation of Indonesians lived. Many changes begun under the Dutch were suddenly accelerated. Against this background, in the urban centres at least, there was opportunity for upward socio-economic mobility among the nationalist elite as well as among the Moslem leaders. Even for the old nobility, new avenues were opened, thus undermining one of the most important sources of support for the Dutch regime.

In the villages the invasion often brought complete disruption, beginning with the Japanese disrespect for the traditional authorities, who were still used as instruments of Japanese policy and so were the agents through whom forced deliveries of rice and other foodstuffs were requisitioned, and forced labour con-scripted. This recruiting of *romusha,* conscripted unskilled labourers sent to other parts of Indonesia and to Japanese-occupied territory on the Asian mainland, was the most serious effect of the invasion. Figures are hard to verify, but the official Japanese estimate was that 270,000 of these hapless villagers were sent overseas. At most, a bare 70,000 of them were ever traced after the war. Recruitment was also carried out among unem-ployed plantation workers on the east coast of Sumatra. The bulk of these *romusha* were from among the ethnic Javanese, and in some parts of Java they were recruited in such numbers that whole areas were depopulated. In many villages only women, children and old men remained. Wide migration took place. After 1945 those ex-*romusha* who survived were among the most turbulent elements in society.

The mass organization of village youth further undermined the traditional structure, and contributed to widespread migration, as many moved into the towns for various training programmes. Even as early as 1942 sheer desperation drove some villagers to revolts, but these were even more ruthlessly repressed than those under the Dutch had been.

Toward Independence

Under the Japanese, old values were questioned, former social relationships were inverted, and in some cases, completely destroyed, new responsibilities were given to those previously denied them, new self-reliance was forced upon those for whom the new situation meant dependence upon their own resources for sheer physical survival. The Japanese emphasis upon physical and military training was particularly important. *Peta,* the

Volunteer Army of Defenders of the Homeland, was the military auxiliary of the nationalist organization, *Putera.* The national Moslem organization, *Masjumi,* which replaced MIAI, also had its military auxiliary, *Hizbullah,* through which the Japanese hoped to mobilize Moslem support for a Holy War against the Allies, difficult because the Japanese government in Indonesia, for all its encouragement to Islam, was itself an infidel government.

Many other military bodies were established by the Japanese in different parts of the country and trained primarily for guerrilla warfare. Smaller semi-independent units were also formed, such as the Black Buffaloes in Java or the Wild Tigers in Sumatra. Many such groups were later incorporated into the Indonesian National Army. As a concession to nationalist feeling the Japanese allowed the use of the national flag and the national anthem but, as a precautionary measure, many units were trained with wooden rifles or bamboo spears rather than with modern weapons.

Another instrument designed for Japanese purposes but used by Indonesians for their own ends was the Japanese propaganda system. All radios were sealed off from overseas broadcasts, except those clandestinely operated by the underground. 'Singing trees' were established even in remote villages. Indonesian was used for such broadcasts, because few Indonesians understood Japanese, despite its compulsory teaching in schools. Indonesian broadcasters, particularly nationalist leaders, were used; and, as few Japanese understood Indonesian, nationalist propaganda disguised in Japanese terms was broadcast. Such radio contact also drew the various districts into a common cultural pattern. This contributed to the villagers' growing political consciousness as did the increased migration of villagers searching for food or employment, conscripted for labour or brought into cities for various training courses. The mass support essential to carry through a successful revolution was now linked to the Western-educated nationalist elite who alone could provide the necessary leadership for it.

Older channels of communication could also be used. In Java the traditional *wayang* or puppet shows[4] were one medium of instruction. Traditional stories could illuminate a contemporary situation without a stranger being any the wiser. Travelling players injected political comment into their performances, increasing an awareness of national identity or of Japanese brutality.

[4] See above, p. 32.

By 1944 the Japanese leaders realized that the war was turning against them. Indonesian leaders, through their concealed radios, also knew this. The Japanese attitude to the national movement began to change. The Japanese authorities were sufficiently divided about the methods and the timing of any concessions to nationalism for the Indonesians to have some room to manoeuvre and gradually to take some of the initiative into their own hands. In September 1944 Premier Koiso of Japan promised Indonesian independence 'in the future'. The naval commander, Admiral Maeda, supported, from navy funds, some of the propaganda tours made by Sukarno and Hatta to different parts of Indonesia, despite army disapproval.

By mid-1945 an Investigating Body for the Preparation of Indonesian Independence had been established in Djakarta with sixty-two members. Of the two secretaries, one Indonesian and one Japanese, the latter spoke no Indonesian, the language of the conference. The Japanese left the agenda open, laying down neither blueprint nor general plan, perhaps hoping they had set the scene for a struggle between various leadership groups which would render the whole exercise fruitless but would keep the Indonesians occupied. Instead the committee proceeded, with remarkable unanimity, to draw up a constitution covering such issues as the territory to be included, citizenship qualifications, religion, and the political structure of the new state.

During the preliminary debates, on 1 June 1945, Sukarno outlined the Five Principles *(Pantja Sila)* now accepted as the state philosophy of Indonesia—Nationalism; Internationalism; Government by Consent; Social Justice; and Belief in God Almighty.[5] He began with a call for independence and concluded with the peroration that 'Independence can only be achieved and owned by a people whose soul is aflame with the determination of *Merdeka,* Independence—or death!' Such sentiments bordered on the revolutionary and yet the Japanese took no action against him, but planned to establish a new body, the Committee for the Preparation of Indonesian Independence, consisting of twenty-one representatives from all parts of Indonesia. (The Investigating Committee had included residents in Java, some of whom were from other ethnic groups, and an investigating committee had also been established in Sumatra.)

On 8 August, two days after the first American atom bomb was dropped on Hiroshima, Sukarno and Hatta flew to the Japanese headquarters at Saigon where, on 11 August, the day after the Japanese surrender terms were accepted, they were

[5] See below, pp. 241-3.

promised independence for 24 August. They returned on 14 August, and although no announcement of the surrender had been made in Indonesia itself, the underground movements knew from their secret radios that surrender terms had been agreed upon. They distrusted the Japanese promise because by 24 August Japan would be in no position to grant independence. Few underground workers wished to accept independence as a Japanese gift, but Sukarno and Hatta argued that they should work through the Committee for the Preparation of Indonesian Independence as a representative body which could speak for the whole of Indonesia. This procedure would avoid any clash with the Japanese who were, after all, not the real enemy once they had surrendered.

The Japanese invasion and the subsequent occupation had 'shaken everything loose from its moorings' in a society which, in the preceding decades, had begun to develop its own sense of national identity. The departure of the Dutch had already given many Indonesians opportunities of which they had dared not previously dream, and the impending departure of the Japanese offered the prospect of consolidating the gains already made. There was a great sense of invincibility, of self confidence and of determination. Independence was within reach and was theirs for the taking.

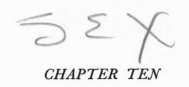

CHAPTER TEN

The Struggle for Independence

There is no hill which cannot be climbed; there is no valley
which cannot be crossed.

Indonesian proverb.

The situation in Djakarta at the time of the Japanese surrender
was greatly confused. It resembled that earlier hiatus when the
British had departed and the Dutch returned at the end of the
Napoleonic Wars, but at the same time circumstances differed
significantly. The returning Dutch had to deal not only with
rulers but with the people at large, and the people at large were
no longer unarmed, nor were they as completely isolated from
the outside world as were the villagers of the preceding century.
The gap between governor and governed, which had widened to
a deep gulf in the period prior to the twentieth century, was
gradually narrowing. Although numerically small and lacking
practical experience, the Dutch-trained elite and the Modernist
Moslems were both bridging the gap by their growing awareness
of the significance of Western technological advances, and they
had contact at last with the mass support they needed for victory
in their struggle.

THE PROCLAMATION OF INDEPENDENCE

In the few days following the return of Sukarno and. Hatta
from Saigon there was the danger that the various groups within
the elite might impede each other's efforts. Sjahrir tried to
persuade Sukarno to declare independence in revolutionary and
anti-Japanese terms, meanwhile rallying six thousand of his
underground supporters, prepared to take over the administration from the Japanese. Sukarno, by now established as the best
known and most influential of the nationalist leaders, was essential to any declaration of independence, and Sukarno hesitated.
Some of the youth groups, including one in which Adam Malik

was a key figure, also attempted to persuade Sukarno and Hatta to take matters into their own hands, even kidnapping the two of them. They too realized that a declaration of independence without Sukarno's endorsement would carry little weight.

On 16 August, when Admiral Maeda attempted to inform Sukarno and Hatta that the surrender had indeed taken place, he discovered that they were missing. Then followed a series of most delicate negotiations, as a result of which the threat of a violent *coup d'état* was averted and Sukarno and Hatta were returned to Djakarta. Late on the evening of 16 August an attempt was made to assemble an unscheduled meeting of the Committee for the Preparation of Indonesian Independence. About fifteen of the twenty-one members, along with some of the Young Generation (*Angkatan Muda*) leaders, met at the house of Admiral Maeda. The site was offered and accepted because it had a degree of extraterritorial status in relation to the Japanese army command and the offer suggested, as Hatta for one believed, that Admiral Maeda may have had personal sympathy for the nationalist aspirations.

By seven the following morning, the final wording of the declaration of independence had been thrashed out. Despite considerable pressure for a strongly worded anti-Japanese declaration, the older leaders, Sukarno and Hatta, finally won consent for a much milder version less likely to lead to open clashes with the Japanese. As a compromise, it was decided that Sukarno and Hatta should sign the proclamation as the 'deputies of the Indonesian nation'. Three hours later, in a simple yet solemn ceremony in the front garden of his private residence in Djakarta, Sukarno read the Proclamation of Independence at ten o'clock on the morning of 17 August 1945:

> We the people of Indonesia hereby declare Indonesia's independence. Matters concerning the transfer of power and other matters will be executed in an orderly manner and in the shortest possible time.
> In the name of the Indonesian people: Sukarno/Hatta.

A soldier in *Peta* uniform hoisted the Red and White flag, specially made for the occasion by Sukarno's wife, Fatmawati, and preserved since as one of the *pusaka* of the new nation; then the national anthem was sung for the first time in an independent Indonesia. Although it was to be another five years before the world at large recognized and accepted the significance of the ceremony, the first step had been taken toward the creation of Great Indonesia.

REACTIONS TO INDEPENDENCE

Nishimura, head of the once-powerful General Affairs Department of the Japanese administration, recorded contemptuously that on 17 August 'about noon a shabby looking and confused Indonesian authority brought a dirty paper on which was written that the Indonesians had proclaimed their independence.' (It is little wonder he appeared 'shabby and confused'. Few participants in the drama of the past few days could have had much sleep, if any, for several nights on end.) The Japanese Army, by the terms of the surrender responsible for maintaining law and order prior to the arrival of the Allies, first tried to prevent news of the proclamation spreading and later became involved in struggles with Indonesians for the control of Japanese arms. Most Japanese were primarily concerned about returning to Japan safely and swiftly and saw the suppression of unrest as a necessary preliminary.

For the Indonesian people this was the long-awaited hour, the culmination of the struggle of the nationalists since the beginning of the century, the achievement of the aim of many heroes of past history throughout the archipelago, the fulfilment for the Javanese, of the ancient prophecy of Djoyoboyo. News of the proclamation spread rapidly through most of Java. Two days later some of the Indonesians sent from Upper Digul to Australia heard that the news had been broadcast in Arabic from a station somewhere in Sumatra. Many Indonesians abroad knew of the proclamation before it was universally known in Indonesia itself. Groups in the United Kingdom, the United States, Australia, and even in the Netherlands itself began to put the Indonesian case to the world at large. By the end of August, when the Sumatran delegates returned from the Committee for the Preparation of Indonesian Independence, confirmation of the proclamation was received in Medan, although no official announcement was made until 17 September. When the Sulawesi delegates returned to Makasar, Dr. Ratulangi, appointed governor of East Indonesia by Sukarno and Hatta, established a branch of the Republican government there. (By April 1946, Dr. Ratulangi had been arrested by the Dutch in the area and exiled in West Irian with seven other families. While there, they assisted the establishment of the Republic-oriented movement for independence headed by Simon Papare.)

Meanwhile in Djakarta the central government of the new Republic was established. On 18 August the first official meeting of the Committee for the Preparation of Indonesian Independence elected Sukarno as President and Hatta as Vice-President of the Republic of Indonesia. By the end of August the provisional Constitution had been ratified and promulgated, a central Indonesian National Committee (*Komite Nasional Indonesia Pusat*—KNIP) of 135 members had been chosen by Sukarno and Hatta to represent the chief ethnic, religious, social and economic groups in Indonesia, and, in the eight provinces established by the Preparatory Committee, arrangements had been made for the establishment of local National Committees. Most Indonesian members of the civil service responded to the Presidential decree to obey them rather than the Japanese, thus leaving their Japanese superiors isolated from contact with the people.

For the people themselves the first reaction was one of excitement and bewilderment. At last they were independent but— what did this mean? One lower-class revolutionary described it in later years as being rather like awakening from a deep sleep and trying to regain one's bearings. The first public response was the wearing of red and white rosettes and the black *petji*, originally Moslem but now of national significance, and the flying of the Indonesian flag. In Medan scuffles broke out as local youths tried to force the Ambonese soldiers, traditional supporters of the Dutch, to wear the red and white. In other cities clashes occurred when attempts were made to replace the Japanese flag by the Indonesian on public buildings. In Djakarta, a huge rally organized by the youth groups took place on 19 September, despite opposition from the Japanese authorities, and the initial reluctance of the Indonesian leaders. At it Sukarno demonstrated his power over such a mass audience not only in his address to them but in their obedience to his injunction to disperse peacefully. The struggle for the control of Japanese weapons continued with varying degrees of success. In all these activities the lead was taken by the *pemuda*—the young people.

When the first British forces landed on 29 September, charged to maintain the *status quo* as at 1942, they were faced with a situation for which they were not prepared. During the six weeks which had elapsed between the surrender of the Japanese and the Allied arrival the Indonesians had established a Republican government with its own civil service, and with extensive militant support among the Indonesian people. Within a fortnight of the British landing the Indonesian national army was formally established (on 5 October) with units from the former *Peta* forces and from youth groups, and *Radio Republik Indonesia* was on the air to present its version of events in Indonesia to the world. The 1942 *status quo* no longer existed to be maintained.

Consequently the British sought to carry out their two main tasks—the rescue of the Allied prisoners of war and the acceptance of the Japanese surrender, along with the removal of Japanese troops—with as little involvement in politics as possible. Yet every effort they made to restore the *status quo* and to assist the return of the Dutch was bitterly resented by the Indonesians; any acknowledgement they made of the existence of the new Republic was equally resented by their allies, the Dutch. In addition, as the British troops were mostly Indian soldiers, India protested because their soldiers were being used to restore colonialism in a fellow Asian country. Some Indian soldiers, mostly Moslem, defected to join the struggle against colonialism, although the Gurkhas supported their British masters.

To Gerbrandy, the wartime Prime Minister of the Netherlands, this Republic of Indonesia was 'a delayed time bomb' left by the Japanese. The charge of 'made in Japan' continued to be levied against the Republic by its real opponents the Dutch. Hatta spoke for his countrymen when he said: 'The Dutch who describe themselves as a democratic people are blaming the Japanese "for not making Indonesian independence impossible". Indeed the Dutch should be covered with shame in that the Japanese went further in recognising Indonesian independence than do the democratic Dutch.' Yet even the most liberal-minded pre-war Dutchmen found it impossible to believe that the declaration of independence represented the opinion of the majority of Indonesians. The Dutch believed implicitly in their own claim that the nationalists were only a small group of disaffected intellectuals and that the majority of the 'natives' needed and wanted Dutch protection, guidance and leadership. To them Britain was 'bailee for Netherlands property' and they bitterly resented the British assessment, that initial Allied landings should not be undertaken by Dutch troops because Indonesian hostility might endanger the evacuation of prisoners of war. Initially Van der Plas, for the Dutch, refused to recognize or to negotiate with 'war criminal' Sukarno and when Van der Plas changed his mind and then found Sukarno understandably reluctant to meet someone who had so branded him, he was indignant that the British refused to *force* Sukarno into negotiation. So the Dutch attitude was the only thing that had remained unchanged since 1942.

The reaction of world opinion to events in Indonesia was to have considerable influence upon the course of events there. When Raffles returned Java to the Dutch, the world outside

Java neither knew nor cared how the Dutch set about re-establishing their authority; when the British of 1945 found themselves in a somewhat similar position, radio and press reported on the attempt, and the world body, the United Nations, acted as a forum for world discussion.

THE BRITISH OCCUPATION. 1945-46

Originally the American Command was to occupy Indonesia. Transfer to the British Command was not finalized until August 24, and the Dutch intelligence service, stationed in Australia, could not join the British invasion because of the shortage of transport. When the first Dutch did land, numerous incidents occurred. The following January, the Republican government, fearing for the safety of its members among the trigger-happy Dutch and Ambonese soldiers in Djakarta, moved to Jogjakarta. Sjahrir narrowly escaped assassination before the move.

In Surabaya the British arrival was believed to be a cover for the Dutch return. In this area, one of the Japanese naval bases, much equipment was in Indonesian hands. The Indonesians maintained their defence for about a fortnight despite fierce opposition from the Gurkha troops, and 10 November, the day the battle began, is celebrated as Heroes' Day. The British, fearing a repetition, were afterwards more cautious in their handling of Indonesian affairs; while the fighting demonstrated to the world at large that the Indonesians were prepared to defend their newly won independence. This brought the whole matter to world attention.

In Manado, north Sulawesi, a predominantly Christian area so strongly influenced by the Dutch that many people called it the Twelfth Province of Holland, rebellion broke out among the Manadonese troops of the Dutch Netherlands Army (KNIL). Although it was quickly suppressed, this shook the Dutch because they had never previously doubted the loyalty of this area of Indonesia.

In Bandung, where the British shared control of the city with the Republican government, the Indonesians, by their control of the countryside, were able to boycott the Dutch at the local markets. To break the boycott, as the Dutch in question were the ex-prisoners of war for whose well-being the British were responsible, the British used Japanese soldiers. This aroused both Indonesian resentment and world criticism. The city soon became divided into two distinct zones, the British, Dutch and Chinese crowded into the northern half, while the Indonesians occupied the southern half. Japanese and Gurkha troops guarded

installations. During December there was fierce fighting, with
the greatest casualties suffered by Moslem auxiliary troops, the
Hizbullah, many of whom, armed only with bamboo spears and
a belief in their own invulnerability, marched upon the tanks of
the Gurkhas shouting 'Allah Akbar—God is great', to be mown
down by machine gun fire. By March the city was divided in half
by sandbags and barbed wire. The northern part was a refugee
camp where people lived out of tins brought by convoy along
the road from Djakarta—an ideal place for ambushes. The
southern part was half-deserted, refugees streaming out into the
surrounding countryside to avoid British air raids. The *pemuda,*
the youth, remained to fight, and the civilian government maintained the Republican presence. On 24 March, after a British
ultimatum, the remaining *pemuda* and civilians left, taking as
many stores as they could and applying a scorched earth policy
to the rest of the southern half of the city wherever possible.
Although a temporary defeat for the Republic, this provided
inspiration to those continuing the struggle elsewhere, and the
song 'Hello, Hello Bandung' became one of the most popular
revolutionary songs:

> 'Tis long since we last met
> But we have resolution firm!
> They have scorched and ravaged you with raging seas of fire
> Comrades, rally, we will return.'

Against this general unrest, attempts were made to begin
negotiations between the returning Dutch and the Republican
leaders. The Dutch at first refused and then demanded to
negotiate with Sukarno, but negotiation was not the role for
which Sukarno was best suited. Instead, in mid-March, a meeting was arranged between Sjahrir, now the first Prime Minister
of the Republic of Indonesia and more acceptable to the Dutch
as a non-collaborator, and van Mook, the Lieutenant Governor.
Although paternalist in outlook, the latter was a Dutch liberal,
and could also realize, as those in the Netherlands could not,
that the Dutch must negotiate: lacking both men and munitions,
they could not yet take back the country by force.

The main problem about any negotiation was that neither
side recognized the basic assumptions of the other. The two
positions were diametrically opposed. The Dutch argued that
they had at no time renounced sovereignty over their Indies
possessions and that the main point at issue was the integrity of
the Kingdom of the Netherlands, of which the Indies were an
integral part. Consequently they recognized neither the validity

of the Indonesian proclamation of independence nor the Republic established on this basis, which they believed was a Japanese creation.

The Indonesians argued, in the words of Hatta, that:

> The Dutch are graciously permitting us entry into the basement while we have climbed all the way to the top floor and up to the attic. Indonesia today has achieved her own administration as a result of her own efforts. And what earthly reason is there for Indonesia to return to her former status as a colony of a foreign nation which did practically nothing to defend her from the Japanese? The Dutch should not remain under the delusion that they can thwart Indonesia's desire to remain independent.

And Sjahrir declared 'We are willing to consider and to welcome Dr van Mook as the first envoy of a foreign but well-known country to discuss with us, we hope, in a most friendly way, the Dutch interests and the Dutch point of view.' Discussion must proceed from the acceptance of the fact that Indonesia was an independent country.

Given such diverging assumptions it was surprising that *any* negotiations could be started, and initially, although Sjahrir and van Mook went a long way toward compromise, each was repudiated by his own government for having gone too far. Yet by the end of April they were able to arrange for talks to be held at Hoge Veluwe in the Netherlands. The Republic would accept *de facto* recognition of its authority in Java-Madura and Sumatra in the areas outside Allied control, and the Dutch would accord such *de facto* recognition, admitting that the Republic did in fact exist but not admitting that it had any legal right to do so. The Republic would be accepted by the Dutch as one partner in the Federal Indonesian Free State which they now proposed to establish within the framework of the Netherlands Kingdom. Neither was prepared to accept any modification of its own position as expressed in the minimal agreement reached by Sjahrir and van Mook at their earlier meetings so the introduction by the Netherlands government of further terms made it clear to the Republican delegation after the first five minutes of the talks that only an initial clarification of opposing viewpoints could be hoped for.

Both the Netherlands and Indonesia faced the difficulties of post-war reconstruction. In the Netherlands government was being restored after the German occupation. Within the Republic a struggle for leadership developed. Tan Malaka, who had returned to Indonesia some time prior to the proclamation of independence, failed, despite his legendary fame as an Indonesian Scarlet Pimpernel, to replace Sukarno as President. Sukarno could control and channel the turbulent revolutionary forces of the *pemuda,* the young people, who otherwise might have swept away everything already achieved in their anxiety to proceed more rapidly along the path of revolution.

The Indonesian armed forces too were showing independence in their relationship with the government. In November, at a meeting of Army commanders, they elected their own Commander-in-Chief, General Sudirman, and their own Minister of Defence, Hamengku Buono IX, Sultan of Jogjakarta. Although the government was able to maintain its right to make its own cabinet appointments, and so did not accept the new Minister of Defence, the Army-appointed Commander-in-Chief was accepted, while the government nominee became Chief of Staff. One factor in the election of Sudirman was his command of the Banjumas district where almost the entire store of Japanese weapons had been successfully transferred to the Indonesians. He controlled the distribution of weapons to districts less successful in obtaining arms. Meanwhile in various areas the army leaders, who were originally political appointees, were being replaced by younger men, closer to the *pemuda* they led. In Bandung the Siliwangi Division came under the leadership of Nasution, one of the few Indonesian army leaders with any pre-war military training, and this division was built up into one of the most powerful in the Indonesian army. Although the National Army worked with the civilian government it was partly independent of it as well.

The Dutch, who in 1942 had rejected any idea of federation for Indonesia in favour of centralized authority, now began to work with great haste to establish a federal Union under Dutch leadership. In July 1946 the Dutch organized the *Malino Conference,* near Makasar. The Republic of Indonesia was not invited to send delegates, allegedly because conditions there were too disturbed for a representative delegation to be chosen. The delegates from the areas represented were elected by members of Dutch-appointed councils and, as a further precaution, the pro-Republican leaders in Dutch-controlled areas were either imprisoned or exiled. The Conference approved the establishment, within five to ten years, of a United States of Indonesia with four component parts—Java, Sumatra, neither of whom were represented, Borneo (Kalimantan) and the Great East. The first two would have split the Republic-controlled area. The Conference also proposed retaining lasting voluntary co-operation with the Netherlands. In October, at Bangka, the *Pangkalpinang Conference,* consisting of representatives of various minority groups, was convened by the Dutch. It approved the general outlines in the Malino plan although the Chinese representatives were unanimous in preferring 'to refrain from any pronouncement of state policy or political problems until the political horizon has again cleared'. Here the Dutch attempted to enlist support from those elements in Indonesian society suspicious of Sukarno and the republic he led.

Despite its six weeks' start, the Republic had lost some initial headway during the British occupation as Dutch administrators (NICA) and soldiers (KNIL), the latter largely trained and equipped by the British, were brought back under British protection, and as the internees, many mentally unbalanced by their three years of imprisonment, were released. Dutch propaganda stressed Dutch willingness to negotiate with moderates, while equating all Republican opposition with 'extremist' activity.

World opinion was already beginning to affect 'The Indonesian Question'. In November 1945, the Arab League recognized the Republic of Indonesia, and in January 1946, the Ukrainian delegate to the Security Council, strongly supported by the Soviet Union, proposed that a Commission of the Security Council should investigate conditions in Indonesia. This the Netherlands immediately opposed as an intervention in her internal affairs but the Ukrainian delegate maintained that the use of Japanese troops by the British authorities against Indonesians was 'contrary to international law, to international political morality and to the declared war aims of the great Powers', referring in particular to the British destruction by fire of the entire town of Bekasi (population 20,000) as a reprisal for the murder of the crew of a British plane forced down there.

LINGGADJATI AGREEMENT. 1947

The last British troops left at the end of November 1946, by which time some 55,000 Dutch troops (KNIL) had already landed in Java. In the following few months Dutch civil administration (NICA) established itself in Djakarta and several other coastal cities. In Bogor (west Java) and Balikpapan (west Kalimantan) Republican officials were imprisoned. Bombing raids on Palembang and Medan (Sumatra) prepared the way for the Dutch occupation of these cities. In east Java, floods near the city of Modjokerto gave the Dutch a pretext to move in to repair the flooded irrigation works. In south Sulawesi the notorious Captain Westerling 'pacified' the area with a death toll of 40,000 in six weeks of bitter fighting. Through the manipulation of licences for import and export the Dutch had virtually blockaded Republican territory, cutting it off from imports of much-needed food, clothing and medical supplies, quite apart from arms and ammunition. In Den Pasar the Dutch called yet another conference early in December 1946 to establish the first of their proposed Federal States, the State of East Indonesia. Here, according to the old formula, Dutch influence could be exercised through the old ruling class, which, unlike its counterparts in Java and Sumatra, had little Western education, and feared the Republic.

In the villages, the social changes begun at the end of the nineteenth century and greatly accelerated under the Japanese, were reaching their culmination. Older village heads and *priyayi* officials were being replaced, with varying degrees of violence or pressure, by members drawn mainly from the new educated elite. On the east coast of Sumatra this revolution took its most violent form as the local non-Malay population overthrew the sultans, who were Malay in origin and supporters of the Dutch.

Against this background of unrest, negotiation proceeded slowly. The Linggadjati Agreement had been drawn up before the departure of the British (15 November, 1946) but was not finally ratified until 25 March, 1947. It represented the greatest compromise either side was prepared to make but so great was the gulf between the two opposing positions that any agreement at all was possible only by slurring over some of the fundamental issues and leaving until later the question of deciding exactly what the agreement meant.

The Netherlands government recognized that the Republic in fact controlled Java, Madura and Sumatra without recognizing that it had any legal right to do so. The Netherlands and the Republic were to co-operate in setting up the United States of Indonesia, a sovereign democratic federal union consisting of the Republic of Indonesia (Java and Sumatra), the State of Kalimantan, and the Great Eastern State. The Dutch had already established the latter without even consulting, let alone co-operating with, the Republic, after the Linggadjati Agreement was drawn up but before it was signed. The Netherlands and the Republic would also co-operate in the formation, no later than 1 January 1949, of a Netherlands-Indonesian Union with the Dutch Queen as its head, to handle foreign affairs and defence as well as some financial and economic matters of common interest. Each side would reduce its armed forces 'as quickly as possible consistent with the maintenance of law and order', and the

Republic was to return foreign properties in its territory to their owners. Any dispute which could not be settled by joint consultation was to be settled by arbitration.

Shortly after the signing of the Linggadjati Agreement the Republic sent Sjahrir to India and Hadji Agus Salim to the Arab countries to put the Indonesian case to them. The Republic could not afford to have only the Dutch version of affairs given to the world. The Dutch protested that this was contrary to the terms of Linggadjati. The Dutch continued to establish more and more federal states, which the Republic argued should be done in co-operation rather than on Dutch initiative. Furthermore some of these states—East Sumatra, Madura and West Java (Pasundan)—were within the area supposedly recognized as being under the *de facto* control of the Republic. The Dutch set up these states because they feared the extension of Republican influence but could not admit this because the whole argument underlying their Federal plan was that it represented the public will,which the Republic did not. Although the Republic branded such states as Dutch puppets and although they were run along the lines of Dutch control which had proved so successful in the 1930s—including 'gentle pressure' and the judicious use of imprisonment and exile—the Dutch found them less amenable to control than they would have liked.

THE FIRST DUTCH MILITARY ACTION. 20 JULY 1947

After the signing of Linggadjati a series of notes, protests, proposals and counterproposals passed back and forth between the Dutch and the Republic. By June the Dutch attitude was hardening, and in July, without making any attempt to resort to arbitration, the Dutch declared that, as the terms of Linggadjati had not been met by the Republic, they no longer held themselves bound by it. On 20 July they launched an attack on Republican territory which they called a 'police action', to restore order in their colonial possessions. The Republic and many others regarded it as open warfare and the Dutch themselves certainly used military terminology in describing their activities.

The Dutch forces, well-trained, well-armed and high in morale, believed they could quickly wipe out 'the pirates' nest at Jogja'.[1] They pushed forward as rapidly as possible into Republican territory and soon controlled most Javanese food-producing areas, the rich estates of East Sumatra and the area around Palembang with its oil and coal. They had overlooked two things which, in combination, caused the final loss of their Dutch empire. They

[1] Jogja (karta) is often thus abbreviated.

had underestimated the extent of support for independence
within Indonesia, and they failed to realize the effect which their
'police action' would have upon world opinion.
Demonstrations occurred in several countries. In Australia and
the Netherlands, dockworkers refused to load ships bound for
Indonesia, while some Dutch troops refused to embark. Several
Asian countries refused landing rights to Dutch planes. Even
Britain, who had been involved with the Netherlands in the
previous Security Council discussion on Indonesia, now brought
the matter before the Security Council. In addition to this,
several adventurous souls, inspired by the struggle for independence, made their own personal contributions by helping
to run the blockade or to put the Indonesian point of view
overseas.[2]
Despite Dutch protests that this was a 'police action' and an
internal matter, her only support at the Security Council came
from the other colonial powers—Belgium, France and Great
Britain—who, of course, had their own future prospects to think
of, and on 4 August 1947 the Security Council, acting on the
Australian resolution, ordered a cease fire and agreed to invite
the Republic of Indonesia's delegate, Sutan Sjahrir, to present
the Republic's case, which he did most tellingly on 14 August.
The Dutch, defeated on the question of admitting a representative of the Republic, then attempted to have representation
of the other states mentioned in the Linggadjati Agreement—
East Indonesia and Kalimantan—but the Security Council
refused them a hearing, arguing that the matter at issue was
between the Dutch and the Republic. The Security Council thus
recognized the Republic as equal partner in the dispute with the
Netherlands. A Good Offices Committee was established. One
member was chosen by the Netherlands (Belgium), one by
Indonesia (Australia), and these two then chose a chairman
(USA). A team of fifty-five military observers (milobs) was sent to
Indonesia to supervise the observance of the cease fire.

THE RENVILLE AGREEMENT. 1948

So deep was the mutual distrust between the two parties after
the cease fire that even any initial agreement about a site for their
meeting could only be reached by the American offer of their
warship, the *Renville*. Meanwhile the Dutch proclaimed the

[2] John Coast, *Recruit to Revolution*, and K'tut Tantri, *Revolt in Paradise*,
give the accounts of an Englishman and an American woman who each
contributed to the cause of Indonesian independence.

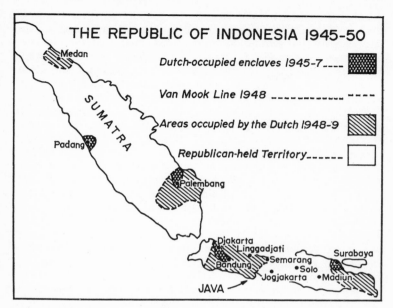

THE REPUBLIC OF INDONESIA 1945-50

Medan

Dutch-occupied enclaves 1945-7___

Van Mook Line 1948 _____

Areas occupied by the Dutch 1948-9

Padang

Republican-held Territory_____

SUMATRA

Palembang

Djakarta
Linggadjati
Bandung
Semarang
•Solo
Jogjakarta •Madiun
Surabaya

JAVA

'Van Mook line' as the Republic's boundary. This line was determined by linking together the isolated Dutch positions at their furthest extent, as if an outstretched hand, representing the Dutch lines of penetration, were enclosed by a line drawn from fingertip to fingertip, the enclosed spaces representing Republic-held areas in which the Dutch, in defiance of the cease fire, proceeded to undertake 'mopping up operations'.

The Renville Agreement, finally signed in January 1948, left the Republic much worse off than before, having lost at least half of its territory in Java and a fifth in Sumatra, in each case the most productive areas. In Java the Republic was virtually encircled by the Dutch and their blockade continued. The terms of the agreement, accepted by the Republic under considerable pressure from the American chairman of the Good Offices Committee, caused much resentment within the Republic itself, while its unity, now that external pressure was slightly reduced, faced threats from within.

The first threat came from the People's Democratic Front *(Front Demokrasi Rakjat)*, established in January 1948 and representing the left-wing Socialist and Communist elements. They were strengthened by Russia's strong stand on Indonesia's behalf in the Security Council. In August 1948, the former Com-

munist leader, Musso, returned to Jogjakarta from Moscow.
Lower-echelon Communist leaders in Madiun, alarmed by the
government's attempts to demobilize their troops and to
strengthen government control of the army as a whole, precipitated the attempted Communist take-over, forcing the Communist leaders to support a badly timed, inadequately organized
uprising or face destruction of the People's Democratic Front.
A People's Republic was proclaimed in Madiun. The revolt was
crushed by the Siliwangi Division, under Nasution. The
Republic's success in coping with this internal threat, although
losing it Russian support, impressed the United States and
answered the charges of some Dutch leaders who claimed the
Republic was not only Japanese-inspired but also Communist-led.

The second threat came from an extremist Moslem group, the
Darul Islam, strongly represented in west Java and Atjeh, which
aimed to establish an Islamic state in Indonesia. Its military
support came from the *Hizbullah* and *Sabilillah* auxiliary Moslem
troops established and trained by the Japanese. By December
1948 the *Darul Islam* was actively anti-Republic, fighting
guerrilla warfare against both Dutch and Republican forces.

United States pressure on the Dutch prevented them from
taking advantage of the Madiun uprising, and the Good Offices
Committee continued its attempts to bring about a satisfactory
settlement.

THE SECOND DUTCH MILITARY ACTION. 1948-49

On 17 December 1948, the Dutch handed Hatta an ultimatum
demanding a reply by the following day, thus allowing Hatta no
time for consultation and barely time to frame any reply. On
the following day the Dutch notified Merle Cochrane, the United
States member of the Good Offices Committee, who was in
Djakarta, of their impending 'police action' but refused to allow
him to notify the other two members, who were in Republican
territory. At 3.30 on the morning of the 19th, the Republican
government, lulled into false security by their belief that the
Dutch would not attack while the Good Offices Committee was
working in the area, received its first intimation of Dutch intentions when Dutch forces bombed the airport of Jogjakarta and
captured Sukarno, Hatta and several other Republican leaders.
The Dutch believed that with the fall of Jogjakarta, the
Republic's capital and the capture of the leaders before they had
even had time to broadcast any last message to their people, the
Republic would cease to exist.

Certainly the situation looked hopeless for the Republic. The Dutch had isolated the Republic so effectively that for some weeks the outside world had no idea of what was happening. Foodstuffs, except the small amount grown locally, clothing, and medical supplies, already in short supply after several years of blockade by the Dutch, were now even scarcer. People scratched a living from backyard gardens and existed on a semi-starvation diet which lowered their resistance to disease—but not to the Dutch. Some people were reduced to wearing sacking. Sterilized banana leaves were used as an unsatisfactory substitute for bandages. Symbolic of the indomitable spirit of his people was General Sudirman himself, suffering so severely from tuberculosis that often he had to be carried by litter and yet continuing to lead the Republican army.

The Dutch troops, despite their military successes and their seeming control of the situation, found themselves facing armed guerrilla resistance and non-co-operation of the civilian population. Peasants bringing in the only meagre food supplies available to Jogjakarta would accept only Republic of Indonesia notes. Copies of the speeches of the leaders were passed from hand to hand and inspired those who remained in Jogjakarta.

In Sumatra, from the Dutch-held enclaves around Medan, Padang and Palembang, Republican supporters moved out into the Sumatran hinterland. From Medan, the Batak population returned to their villages. The large Minangkabau community from the west coast of Sumatra, who felt, as Moslems, less at home in the Christian villages of the Bataks, moved either to Atjeh in the north or back to their villages in Minangkabau. The movement of population to the cities was so recent, and family ties within the different ethnic groups were so extensive, that even third generation city dwellers would have village communities to which they 'belonged' and to which they could return. Many undertook the long journey on foot, across the mountain range which forms the backbone of Sumatra, facing the danger of jungle tigers rather than falling into Dutch hands. Whole families, from grandmothers to babes in arms, made such journeys in the wake of the young men who had usually already gone ahead to join the resistance forces.

The interim government of the Republic was established in Minangkabau under the former Minister of Finance, Sjafruddin Prawiranegara, who, before he left for Sumatra had been given a mandate to take over leadership should the need arise. Hatta had been surprised by the timing of the attack but not by the attack itself, and had prepared in advance for the continuity of the Republic's government.

Dutch propaganda had led many of the troops to believe that they were going to Jogjakarta to free the Sultan from his captors, the 'extremist' rebel Republic. To their surprise, when they attempted to negotiate with the Sultan, hoping to use him as head of yet another federal state, the Sultan retired into his *kraton* and refused to have any dealings with them at all until the Dutch threatened to force their way into the *kraton* by tank. Then the Sultan granted a ten-minute interview but was prepared to discuss only one subject—the withdrawal of Dutch troops from Jogjakarta. At the end of the ten minutes he indicated that the audience was concluded and again withdrew to his residence inside the *kraton*.[3]

The Dutch attack stiffened the resistance of the Republic, and when news of it reached the outside world, it aroused great hostility. Nehru, who had responded to the first military action by calling it 'an astounding thing which the new spirit of Asia will not tolerate', responded to the second by refusing transit rights to Dutch planes and by calling an all-Asian conference at New Delhi to consider the matter. American pressures on the Dutch increased. The United States postponed the granting of Marshall Aid for the rehabilitation of the Netherlands post-war economy. Perhaps even more disturbing to the Dutch in Indonesia was the criticism from the Federal states. In Pasundan (western Java) and East Indonesia, the Federalist governments resigned in protest. They knew how much they depended on successful resistance by the Republic for further advances of their own.

The United Nations expressed growing criticism of the Dutch, who had flouted the Good Offices Committee, who had never accepted the United Nations' right to intervene, and who ignored the cease fire called for by the Security Council. A very bad impression was made when the Dutch representative, misinformed by his own side's propaganda, wrongly declared that the Republic leaders, although still detained in Bangka, had the freedom of the island. The Good Offices Committee found that the six leaders were confined to a heavily guarded barbed wire enclosure of not particularly ample dimensions. The military

[3] Part of the *kraton* buildings had already been handed over by the Sultan to the University of Gadjah Mada, established in March 1946. During the Dutch military action many students joined the guerrilla forces or set up small armaments factories to supplement the dwindling ammunition of the Republic.

victory proved hollow compared with the moral victory of their opponents. The tragedy was that the Dutch, who believed in their own propaganda, were most deeply hurt by the doubts cast upon their sincerity in the councils of the world. The very characteristics which had gained for them the reputation of being good colonizers, their paternalism, their concern for order and efficiency, made them obstinate and inflexible in the face of change. Their close identity with their colony made their rejec- tion first by the Republic and later by the Federalists the harder to bear. They thought they understood the 'native' mind; they discovered that they did not. Their disillusionment was a bitter one.

THE ROUND TABLE CONFERENCE AND THE TRANSFER OF SOVEREIGNTY. 1949

In May 1949 the two parties we.e brought to negotiate again. At the Roem-van Royen talks, the Dutch finally agreed to draw back to the 'Van Mook Line', which meant that relations were re-established along the lines of the Renville Agreement. Arrangements were then made for a Round Table Conference of delegates from the Republic, the Federated States and the Netherlands to work out the terms for the transfer of sovereignty to a Republic of the United States of Indonesia. The Federalists realized that they must come to terms with both the Dutch and the Republic, which had shown its ability to match forces with the Dutch. The Dutch themselves, who had launched the second military action confident of a quick and successful campaign, had learned to respect the Republican troops as opponents who simply did not recognize when they were beaten. The United States made it clear that they would apply economic sanctions if the Dutch continued to defy the Security Council.

The Round Table Conference at the Hague was held between 23 August and 2 November 1949. With the assistance of the United Nations Commission for Indonesia the three delegations finally reached sufficient agreement for all parties to be prepared to endorse it.

From the Netherlands point of view the greatest concessions were the transfer of sovereignty of the Republic of the United States of Indonesia and the loose form of Netherlands-Indonesian Union established. For the Republic the greatest concessions were the debt assumed by the new Republic, and the deferred decision on the status of West Irian. The Republic was particu- larly reluctant to accept that part of the debt incurred through military actions against the Republic, arguing that it should only accept debts incurred to benefit the Indonesian people. On this basis it argued that the Netherlands would actually owe over 500,000,000 guilders to the Republic. Yet the Indonesians were ultimately forced to accept a debt of 4,300,000 guilders, including most of the costs incurred by the Netherlands in their military actions against the Republic. The Federalists were particularly concerned about the West Irian question, but the decision on its status was deferred when the Dutch indicated that, without such a clause, it would be impossible to have the agreement ratified by the Dutch parliament.

On 27 December 1949 at Amsterdam, Queen Juliana signed the document 'unconditionally and irrevocably' transferring sovereignty over the former Netherlands East Indies to the new Republic of the United States of Indonesia, and recognizing the latter as an independent and sovereign state. In Djakarta on that day crowds listened to the radio broadcast from Holland and the speeches of Queen Juliana and Vice-President Hatta. Above the former residence of the Governor-General the Dutch flag was lowered and in its place the Indonesian flag was raised. It was a solemn moment, the crowning achievement of decades of struggle. In Jogjakarta President Sukarno, Bung Karno, the great leader of the struggle, prepared to return in triumph to Djakarta, flying by Garuda Indonesian Airways plane. He arrived at Kemajoran Airport, Djakarta, to be greeted by a sea of people lining the several miles between the airport and the palace. Outside the Presidential palace he addressed the Djakarta crowd:

> Thanks be to God, today I have trod under foot again the soil of Djakarta after being separated from it for almost a full four years. Four years, four long years I have been divided from the people of Djakarta. Today I greet you all, the heroes, the soldiers of our army, the civil servants, our brothers of the *marhaen,* our brothers the *betjak* drivers, our brothers the vegetable sellers, the humblest employee, not one of you is excepted. To all of you I give my thanks.

By Independence Day, 17 August 1950, the Republic of the United States of Indonesia had exercised its right as an independent sovereign state and had become the unitary Republic of Indonesia. In the following month, with Australia and India as its sponsors, the Republic of Indonesia became the sixtieth member of the United Nations, whose intervention had contributed to the birth and survival of the new nation.

CHAPTER ELEVEN

After Independence

Do not imagine that with the existence of the state of Free Indonesia our struggle is at an end. No! I even say: Within that free Indonesia our struggle must continue, only its character will be different from that of the present struggle, its characteristic will be different. Together as a united people we shall continue our struggle to realize our ideas contained in *Pantja Sila*.'

Sukarno, 'The Birth of *Pantja Sila*', 1 June 1945.

(Speech to the Investigating Body for the Preparation of Independence.)

With the transfer of sovereignty and the end of the physical struggle for independence, Indonesians looked forward to a new era in which they would at last be the masters of their own fate. It was a period of tremendous optimism and high hopes. The Javanese peasants who made up almost 85% of Java's population believed that the departure of the white buffalo (the Dutch) and the little yellow chicken (the Japanese) would lead to the coming of the *Ratu Adil*, the Just Ruler, who would introduce the Utopia familiar from *wayang* stories, a kingdom where bounteous harvests sprang from fertile ricefields, where prices were low and goods plentiful, and where the spirit of mutual co-operation (*gotong royong*) would prevail in all human relationships; a time of 'order, peace, joyous labour, prosperity and fertility'. Many among the Western-educated elite, that 2% of Indonesian society in whose hands the instruments of governmental power now lay, shared this optimism, even while recognizing that many problems still remained to be solved.

Several urgent tasks faced the governing authorities. They needed a basis of consent upon which to govern. Even had they wished, they could not rule with 'the whip and the club', in the old style, yet needed to restore order and to curb the smuggling and black market activities which had earlier worked in favour of the Republic but which now, although still as profitable to

239

those involved, were detrimental to government interests. They needed to rebuild an economy shattered by the cumulative effects of the preceding twenty years of depression, occupation and revolution.

The trend toward increasing population and diminishing welfare, noted as early as 1901 and a matter of concern then to the Ethici, still continued, and if anything, accelerated. The new government, like Alice in Looking Glass Land, needed to run as hard as possible just to remain in the same spot. Increased production, especially of rice and other foodstuffs, clothing and household goods, had not simply to keep pace with the annual increase in population, about 2.3% or an addition of about four thousand mouths to feed and bodies to clothe each day, but to overtake it, or welfare would continue diminishing. The government also faced the problem of providing schools and teachers for an ever-increasing school age population, promised an equal right to educational opportunity with all other citizens, including those adults who wished to attain a basic standard of literacy.

The educated elite of the post-war period outnumbered the total Dutch population of colonial times, including those Dutchmen who had held the top government positions, who had run the community's business life, managing plantations, controlling inter-island shipping, banks, and import-export firms. Many still continued in the latter positions. There were qualified Indonesians to fill the top level government posts, but insufficient numbers with practical experience in such positions and a serious lack of trained personnel at the middle levels of government. Technologists, technicians, accountants, typists with sufficient training, practical experience and self-confidence to accept responsibility were all in short supply.

In the early years of independence, at almost all levels of government, people were doing jobs for which they were, through no fault of their own, inadequately prepared by formal education, by practical experience, or both. This gave many a sense of insecurity particularly when, within the next few decades, better-educated junior people returned from study overseas. Within the army the same process was at work, as attempts were made to replace older, less well-trained officers with younger, better qualified men. Many of these less qualified men saw their position as a just reward for loyal service to the Republican cause, and resented any effort to achieve greater efficiency if it threatened their own position. Within both army and civil service the provisions for accepting Indonesians who had previously worked for the Dutch, or who had remained aloof from the revolutionary struggle, led to a certain amount of friction and bitterness.

Resistance to the Dutch military attacks was a strong force binding the Republic together in its first five years. With the cessation of hostility and the removal of this external pressure, the divisions within Indonesian society began to reassert themselves.

UNITY IN DIVERSITY—THE UNITARY REPUBLIC. 1950-59

Many people, including President Sukarno, believed that the Republic's first task was to consolidate unity. Before examining the diversity within Indonesian society and the challenges to unity, it is worth looking again at the basis of unity hammered out by the Investigating Body for the Preparation of Independence in the middle of 1945, particularly the concept of *Pantja Sila*—the Five Principles, presented by Sukarno to the Investigating Body and accepted by them as the philosophical basis for independent Indonesia.

(a) *Pantja Sila—The Five Principles of State*

Sukarno himself has said of his formulation of these Five Principles: 'I do not feel that I made *Pantja Sila*; do not feel that I created *Pantja Sila* . . . I merely put into words some feelings existing amongst the people, to which I gave the name *"Pantja Sila"* . . . I merely formulated it, because these five feelings had already lived for scores of years, even for hundreds of years, in our innermost hearts.'

The first principle, as formulated by Sukarno, was that of *nationalism,* an Indonesian national state stretching from Sabang (in north Sumatra) to Merauke (in West Irian) based on the desire to be united. He traced such a state back to its predecessors, the Kingdoms of Madjapahit and Srividjaya, and claimed that 'if all our people, the Indonesian people, are ready to die to defend our country Indonesia, though it be with bamboo spears, then at that moment the people of Indonesia are ripe for independence'. This nationalism, he said, must not develop into chauvinism, a warlike patriotism with no respect for the national sentiments of others, but must be modified by the second principle, *internationalism,* or the *principle of humanity.* He distinguished this from cosmopolitanism, which would substitute a world citizenship for nationalism, and said: 'Internationalism cannot flourish if it is not rooted in the soil of nationalism. Nationalism cannot flourish if it does not grow in the flower-garden of internationalism.'

The third principle he defined as that of *unanimity, repre-sentation* and *deliberation among representatives,* or *sovereignty* of the people, and argued that in a body representative of the people, the Islamic group should bring forward the demands of Islam. He linked this third principle with the fourth, *social justice,* claiming that equal political rights were valueless without equality in the economic field too. Social well-being must go hand in hand with political justice. There must be social justice too for the *marhaen,* 'the little man', Sukarno's description of the typical Indonesian peasant, who is not a member of the proletariat, for in strictly Marxist terms the proletariat has nothing to sell but his labour and owns none of the means of production. The *marhaen* may own a small plot of land or share the communal land of the village, and also owns his means of production, a simple hoe, a harvesting knife, but is nevertheless poor, a 'not enough' rather than a 'have-not', one of the 85% *marhaen* making up the bulk of the Indonesian nation.

The fifth and final principle was 'to build *Indonesia Merdeka* in awe of the One, Supreme God', *belief in God* with mutual respect for one another, a state in which every person can worship his own God as he likes without religious egotism. When later the Islamic groups claimed that Sukarno did not dig deeply enough into the spirit and the identity of the Indonesian nation, for if he had, he would have found Islam rather than the *Pantja Sila,* he claimed that, although a Moslem himself, 'my digging went to the era before the religion of Islam existed; I dug to the Hindu period and to the pre-Hindu period', and found at each layer, 'the Indonesian nation has always lived in a world of adoration for something in which it lays all its hopes, its faith'.

Having enunciated these five principles, Sukarno continued: 'I like symbolism, the symbolism of numbers also. The fundamental obligations of Islam are five in number;[1] our fingers are five on each hand; we have five senses; the Pendawa [the heroes of the Hindu epic, Mahabharata, on which many *wayang* stories are based] also are five persons. And now the number of principles: nationalism, internationalism, consensus after deliberation, well-being, and belief in God—also five in number.' Or he would compress these five into three principles—the first two becom-ing socio-nationalism, the second two, socio-democracy and the third, belief in God. If they wanted just one principle it would be the principle of *gotong royong* or mutual co-operation, the establishment of a *Gotong Royong State. Gotong royong* is the principle of mutual self help upon which the Indonesian village

[1] See pp. 55-6, above.

functions as a social unit, combining forces to complete some community undertaking, or assisting with one man's harvesting or house building in the knowledge that he will extend the same mutual co-operation in his turn. '*Gotong royong*,' said Sukarno, means 'toiling hard together, sweating hard together, a joint struggle to help one another, acts of service by all for the interest of all—One, two, three, heave! for the common interest.'[2] This suggests the interrelationship between the five principles. The five are interwoven, each one in turn conditioning or modifying the other four.

The Five Principles *(Pantja Sila)* have been accepted by the majority of Indonesians as the basis for their state and woven into the symbolism of the national emblem. This depicts a modernized version of the legendary *garuda*-bird related to the eagle and the phoenix, the steed of Kresna's son in the *wayang* stories, and endowed with human speech. The *garuda* of modern Indonesian heraldry has seventeen wing feathers and eight tail feathers, symbolising the date of the proclamation of Indonesian independence. Round his neck he wears a shield divided into four quarters, alternately red and white. Superimposed on these is a smaller black shield surmounted by a five-pointed gold star, representing what is now the first principle of *Pantja Sila*— *Belief in God*. Behind it on the upper left hand quarter of the larger shield, against a red background, is the head of the *banteng*, or wild buffalo, patient and not easily roused, but once roused, prepared to fight to the death to protect his herd. This symbolizes *Sovereignty of the People*, government by the people whom the *banteng* represents. On the upper right hand, against a white background, is a *waringen* or banyan tree, a kind of giant fig tree, whose branches, on touching the ground, become new roots. It has been revered from earliest times, and represents *Nationalism*. Below the thick black line dividing the shield horizontally and representing the equator, is the white quarter on the left, with a spray of cotton and a stalk of rice, the basic necessities of life, *Social Justice* for all; and the right hand quarter, against a red background, has a continuous gold chain with alternate square and round links, symbolizing the principle of *Internationalism or Humanity*, woman and man linked in a never-ending human circle which joins all nations in the one common humanity. In his claws the golden *garuda* bears a scroll emblazoned with the words '*Bhinneka Tunggal Ika*', the Indo-

[2] This is also related to the Indonesian saying 'Sama rata, sama rasa', 'Equal status, equal opportunity', sharing alike in good and bad times, which William Marsden commented on in 1811 as typical of Sumatran democratic theory.

nesian motto, though the words are Sanskrit (comparable to our use of Latin for mottoes). The meaning is 'They are many; they are one' or, as it is more commonly translated, 'Unity in Diversity'.

(b) *Potentially Divisive Elements*

Yet despite the unifying effects of the revolutionary struggle, and the symbols of unity—the red and white flag tracing its origin to the red and white regalia of Madjapahit; the national headdress, the *petji* or modified fez, tracing its origin to Islam, but worn today by any nationalist regardless of his religion; the national anthem expressing the aspirations of the nationalist movement of the twentieth century; the national language and the Five Principles (*Pantja Sila*) claimed by Sukarno to be 'the highest common factor and lowest common multiple of Indonesian thought'—there were still many potentially divisive elements within Indonesian society.

(i) Currents of thought

First were the different currents or streams of thought. Fluid and at times merging with one another, yet distinguishable as differing in origin, they underlie the conscious and unconscious thoughts and reactions of individual Indonesians. We can try to separate them in order to distinguish between them, but it would make little sense to most Indonesians to ask 'What stream of thought do you follow?' because this would really be asking 'Which of the historical forces which have shaped modern Indonesia has influenced you most strongly?' Not many people could answer such a question about themselves.

The first current of thought in point of time is the *Javanese Tradition*, an important influence particularly on the ethnic Javanese, although it has also influenced such a person as the Minangkabau poet and historian, Mohammad Yamin, who designed the Indonesian national emblem. It stresses the importance of continuity and order, of a right relationship between the inner life of a man and the outer order of the cosmos, and encourages a belief in and a search for the magic formula, the key providing the clue to the mystery of the universe, which, once found, will usher in the golden age of the Just Ruler. The element of messianic hope, although not unknown in Moslem tradition and in both Christianity and Marxism, is particularly strong in the Javanese tradition.

Within the tradition can be distinguished influences arising from the *kraton* and felt most strongly by the Javanese *priyayi*

The Indonesian Coat of Arms, symbolizing the proclamation of
independence and the Five Principles (*Pantja Sila*) of the
Indonesian nation (pp. 241-3)

Djakarta became a city of slogans during the General Election of
1955 (pp. 250-4)

Election candidates with their picturegrams above their heads, 1955

Preparing the ballot papers for the 1955 General Election

or aristocratic class, with an emphasis on refinement and on the formal etiquette which Kartini in her day found so terrifying and which has been modified to some extent since then; and that of the *abangan*, the Javanese peasant, affected most strongly by the communal life of the village, with its festivals, its superstitions and its mutual co-operation. Common to both is a belief that inner feelings are more important than any overt actions, coupled with a preference to be passive, to be acted upon rather than to act. It is linked with the desire for consensus of opinion, reached by mutual discussion and with the minimum of friction. For all those influenced by the Javanese tradition, the *wayang* is important in moulding thought patterns and in inculcating moral virtues, particularly those of harmony and continuity.

The second current of thought is that of *Moslem tradition*, which in different parts of Indonesia, not only in Java, conflicted with some patterns of behaviour sanctioned by local *adat*, or customary law and tradition. Many of the early manifestations of opposition to Dutch rule derived their impetus from the teaching of Islam. The orthodox Moslem knows no distinction between secular and sacred in everyday life, so for many Moslems the Five Principles *(Pantja Sila)* fell short of the requirements of the Islamic state which Moslem teaching advocated.

Within Islam are three currents of thought, although again the one person may be influenced by more than one such current. Moslems influenced by Modernism more frequently come from the urban middle classes, seeking to come to terms with, and reap the benefit of, the modern technological and scientific advances of highly industrialized countries while retaining a distinctively Moslem outlook on life. There are the Moslems whose orthodoxy can more easily accommodate itself to the conservative older generation, particularly in rural areas, represented in Java for example by the village *kiyayi*, the traditional theologians, interpreters of Moslem law, and teachers, but also found in other areas. There are also the militants, whose advocacy of an Islamic state led them, from 1950 to 1962, to proclaim the establishment of such a state, *Darul Islam* (The Domain of Islam) and to fight a continuing guerrilla war on its behalf.[3]

The third current of thought, again with its own diverse currents, stems from *Western tradition:* all those influences on Indonesian thought since the establishment of Western domination, which have been transmitted through its influence. The

[3] See below, pp. 249-50.

earliest was Christianity, which left its main imprint upon
Minahasa, in North Sulawesi, an area where 90% of the population is Christian, the so-called 'Twelfth Province of Holland';
upon Ambon, in the Moluccas, where about 50% of the population became Christian; on Flores where there are many Roman
Catholics; and in the Batak district, particularly around Lake
Toba in North Sumatra, where German Lutheran missions in
the nineteenth century converted these former animists. Equally
regarded as a Western influence is Marxism, or Socialism, whose
influence has spread more widely, although sometimes in rather
diluted form, than membership of the left wing parties would
suggest. Hadji Agus Salim, for example, was influenced quite
strongly by Socialism although within the Moslem current of
thought. Less influential than the other two, and yet with considerable influence upon small sections of the Western educated
elite, is rationalism or secular humanism, which served as Kartini
feared it might, and as Sjahrir admitted it did, to cut them off
from the masses whom they sought to serve and to lead.

Although the differences may be rather blurred at the edges,
and although it may, in many cases, be difficult to place anyone
firmly within one current of thought rather than another, these
divisions are a real threat to the political unity of society, so
that increasingly the formulation represented by *Pantja Sila* has
been seen as an instrument of unity.

(ii) Regional differences

At times cutting across, and at times reinforcing, these different
currents of thought, were the regional differences which have
existed from time immemorial within the Indonesian archipelago.
It is tremendously important in Indonesian national life that
Java-Madura contained 65% of the total population of Indonesia
but barely one-fourteenth of the total land area, while Sumatra
and Sulawesi between them provided about 85% of the foreign
exports upon which Indonesia's badly needed foreign currency
reserves depended. The old rivalries which once existed between
sea-based, trade-oriented Srividjaya and land-based agricultural
Madjapahit continued but were accentuated because the land-
based agricultural area was no longer an area with rice surplus
for export but had to import it instead. Growing resentment
arose in the foreign income earning areas because they believed
that a disproportionate amount of their earnings were being
spent on Java. It was tempting to continue the barter trade (a
polite name for smuggling) which began during the blockades
of the 1940s.

Coupled with this jealousy of Java was a resentment of centralized control exercised from Djakarta. Some was the inevitable result of poor communications with the Outer Islands, and some resulted from the inevitable inefficiency of a newly created bureaucracy. Government employees in the Outer Islands were understandably resentful when letters of appointment upon which the payment of salary depended, arrived months or even years after the employee had been appointed. The resentment in the provinces against centralized control was matched by the eagerness with which many employees sought to be transferred to the centre of power at Djakarta.

Antipathies also existed between different districts and different ethnic groups, at times no more (and no less) serious than local football rivalries can be, but at times of tension deeply divisive. For example there was often bitter resentment against those Ambonese who had been members of the Royal Netherlands Indies Army (KNIL) and who had fought on the Dutch side in the struggle for independence. Not all Ambonese had done so; but the Ambonese as a whole sometimes suffered from the hostility directed against the Ambonese soldiers. Many non-Javanese are suspicious of the Javanese, the largest ethnic group, fearing a form of Javanese imperialism leading to Javanese domination in politics and culture, and they complain among themselves about Javanese arrogance and feudal class consciousness. In some districts local cleavages between related ethnic groups are significant. To understand events in Medan (north Sumatra) it is necessary to know that the Toba Bataks, predominantly Christian, are rivals of both the Karo Bataks and those from Mendeling who, although ethnically Batak, prefer, because they are Moslems, to be called Mendeling. Just as the British have their stereotypes—the feckless Irishman; the dour, skinflint Scot; the reserved, arrogant Englishman; Taffy, Welshman and thief—so the Indonesians have theirs. And in each case, when someone from a given district does something which fits his particular stereotype, this is remembered when his 'atypical' deeds and actions may be forgotten.

Indonesians are strongly aware of these ethnic and regional differences, and although their importance should not be exaggerated, it should not be minimized either. Yet it may not always be tactful to ask an Indonesian 'Where do you come from? What is your ethnic group?' for, while many may readily answer, 'I am Javanese', 'I am Batak', others may say, 'I am an Indonesian. What does it matter what district I come from?' When introduced to another Indonesian who is a stranger to him, an Indonesian will not ask this question of his new acquaintance but if, at the end of the meeting, he has not managed to discover the man's ethnic group—from his accent or from the general conversation—this is likely to be the first question he will ask about him once he is out of earshot. President Sukarno, himself part Javanese and part Balinese, took every opportunity, when speaking to groups of young people, to encourage them to marry those of different ethnic origin, seeing in such inter-ethnic marriages the surest basis for an Indonesian nation where ethnic differences would unite rather than divide.

(iii)   Divisions among the elite

Many of these wider differences in Indonesian society also existed among the leadership. Sukarno's abilities as a leader—his skilful use of symbols, his powerful and inspiring use of language to communicate with Indonesians at all levels of society, his personal charm and *semangat*—needed the balance provided by the more sober talents of Hatta and his fellow negotiators. Sukarno, self-educated in the social sciences, had read widely but without the discipline imposed by formal study. He was also one of the few Indonesian leaders who had not, at some time, studied overseas, so he knew the Dutch only in their worst aspect as colonizers, without any experience of life in the more liberal atmosphere of the Netherlands to balance his view of them. This made his outlook comparatively provincial and his nationalism more radical, though certainly not any more sincere, than that of either Hatta or Sjahrir, for example. He drew more fully upon the Javanese current of thought, which helps to account for his closeness to the common people to whom and on whose behalf he spoke. He drew also upon the Moslem current of thought, and upon the Western current of thought represented by Marxism and by Socialist writings, and translated into his theory of the *marhaen*. This ability to blend the different elements into a seemingly harmonious whole and his skilful handling both of crowds and of individuals fitted him for his role as preserver of unity.

Yet the top leadership of the Republic was drawn from a very small group, perhaps about two hundred highly educated Indonesians of much the same age who had studied together either in Indonesia, in the Netherlands or in Cairo. They knew each other well, as classmates do, and they knew both the strength and weakness of their contemporaries. Within this group, Sukarno did not inspire the same reverence that he did among the masses.

They knew his weaknesses although they may have underestimated his strength.

The negotiators, led by Mohammad Hatta, Sjahrir, and Mohammad Roem, hammered out the agreements on which international acceptance of a free Indonesia rested, and they had to compromise to reach any agreement at all. To some extent this compromise discredited them, while Sukarno could dissociate himself from the unpleasant aspects of the agreements. Yet as Vice-President, Hatta balanced the inspiring romanticism of Sukarno with a solid and realistic awareness of the problems, particularly the economic problems, which lay ahead.

Hatta represented the negotiators. As an economist by training, he was one of the planners whose utmost efforts would be needed to restore order to the economic chaos facing the new nation. As a Sumatran he represented the non-Javanese of the Outer Islands, and as a devout Moslem he was a more acceptable representative of other devout Moslems than was Sukarno with his more syncretic[4] religious approach. When Hatta resigned late in 1956 because he no longer agreed with the policies being put forward by President Sukarno, it marked for many people a decisive split within the leadership. Those who believed that any political solution was bound to fail as long as the underlying economic problems remained unsolved, found that their warnings fell upon deaf ears. President Sukarno, as he himself was the first to admit, was no economist and paid little attention to the recommendations of those who were. He preferred to look first for a political solution, uniting people through their pride in Indonesia both past and present.

(c) *Challenges to Unity*

Several specific challenges to unity arose after independence, related to the underlying diversity in the country.

(i) *Darul Islam*—The Islamic Domain

First was the challenge of the *Darul Islam* movement, which rebelled against the Republic during the second Dutch Military action. In west Java and Atjeh, the Islamic State of Indonesia was proclaimed as an alternative to the Djakarta government. The other areas of *Darul Islam* strength were south Sulawesi and Kalimantan. These four areas had been traditional centres of Moslem protest against infidel rule in Dutch times.

[4] Attempting to unite Islam and the older Hindu-Buddhist teachings by emphasizing their common elements.

Throughout the 1950s, and up to 1962, *Darul Islam* continued indecisive guerrilla war, making it unsafe for travellers to venture far outside west Javanese cities alone after nightfall. Some of those loosely associated with *Darul Islam* were local bandits taking advantage of the troubled times, but the hard core were supporters of an Islamic state, unwilling to work through the representative institutions of a *Pantja Sila* state to achieve their aims, and seeking to achieve them by force through the Islamic Army of Indonesia, descended from the former *Hizbullah* and *Sabilillah* units of Japanese days.

(ii)   Colonial Aftermath

In the early years of the Republic there were at least two Dutch-supported challenges to its unity which originated with those elements of society whose fortunes had been most closely linked with those of the colonial rulers. The first was the attempt of Sultan Hamid II of Pontianak (Kalimantan), a leading Federalist, to stage a *coup d'état* in alliance with the notorious Dutchman, 'Turk' Westerling, and a force composed of former Netherlands Indies troops. Westerling and his followers attacked Bandung and later planned a coup in Djakarta. The plot failed. The Sultan was imprisoned until 1958 and Westerling, with Dutch connivance, escaped via Singapore.

The second threat was the attempt by a group of Ambonese, former members of the Royal Netherlands Indies Army (KNIL), to establish an independent Republic of South Moluccas with its headquarters on the island of Ambon. The Republic had to turn reluctantly to force and the self-styled 'Republic of the South Moluccas' subsequently set up its government-in-exile at The Hague, where it continued its propaganda for a decade or more.

(iii)   The General Elections

Indonesians hoped that the General Elections, scheduled finally for 1955, would be a turning point at last into a new era. These elections involved considerable organization. First voters had to be registered—all Indonesian citizens, male and female, eighteen years and over, as well as any married citizens under that age. (This had enfranchised a greater percentage of the female than of the male population, for although many Indonesians of both sexes, particularly among the poorer classes, married before the age of eighteen, girls on the whole married younger than did boys.) The registration of voters and the distribution of ballot papers to the villages throughout Indonesia, given the lack of communications in the Outer Islands, were extensive under-takings. So was the massive educational campaign, carried out largely by means of radio, to inform the village people about their rights, privileges and duties as voters.

These preparations took over two years to complete and, dur-ing this time, the many political parties undertook intensive campaigns for support both in the cities and at the village level. Each party, and there were over forty of them throughout the whole country, had its own symbol which appeared on the ballot paper. A single ballot paper was about the size of a double sheet of newsprint. The paper had to be intelligible to illiterate voters, almost half of the total number of electors; and most people voted for the party of their choice by piercing the appropriate party symbol. An alternative method of voting available to the literate voter was to write in the name of a particular candidate. On election day each polling booth was equipped with a pencil for writing and a nail for piercing the party symbol. Much of the pre-selection campaigning centred around the recognition of these party symbols.

By mid-1955 Djakarta had become a city of symbols, as each party erected its own billboards at strategic crossroads or outside railway and bus stations. The Indonesian Nationalist Party (PNI) had an equilateral triangle enclosing the head of a magnificently horned buffalo;[5] the Modernist Moslem Party (*Masjumi*) had the crescent moon and star, traditional symbol of Islam; the Islamic Theologian's Party (NU) a globe of the world and nine stars for the missionary pioneers of Islam in Java; and the Communist Party (PKI), the hammer and sickle. Sjahrir's Indonesian Socialist Party (PSI) was represented by a five-pointed star. One huge Communist signboard outside the big Gambir railway station in Djakarta bore the legend 'Election sign for the Communist Party of Indonesia and for electors who have no party', a piece of deception which infuriated many non-Communists.

Indonesia was divided into sixteen electoral districts, one of which included West Irian, although, as this was still under Dutch control, it was recognized that neither campaigning nor voting (nor even registration of voters) could be undertaken there. For every 150,000 inhabitants of Indonesian citizenship, parliamentary representation allowed one member for the Con-stituent Assembly, the body elected to determine the final form

[5] One piece of evidence supporting the effectiveness of the PNI campaign has been the tendency of many Indonesians to think that the *banteng* on the national emblem stands for nationalism instead of sovereignty of the people. The use of the *banteng* as a symbol of the PNI pre-dated its incorporation in the State emblem.

of the Indonesian constitution; and one member for every
300,000 citizens for the People's Representative Council (D.P.R.),
the one-house Parliament. Although voting was not compulsory, it has been estimated that only about 6% of those
eligible to vote did not do so. There was a widespread feeling
of community obligation, and of taking part in a ritual marking
a ceremonial occasion of great significance. The publicity campaign of the preceding three years, and the propaganda campaigns of the different parties had stressed successfully that the
elections were part of independence and that they were a means
to the achievement of a better society.

Election Day, 29 September 1955 had the atmosphere of a
solemn festival with a strong undercurrent of excitement and
vague expectation. An eyewitness reported that in Djakarta at
seven that morning—the usual peak period for office-bound
workers, when the city traffic is at its most chaotic, a seething
mass of buses, bicycles, jeeps, *betjak,* cars and pedestrians moving slowly from bottleneck to bottleneck—there was scarcely a
person or a vehicle to be seen. Streets were deserted, and not a
betjak was in sight as people went to their polling booths, joining the long queues of men and women waiting patiently to
register their votes. Some were still waiting five or six hours
later, and even though there were no undue delays, a wait of
two or three hours was not uncommon. The women heightened
the festive air by wearing their best clothes for the occasion, and
many had babies which they nursed during the long wait in the
steamy heat under the fierce rays of the tropical sun. Observers
were impressed with the courtesy of the officials, the endurance
of the voters, and the patience of both, as well as with the
quietness and orderliness of the proceedings, especially as there
had been many vague fears beforehand that tension might lead
to disorder.

When at last the electoral results were known it became clear
that the four main parties were the Nationalist Party (PNI) with
22.3% of the valid votes cast, the Modernist Moslem Party (*Masjumi*) with 20.9%, the Moslem Theologians' Party (NU) with
18.4% and the Communist Party (PKI) with 16.4%. Between
them they shared 78% of the valid votes. The next four parties,
with about 2% of the votes each, were: the lineal descendant
of the old *Sarekat Islam* (Islamic Union), the *Partai Sarekat
Islam Indonesia* (PSII), the Protestant Christian Party (*Parkindo*),
the Roman Catholic Party (*Partai Katolik*) and, to the surprise
of many observers that it should have polled so poorly, Sjahrir's
Partai Sosialis Indonesia (PSI).

The voting revealed that the main support for the Nationalists (PNI), the Moslem Theologians (NU) and the Communists (PKI) came from central and east Java. The Modernist Islamic Party (*Masjumi*) obtained almost half its support from outside Java, and only about a quarter from the ethnic Javanese areas of east and central Java. The voting pattern thus emphasized the strength and nature of regional divisions within the country, particularly as the same pattern could be observed in regard to the support for some of the smaller parties. The two Christian parties, for example, received their main support from regions in the Outer Islands. (Not all Christians necessarily voted for the Christian parties, just as not all Moslems necessarily voted for specifically Islamic parties.)

The state of the parties revealed the depth of division between different groups in society, particularly the threefold division between nationalist, religious and socialist groups. In retrospect, the General Elections of which so much had been hoped were a further divisive element within Indonesian society, by making clear the divisions which in fact existed and by forcing a choice upon the people, as well as by the cumulative effect of the preceding years of campaigning by the parties, accompanied, in many cases, by a growth of corruption in the interests of the different parties.[6]

In the years following the General Elections, disillusionment with the party system and with Western-style liberal democratic government became widespread. The 1955 elections created a Constituent Assembly as well as a People's Representative Council, but in the Constituent Assembly, where the rival groups were much more evenly balanced than they had been in the Investigating Body in 1945, the discussion between advocates of *Pantja Sila* and those wanting a more specifically Islamic state was reopened. So even was the balance that neither could hope to achieve the necessary two-thirds majority required to ratify the Constitution. In the People's Representative Council (DPR) cabinets were formed and fell with almost the same rapidity as in the pre-election period, each representing some slight change of grouping between competing parties who could only form unstable coalition governments. These parties, and the small group of leaders became more absorbed in the problem of political survival than in broader questions of administration and government. Economic reforms, bound to cut across the

[6] H. Feith, *The Decline of Constitutional Democracy in Indonesia*, pp. 424-37 gives a good analysis and account of the elections. Like C. Geertz, *The Religion of Java*, this is a book into which you may wish to dip. See also R. McVey, *Indonesia*, pp. 334, 345, 365.

economic interests of supporters of the various parties, were shelved because their implementation would threaten the party in power at the time.

By 1956 President Sukarno criticized parliamentary democracy, suggesting a system more suited to the Indonesian national character than this 'liberal, free-fight, half-plus-one-majority, oppose-for-the-sake-of-opposition democracy, that caricature of real participation by the people in the act of governing.' Its most serious weakness was that it was 'based upon inherent conflict', thus running counter to the Indonesian concept of harmony as the natural state of human relationships. President Sukarno sought a system more in keeping with this desire for harmony, and drew upon the traditional village system of discussion and deliberation upon a problem in an attempt to find common ground and consensus of opinion (*musjawarah* and *mufakat*). He wanted to apply at national level the deliberative processes familiar in village government under the guidance of the village elders. Upon the basis of the election results he argued that the threefold division, *Nas*ionalism, Religion (*A*gama) and *Kom*unism, should be blended into a co-operative government, or what he called a *Nasakom* government. It was much easier to coin the word than to gain common acceptance for the proposal.

It was clear by the late 1950s that Dutch-educated leaders, working on what was in fact a Dutch-inspired blueprint to establish a parliamentary democracy based upon the multi-party system of the Netherlands, were achieving neither unity nor stability. Many believed that greater guidance and stronger leadership were needed if the Indonesian government were to have the authority necessary to set its house in order. Yet many did not wish to accept the guided democracy proposed by the President.

(iv)   The Rebellions in Sumatra and Sulawesi: PRRI/Permesta 1956-8

The most serious challenge to the unity of Indonesia in the 1950s was the establishment in Sumatra in February 1958 of a revolutionary council designed to be an alternative to the government established in Djakarta. This was linked with support for Hatta and opposition to the new political concepts of President Sukarno, and with a growing regional hostility to the mismanagement, inefficiency and corruption in the central government. It differed from the attempt to establish an independent

Republic of the South Moluccas because at no time was it a secession movement. Despite their support of regional grievances against the central government its supporters wished to preserve the unity of the Republic of Indonesia. It was a more serious challenge because it represented a division among those nationalists who had led the fight against the Dutch.

Behind this action lay a history of struggle between the army and the parliament for control of military matters and a continuing struggle within the army between the supporters and opponents of Abdul Haris Nasution, for internal control of the army. On 17 October 1952, sections of the army demonstrated against the power of parliament, unsuccessfully urging the President to dissolve parliament. This the President was not prepared to do. While both Army and Parliament were rival power groups, the President, as arbiter between the two, could maintain his position, without being fully dependent on either, by balancing one against the other.

The Army was divided over the 'October 17th Affair'. For his role in it, General Nasution was suspended as Chief of Staff. Unity was not restored within the Army until February 1955, but once it was, the Army was able to assert its authority against that of Cabinet in the appointment of a new Chief of Staff. With Army support General Nasution was reinstated and he then took steps to establish greater central control in the Army. To achieve this he planned to transfer certain officers from areas in which they had already built up a considerable personal following at the expense of central government control. In December 1956 regional commanders in Sumatra openly engaged in smuggling or barter trade with Singapore to divert foreign currency earnings to their own districts, and they took control of local civil administration. They recognized President Sukarno but not the central government's cabinet. This was part of the internal army struggle, but also a protest against the Djakarta civilian government.

Against this background President Sukarno announced his new conception of government to replace liberal (free-fight) parliamentary government. A National Council would represent not only parties but also functional groups within society— workers, farmers, the armed forces, Islamic authorities, youth, women, intellectuals—with the President as its head, and a Cabinet representing the four main parties, a Nationalist-Religious-Communist (*Nasakom*) Cabinet. He was supported by the Nationalists (PNI) and Communists (PKI) and a few small parties, but the plan was opposed by the two Moslem parties, the Modernists (*Masjumi*) and the Theologians (NU).

Further opposition was expressed in the Outer Islands when in early March 1957 other colonels declared martial law and took control from the civil authorities representing the central government. On 14 March 1957, President Sukarno declared a state of war and siege, legalizing the existing situation in the provinces where the military leaders had already taken over the government, but also increasing the powers of the president. He also formed a presidential cabinet, led by a non-party man, Dr. Djuanda, like Sukarno an engineer by training, but unlike Sukarno, widely read in economics as well, and universally respected.

After Hatta's resignation, and the publicizing of the President's new conception, the lines of division within Indonesia came increasingly to be between those supporting and those opposing the President. Sukarno without Hatta was no longer a unifying symbol for many groups in society, although he increasingly stressed his own role as leader, as voice of the people, and sought to impose unity where he could no longer, as in earlier days, inspire it. In many people he still inspired it, but he had begun to arouse bitter antagonism; and in November 1957 this became evident when a group of youths, advocates of a Federal State based on Islam, attempted to assassinate Sukarno as he was leaving a social function at the primary school his children attended. The grenades designed for the President narrowly missed their target and killed eleven bystanders, including some of the children crowding round to bid him farewell. This was the first of five attempts in the following six years, each of which further convinced him that, by divine intervention, he was being preserved to fulfil the role of leader for which he had been preordained.

Early in 1958, when Sukarno left Indonesia for a 'rest cure' in eastern Europe, the Middle East and Asia, the men associated with the regional protest movements presented an ultimatum calling for the resignation of the Cabinet and its replacement by one led by Hatta and the Sultan of Jogjakarta. If not, they would form a new government in Sumatra. On 15 February, the Revolutionary Government of the Republic of Indonesia (PRRI) under Sjafruddin Prawiranegara[7] was proclaimed in Padang. Central Sumatra had become the gathering place of various

---

[7] Who had previously led the Republic from western Sumatra during the second Dutch military action, see p. 235, above.

people opposed to Sukarno and the central government: some leaders of the Modernist Moslem Party (*Masjumi*); Professor Sumitro (former Minister of Finance and an outspoken critic of Sukarno's lack of any economic policy); and others, who were in contact with the other main centre of opposition, the Minahassa region of north Sulawesi.

Apart from any personal reasons for opposing Sukarno or feeling threatened by his opposition to them, they were critical of the growing influence of the Communist Party (PKI), whose main support came from central and east Java, and whose support of Sukarno's Conception was bringing it into increasing favour with him. Their ultimatum was a bluff, however. They thought the central government would not risk civil war by using force against them, and so were totally unprepared for the central government's decision to launch an attack.

The revolt collapsed quickly. The widespread sympathy for the rebels was passive rather than active. Too many people had friends and relations on both sides of the struggle and were reluctant to become involved in civil war. The rebels also lost a good deal of sympathy because they sought foreign intervention and support.

By mid-1958, apart from sporadic guerrilla activity, the revolt was virtually over. The central government army was strengthened because of its quick and efficient suppression of the revolt and its closing of ranks against the rebels. Those parties more closely identified with the rebels were discredited, in particular the Modernist Moslems (*Masjumi*) and the Socialist Party (PSI) both of which, by 1960, were banned for refusing to denounce their rebel members.

Above all, the rebellion marked the success of the pro-Sukarno elements who emphasized the need for solidarity through political means. Among the supporters of Sukarno to benefit were the Communists, because they had been one target of criticism for his opponents. The anti-Sukarno elements were discredited. Their first priority was economic stability and administrative decentralization to cope with the real and continuing grievances of the provinces. Now political solidarity became first priority.

UNITY WITHOUT DIVERSITY—THE PERIOD OF GUIDANCE. 1958-65

In October 1956, Sukarno began advocating the abolition of political parties. The Constituent Assembly, split along party lines, was still deadlocked in its discussion about *Pantja Sila* versus Islam as the basis of the Indonesian State. Addressing an assembly of young people he said: 'Do you know, brothers and sisters, what my dream is as I speak to you now? ... My dream is that the leaders of the parties would meet, would consult together with one another, and then come together to the decision "Let us now join together to bury all parties".' By February 1959, the President advocated a return to the 1945 Constitution and declared himself prepared to accept the responsibility for the big changes involved in implementing Guided Democracy.

The difference between the Constitution of 1945 and the Constitution of 1950 was that the former gave the elected President the power to appoint and dismiss members of the Cabinet, while the latter gave Parliament full power to appoint and dismiss the government. The earlier constitution did not give absolute power to the President, as sovereignty lay with the people as represented in their Consultative Assembly, and this Assembly was to appoint both President and Vice-President and to outline the government's policy. This Assembly was to meet only once in five years, and this left a good deal of actual power in the hands of the President, working through the Cabinet which he appointed.

On 2 June, for the third time the Constituent Assembly rejected a motion advocating a return to the 1945 Constitution. The voting was 263 in favour and 203 against, falling short of the required two-thirds majority by almost 50 votes. Sukarno, on his return from abroad, said that he would act according to the wishes of the majority and so, on 5 July 1959, by Presidential decree, Indonesia returned to the 1945 Constitution. The Constituent Assembly was dissolved.

On 9 July, the President announced the appointment of an Inner Cabinet of nine men and three days later an Outer Cabinet of twenty-three. On 30 July, he announced the appointment of the forty-five members of a Supreme Advisory Council (*Dewan Pertimbangan Agung*—DPA), including two Communist members, Aidit and Njoto; and also announced the twenty-seven members of the National Planning Council (*Depernas*) under the chairmanship not of an economist but of poet and historian, Mohammad Yamin, although the three-point programme of *Depernas* involved first the provision of sufficient food and clothing for all; second, security; and third, the implementation of the struggle against economic and political imperialism. Yet the appointees were not simply 'yes' men, although at the same time Sukarno's most outspoken critics were not included.

The implementation of Guided Democracy must be seen against the general background of growing unrest in Indonesia at the end of the 1950s. The rebellions in the Outer Islands, although reduced to guerrilla warfare by 1959, still disrupted trade and reduced the central government's foreign earnings; and the campaign for the recovery of West Irian was reaching its climax, leading in 1957 to the take-over of many Dutch enterprises, which in turn led to initial disruption during the actual changeover.

Part of the symbolism of the Republic has centred, as it does in any nation, around the celebration of anniversaries of national significance, particularly 17 August, Independence Day. So it was on 17 August 1959, in his Independence Day speech, that Sukarno presented his Political Manifesto to the Indonesian people. Known as *Manipol—USDEK,* it became the 'broad lines of the policy of the state'. It was endorsed in November by the President, acting as Head of the State, Supreme Commander of the Armed Forces and Prime Minister. Then in the first session of the (Provisional) People's Consultative Assembly *(Madjelis Permusjawaratan Rakjat (Sementara)—*MPR(S), held in November of the following year, it was again ratified by the supreme organ of the State, which according to the 1945 Constitution has the task of determining the broad lines of state policy.

The Political Manifesto *(Manipol—USDEK),* was explained by Sukarno as being 'the rediscovery of our revolution' and a 'return to the rails of the revolution'. The five letters, U S D E K, stood for the initial letters of the five clauses of the Manifesto. (Once again Sukarno was showing his love for the symbolism of numbers.)

U referred to the *return to the 1945 Constitution* and with it a return to the idea of continuing revolution; *S* referred to *'socialisme à la Indonesia'* under which every citizen would be assured of work, food and clothing, housing and the opportunity to enjoy an adequate cultural and spiritual life; *D* to *guided democracy,* described by Sukarno as 'the democracy of the family system, without the anarchy of liberalism, without the autocracy of dictatorship', and this guidance was to be provided not by a person but by the ideals of *Pantja Sila,* the Five Principles; *E* stood for *guided economy* aimed at the abolition of inequalities remaining from the old colonial days and the reorganization of the economy 'as a common endeavour based upon the principle of the family system' and seeking the prosperity of the community rather than the prosperity of the individual; while *K* referred to *national identity,* the preservation of Indonesia's national heritage, and the creation from the diverse cultural elements within society of a specifically Indonesian culture, and 'a nation which stands on its own identity'.

Under Guided Democracy, Sukarno saw himself increasingly as the embodiment of the nation, and each year on Independence Day he held a dialogue with his people, whose titles, each with its own acronym,[8] suggest the particular emphasis he was attempting to achieve. After the introduction of the Political Manifesto *(Manipol—USDEK)* in 1959, he spoke in 1960 of 'The March of our Revolution' *(Djarek),* in 1961 of 'Revolution, Indonesian Socialism and National Leadership' *(Resopim),* in 1962, the year of the transfer of West Irian to the Republic, his title was 'A Year of Triumph' *(Takem),* in 1963, 'The Resounding Voice of the Indonesian Revolution' *(Gesuri)*[9], in 1964, during the course of Indonesian confrontation with Malaysia, 'A Year of Living Dangerously' *(Tavip),* in 1965, after Indonesia had withdrawn from the United Nations, 'The Year of Self-Reliance, of Standing on One's Own Feet' *(Takari).*

One element in the President's complex character was his own rise to eminence, partly through his combination of talents but partly because he was born at that particular time in his country's history. In 1956 when he made his first visit to a Western country, he told the American crowd which welcomed him in Washington, 'A man's life is unpredictable, indeed. I am the son of poor parents. My father was a small teacher who earned 25 guilders a month. This is ten dollars. I am the child of common people. Thirteen years of my life were passed in prison and exile. Now I am honoured by you. I am received by you with great hospitality, not only as the man Sukarno, but as the President of the Republic of Indonesia.' He saw his own place in the world as symbolic of the sense of human dignity which was the most precious gift of independence to those who had suffered the indignities of being 'a nation of coolies and a coolie among nations' in the old colonial days.

Some people have seen this period of Guided Democracy as a return to *kraton*-style government where the main contact of the common people with the god-king was through their share in and their contribution to the ritual of the state, or the glimpse they caught of the ruler as he toured different parts of the realm.[10] The monuments and buildings, which were given a higher priority than the less spectacular but more urgent task of provid-

[8] A name formed from the initial letter(s) of the key words in the title— e.g. Nasakom from *Na*sionalism, *A*gama (religion) , and *Kom*unism.
[9] For a description of this occasion see Ivan Southall, *Indonesian Journey,* pp. 46-50, and *Indonesia Face to Face,* pp. 244-6, though you might also read on to the end.
[10] For a description of such a glimpse, see M. Williams, *Five Journeys from Jakarta,* pp. 336-44.

President Sukarno addressing a mass rally

Independence Day, 1963, showing part of the crowd which listened to
President Sukarno in the Asian Games Stadium at Djakarta

Seventeenth century Batavia (Johan Nieuhof: *Zee en Landreise*, 1682)

Twentieth century Djakarta—Pasar Senen Square

ing sufficient food and clothing for all, might then represent the modern-day equivalent of the building of Borobudur, earning merit for both ruler and people, while Sukarno's visits overseas and his invitations to overseas guests represent the older missions from ruler to ruler in modern guise.

In the course of establishing Guided Democracy, the President had managed to render politically ineffective those men of his own generation who were a threat to his power, particularly by banning the Modernist Moslem Party *(Masjumi)* and Indonesian Socialist Party (PSI) in 1960. Although their political and personal freedom was limited, these men were not treated harshly. Those who did not choose to live in exile, a choice which some of the leading figures in the Revolutionary government (PRRI) thought it wise to make, were kept under house arrest. Sjahrir, for example, was under house arrest during the early 1960s. After his death in 1966, which was also after the coup which marked the beginning of Sukarno's decline in power, Mohammad Hatta, Sjahrir's old comrade from Upper Digul days, emerged momentarily from his obscurity as a private citizen to make a funeral oration reminiscent in tone to that which Shakespeare put into the mouth of Mark Antony.

As a democratic socialist Sutan Sjahrir had as his ideal that the people of Indonesia be free in all their undertakings. . . . He struggled for a free Indonesia . . . but he became ill and died under arrest in the independent Republic of Indonesia. Sutan Sjahrir suffered more at the hands of the Indonesian Republic than ever he did at the hands of the Dutch colonial government that he opposed. During Dutch rule, after a year of preventive detention, it was decided that he should spend the rest of his life in exile. This was the sentence of a cruel foe, and its attitudes and habits could have been foreseen. But in the Republic of Indonesia based on *Pantja Sila*, which should hold in high esteem truth, justice and humanity, he was arrested and imprisoned without any grounds of truth and justice, and with scant regard for humanity.

Here Hatta was not talking of physical privation. Of Sjahrir, Sukarno said: 'He was vicious. He did nothing for the Republic except criticize me'; and Sukarno's failure to recognize that this criticism indeed could have been a service to the Republic was a reflection on the nature of the democracy which developed under his guidance.

Yet it is important to realize that the majority of those who disagreed with Sukarno's conception nevertheless agreed with him that Indonesia needed a more authoritarian form of government, with sufficient power and authority to introduce changes bound to be unpopular with certain influential sections of the community. The task of economic reconstruction in particular was at no time an easy one, potentially a divisive one, and one which became more difficult the longer it was delayed.

By 1962 the decline in welfare was noticeable. One visitor, comparing conditions in 1962 with those ten years earlier, commented that clothes were of a poorer quality and that government employees were now often forced to wear to the office clothes which had been patched or darned. More servants were wearing Western dress, which took much less material than the traditional but increasingly expensive *kain batik,* a piece of cloth one metre (39 inches) by 2½ metres. One friend, a government employee in Djakarta, had begun to grow backyard vegetables in an attempt to beat inflation. Another friend in Bandung had six different jobs, but still the bulk of the family's earnings was absorbed by the continuing rise in the cost of food. In Djakarta by 1961 food prices were slightly over *ten times* those of 1958. Outside Djakarta, in the villages and the Outer Islands, economic conditions seemed better than in the urban centres.

President Sukarno, although he often talked as if he held absolute power, actually depended for his position upon the balance between the different power groups within society. The two most powerful of these were now the Communist Party (PKI) and the Army. Both had benefited from the internal and external situation in the 1950s. The Sumatran leaders had been anti-Communist and their outside support, both moral and material, came from non-Communist sources, so their failure enhanced the position of the Communists. The Communist Party (PKI) also gained prestige from the support Communist countries gave the West Irian campaign. The Army was strengthened by its success in ensuring internal security, which had been achieved by 1962, and by its growing importance as Indonesia moved toward a show of force to regain West Irian.[11]

The Communist Party leaders from Sukarno's generation had been killed or discredited in the Madium revolt of 1948,[12] and its leaders in the 1950s, Aidit and Njoto, were younger men prepared to support the President's programmes in return for Presidential protection from their chief rivals for power, the Army leadership. This Army leadership was drawn mainly from the *pemuda* generation of 1945, men in their forties by 1960. Sukarno, who turned fifty-nine in that year, could see his

[11] See below, pp. 263-6.
[12] See above, pp. 233-4.

relationship to both groups as that of an elder brother, even a father figure. As long as he could maintain this balance between opposing forces within society, he was protected and maintained by these divisions which emphasized his role as Great Leader of the Revolution and preserver of the unity of the nation.

INDONESIA'S RELATIONS WITH THE WORLD

Before looking at the events which led to the collapse of Guided Democracy, we must consider the role of Indonesia as an independent nation. There has been a greater consensus of opinion about aims and attitudes in foreign than in internal policy though not always about the best methods by which to achieve such aims.

(a)   *The Netherlands.* 1950-63

From the moment of the Proclamation of Independence on 17 August 1945, Indonesians regarded the Netherlands, in Sjahrir's words, as a 'foreign but well known country'. The negotiations leading to the transfer of sovereignty—the talks at Hoge Veluwe, the Linggadjati Agreement, the Renville Agreement and the final Round Table Agreement—did little to remove the distrust on both sides. When the Indonesians established the Unitary Republic of Indonesia in 1950 by dissolving the Federal Republic of the United States of Indonesia established at the Round Table Conference, the Dutch regarded this as contrary to the terms of the agreement; when the Dutch retained West Irian and, in 1952, incorporated it within the Kingdom of the Netherlands under the title of 'Netherlands New Guinea', the Indonesians regarded this as contrary to the clause of the Agreement which said: 'The *status quo* of the residency of New Guinea shall be maintained with the stipulation that in a year the question of the political status of New Guinea be determined through negotiations between the Republic of the United States of Indonesia and the Kingdom of the Netherlands.'

There was no agreement about what this *status quo* actually was. The Dutch held that it remained a Dutch possession. The Indonesians believed it to be an integral part of Indonesia. In their eyes all that had to be arranged was *when* it should be returned to the Republic. The Dutch believed the discussion to be concerned with *whether* it should be handed over to the Republic at all.

For both countries the question was a matter of national pride. West Irian, one-fifth of the total land area of Indonesia, was infertile and inhospitable country, consisting of lowland swamps and impenetrable highlands—where there lived isolated and scattered tribesmen whose number had never been accurately ascertained—and a few coastal settlements, the earliest Dutch ones dating back to 1901 and the rest made between 1921 and 1936. So far the vague hope of undiscovered mineral wealth has been unfulfilled. The Dutch argued that racially and culturally the Irianese were different from the peoples in the rest of Indonesia, particularly those strongest in the central government, and that they believed it to be their mission to prepare the Irianese for 'self-determination' under Dutch guidance. For the Indonesians the Dutch retention of West Irian was a continuing reminder that the independence which they proclaimed was still not finally achieved. The Indonesians also argued that they were ethnically closer to the Irianese than were the Dutch and that Indonesia was already a land of wide ethnic diversity.

There were other reasons beside that of national pride. The Dutch argued that they were financially better able to develop the area than was Indonesia. The Indonesians argued that they were better equipped to develop the area because of their experience with tribal groups in other parts of Indonesia and also because they would provide immediate participation in self-government along with representation in the central government, and educational opportunities for the Irianese on a par with those in the rest of the Republic, rather than Dutch-oriented education for a small elite.

Efforts at negotiation between 1950 and 1953 failed and opinions on both sides hardened, despite growing criticism from Dutch business interests in other parts of Indonesia who feared the loss of profitable investments for the sake of retaining an unprofitable liability.

Between 1954 and 1957, Indonesia made repeated attempts to persuade the General Assembly to press the Netherlands to negotiate on the issue, although the Netherlands maintained, after 1952, that there was nothing calling for negotiation. Although on each occasion the Indonesians received a majority of votes, representing, as President Sukarno was quick to point out, an overwhelming majority of the world's population, they could not achieve the required two-thirds majority. During this period, the West Irian dispute became an issue around which colonial and anti-colonial forces grouped themselves. In 1955 the Bandung Conference of Afro-Asian countries gave unanimous support to a motion calling on the Netherlands to resume negotiations with Indonesia on West Irian, and this vote indicated that Indonesia also had the support of Communist China to her claim, while Nationalist China had been the only Asian country to cast its vote in the United Nations with the colonial powers. Continuing deadlock led Indonesia to withdraw from the Dutch-Indonesian union in 1956 and to refuse to pay the Netherlands' 'internal debts' incurred during the military actions of 1947 and 1948-9.

Indonesia's final appeal to the United Nations was made late in 1957. In the preceding months, both sides were engaged in lobbying for support. From August to November there was increasing tension in Indonesia. The Constitutional Assembly, split on many other issues, was unanimous about the first clause of the new constitution, which defined Indonesian territory as including West Irian, and although some foreign observers argued that the West Irian problem was emphasized in order to create unity and to divert attention from problems at home, this was, in the words of one more perceptive commentator, 'misleading and dangerous' because it led the foreign press to underestimate the extent of Indonesian sentiment on this matter.

When Indonesia again failed to achieve the necessary two-thirds majority, the Indonesian delegate, Dr. Subandrio, said they would make no further appeal to the world body but would seek their own solution of the matter. Within the next month the pressure upon the remaining Dutch economic interests within Indonesia intensified. On 2 December, a 24-hour general strike was held against Dutch enterprises, followed by the unauthorized seizure of Dutch firms by youth groups, and left-wing unionist employees. The Army then took protective control of these businesses, pending government moves to nationalize them and to work out compensation terms. The Dutch airline, KLM, was denied landing rights in Indonesia; Dutch publications were banned, and measures were taken to repatriate 'unemployed and superfluous' Dutch citizens. The Dutch government retaliated by urging a mass exodus and over 40,000 Dutch citizens left Indonesia in the next few weeks.

Indonesians now believed that at last they were about to reach the long expected turning point. Once the revolution had been completed and West Irian restored to the Republic, *then* the promise unfulfilled by the Proclamation, by the transfer of sovereignty or by the general elections would finally be fulfilled, and the new era would dawn.

By 17 August 1958, President Sukarno was talking of 'another solution' to the problem of West Irian. On 17 August 1960, Indonesia broke off diplomatic relations with the Dutch, and, in that September, President Sukarno, addressing the United

Nations, said: 'Hope evaporates; patience dries up; even toler-
ance reaches an end. They have all run out now, and the Netherlands has left us no alternative but to stiffen our attitude.' In
1961, a build-up of Dutch defences in West Irian began and in
April, as a stage toward self-determination for the Irianese, the
Dutch introduced a Papuan Council, and a Papuan flag and
national anthem. During 1961 the Indonesians began acquiring
Russian-built ships and planes. Against this background of growing tension, the Dutch referred the dispute to the United
Nations, while Sukarno, in December, issued his People's Triple
Command (*Trikora*) to prevent the establishment of the State of
Papua, to hoist the Red and White flag in West Irian, and to
prepare for general mobilization. Early in 1962 small groups of
paratroopers landed in West Irian; the Dutch sank an Indonesian torpedo boat in neighbouring waters.

In the face of the Indonesian threat to resort to arms the
United Nations and the United States finally moved from a
neutral position. Once again revolutionary action had succeeded
where the attempt to negotiate had failed. The lesson was clear
to Indonesia. The colonial powers, the old established order in
the world, responded to force rather than to negotiation. In
Washington secret talks between the Netherlands and Indonesia,
presided over by Ellsworth Bunker, as representative of the Secretary General of the United Nations, led to the signing of an
agreement on 15 August, and two days later President Sukarno,
in his 17 August address, spoke of 'A Year of Triumph'.

By the agreement, the territory would be handed by the Dutch
to a United Nations Temporary Executive Authority and, after
a suitable interval the United Nations would transfer it to Indonesia. The Dutch and United Nations flags would fly side by side
until 31 December 1962, and on 1 January 1963, the Dutch flag
would be replaced by the Indonesian. Transfer of authority from
the United Nations to Indonesia was to be effected as soon as
possible after 1 May 1963, and provision was made for the
Irianese to participate in an act of self-determination under
United Nations auspices, before the end of 1969. It was also agreed
that after the signing of this agreement the Indonesian-Dutch
diplomatic relations, broken off in 1960, would be renewed.

(b) *Indonesian Foreign Policy—From Non-Alignment to Confrontation.* 1950-65

Indonesian foreign policy and her reactions to the outside
world were shaped by the attitudes of foreign nations to her own

national aspirations in West Irian. It was clear that, in the final 'year of triumph', Indonesia had achieved victory because she was prepared to back her claims with force. Her experience of the United Nations had convinced many Indonesians, as it had other observers, that the decisions within that body reflected, not the justice of any particular case, but the particular interests of the Great Powers. On the whole, the United States had followed a policy of neutrality which in fact favoured the continuance of the existing situation in West Irian and so favoured the Dutch, because the United States had to consider not only its image in south-east Asia but also its relationships with the Western allies, among whom were the old colonial powers. The Soviet Union, on the other hand, had supported Indonesian claims, and, when it became clear in 1957 and again in 1960, that America's neutrality included the refusal to sell arms to Indonesia, the Indonesians were forced, reluctantly in the case of some of the anti-Communist army leaders, to buy arms from eastern Europe and the Soviet Union. The failure of the United Nations to act, the line-up of the colonial powers and with them Nationalist China, the neutrality of the United States, the support of the Communist countries, all influenced both Indonesia's attitude to the world body, and her view of foreign affairs in general.

To 1960, Indonesia followed a non-aligned, independent and free foreign policy aimed at the establishment of solidarity among the Afro-Asian nations who were, on the whole, not committed to either the Russian or the American side of the Cold War. For them, the real issues were only indirectly related to the struggle between Communism and Capitalism. The dividing line was drawn between colonialism and anti-colonialism, the basis of agreement between the members of the Afro-Asian Conference held at Bandung in 1955, where it seemed possible that they might emerge as a third bloc, capable of reducing the tensions of the Cold War. Twenty-nine nations from Africa and Asia sent delegates to the conference, sponsored by the Prime Ministers of India, Pakistan, Ceylon, Burma and Indonesia and initiated by the Indonesian Prime Minister at the time, Ali Sastroamidjojo. The actual organization and administration of the conference, including the necessary security arrangements, were a triumph for the host nation, and enhanced Indonesia's international prestige.[13]

[13] Richard Wright, *The Color Curtain*, gives an account of this conference as seen by an American Negro journalist observer.

In 1956 when President Sukarno made his first State visit to a foreign country and his first visit at all to a Western country, it was, significantly, to the United States that he went and, having paid tribute in his address to the Congress to America as 'the first product of nationalism, or anti-colonialism and of the principle of independence', he spoke on the following day to the National Press Club in Washington. 'You who have never known colonialism can never appreciate what it does to man . . . In any case, whether all the world approves or not, the fact is that nationalism and the liberation of nations are realities. They are the reality of international life.'

By 1960, from his experience during the struggle for West Irian, President Sukarno was evolving a new interpretation of the world in which Indonesia found itself. Rather than a three-fold division, he saw the world as divided into those who sought to preserve the existing state of affairs, and those who sought to 'build the world anew', divisions which cut across those of the Cold War. On his return from the Belgrade Conference of Non-Aligned Nations in 1961, President Sukarno began to develop this analysis, although much of it was already implicit in his earlier statements.

Yet for a brief period in 1963, with West Irian returned, and with the forces of revolt within Indonesia—both *Darul Islam* and the revolts in Sumatra and Sulawesi—defeated, it looked as if Indonesia's energies might be directed to the achievement of the just and prosperous society. Instead she became involved in opposition to the newly formed federation of Malaysia, an involvement stemming directly from the analysis of the world situation propounded by President Sukarno, like *Pantja Sila*, an analysis deriving from and making articulate a wider Indonesian sentiment. He saw the international scene as representing a struggle between the Old Established Forces (*Oldefos*), the colonial countries and their allies; and the New Emerging Forces (*Nefos*), anti-colonial, newly independent countries and their allies.

The British in Malaya, approaching the colonial problem more flexibly than had the Dutch, had granted political independence to the peninsula, while hoping to retain control both of their strategic naval base at Singapore and those sectors of the Malaysian economy which contributed to the wealth of Great Britain—tin, rubber and other enterprises. In May 1961 Tunku Abdul Rahman, Prime Minister of Malaya, made public a proposal, first suggested by the British as early as 1887, but receiving serious consideration only in the post-war period, for the creation of a federal union among the former British colonial possessions in Malaya and north Borneo (north Kalimantan). Initially Indonesia did not oppose this, but her own background of independence through struggle made her suspicious of any proposals by the colonial powers to grant independence and when, in 1962, a revolt occurred in Brunei, Indonesia began to query whether the proposed merger was indeed based on the wishes of the people or whether it was a 'neo-colonial plot' to retain ultimate control.

Fresh from a victorious struggle against the continuing power of colonialism within Indonesia, she was apprehensive about the existence of neo-colonialism within the region and suspicious of the existence of foreign bases in Singapore and the Philippines. With growing hostility towards Indonesia's alleged expansionist policies in the Australian press, in Sukarno's view the lackey of the Old Established Order, many Indonesians saw themselves as being dangerously encircled by the forces of *Nekolim* (*Neo*-colonialism, *Colo*nialism, and *Im*perialism), a theme constantly emphasized by President Sukarno. Indonesia did not claim sovereignty over any of the north Kalimantan states although the Philippines, her ally, did lay claim to part of Sabah.

During 1963, meetings were held between the *Maphilindo* powers (*Ma*laya, the *Phil*ippines and *Indo*nesia), seeking ways of settling the conflicting issues peacefully; and it looked for a while as if the three might be able to co-operate with each other in a regional group. Instead, Britain and Malaya went ahead with the plans for Malaysia, making it clear that they would not wait for the results of the United Nations survey of popular feeling in north Kalimantan required by Indonesia and the Philippines before they accepted the new federation.[14] Demonstrations and counter-demonstrations in Djakarta and Kuala Lumpur led finally to the burning of the British embassy in Djakarta and the cutting off of trade relations with Britain.

In 1963, Indonesia launched an active 'confrontation' against Malaysia. This actually prolonged the British presence in the area, and, although it was directed primarily against Britain, it provided for the rather shaky federation an external enemy that perhaps did more to create Malaysian unity than did any other single factor. Ironically too, President Sukarno, by rousing support for Malaysia from fellow Commonwealth countries, helped

[14] The findings supported the earlier survey undertaken by Britain, and Britain and Malaya acted on the assumption that this would be the case.

to create the very situation which he feared, an encirclement of Indonesia and its growing isolation from the rest of the world, symbolized in January 1965 by Indonesia's withdrawal from the United Nations because Malaysia was given a seat on the Security Council.

Even Indonesians who doubted the wisdom of the course the President was pursuing admired the self-confidence, the boldness and the shrewdness with which he pitted himself against the representatives of the Great Powers. As confrontation failed to 'crush' Malaysia, those who doubted its wisdom increased. Sukarno's policy was based on a belief in the Indonesian ability to triumph abroad as she had in her revolutionary struggle at home, to 'reach to the stars', to 'build the world anew', to crush the forces of *Nekolim* throughout the world. This policy drew Indonesia more closely toward that other great power in isolation from the world, the People's Republic of China, and increased the prestige of the party most closely in sympathy with China's ideology—the Communist Party (PKI)—whose opposition to *Nekolim* was as outspoken as that of Sukarno himself.

(c) *Indonesia's Relationships with China. 1955-65*

China, throughout recorded history, has had a continuing influence on Indonesian history. The first written records, dating back to 200 B.C., show that trade relations existed between the two.[15] In 1292, Chinese intervention in Java proved decisive in determining the course of the succession.[16] Under Dutch colonialism the privileged place of the Chinese within the economic system aroused Indonesian resentment. During the Japanese period, their position became more precarious and the majority of them welcomed the Dutch back eagerly. Most Chinese during the Revolution remained aloof, as expressed in the Chinese resolution at the Pangkalpinang Conference.[17] In Medan, for example, most Chinese laughed at the revolutionaries, saying, 'You'll never get your independence in a thousand years'; a miscalculation which, along with the extortion and market manipulations practised by some Chinese, was to cost many of them dearly when Indonesians were in control of their own destiny once more. Yet despite much resentment toward the Chinese in Indonesia, there was a grudging admiration for the strides made by the New China, a fellow Asian nation. At the Bandung Conference in 1955, Communist China was recognized by the other participants as a reality and a permanent part of the Asian scene to be both feared and respected.

One of Indonesia's diplomatic triumphs at the Bandung Conference was the drawing up of an agreement with China on the question of dual nationality. Up to that time, overseas Chinese, whether or not they became citizens of the country in which they settled, were still claimed by China as its nationals, even after several generations of residence. The terms of the dual nationality agreement provided for an active choice on the part of Chinese residents in Indonesia who wished to become Indonesian citizens. If, within two years, they made no choice they would be regarded as Chinese; if they chose to be Indonesian, China would renounce all claim to them.

In 1958, while efforts were being made as part of the West Irian campaign to remove the Dutch from their privileged position in Indonesian economic life, attempts were also made to remove alien Chinese from their dominant position in the retail trade. As part of the programme of Guided Economy, a ban was placed on foreign traders operating in rural areas or in towns of less than about 15,000 inhabitants. This was directed against those Chinese who had not opted for Indonesian citizenship, and was particularly popular among members of the conservative Moslem Theologian's Party (NU), many of whose members were in competition with rural Chinese traders. When questionnaires were distributed asking alien traders whether they intended to close down, to transfer their businesses to Indonesian citizens, or to move to larger towns, those who did answer, less than 25%, mostly said that they wanted to continue business as usual, which was not one of the options offered them.

It is doubtful whether the ban removed village retail trade from Chinese control, but it certainly led to tension between the governments of Indonesia and China. Some Chinese embassy officials issued instructions to alien Chinese to disobey the local officials attempting to implement the shifting of Chinese activities from trade to production. Notes were exchanged between the two governments, and the Indonesian Foreign Minister pointed out that the Chinese community in Indonesia 'through every sort of manipulation have succeeded in dominating the economy of the Indonesian people'. Groups of overseas Chinese 'through smuggling, hoarding and speculation . . . have been opposing the growth toward economic stability in Indonesia'.

The Chinese government protested against attacks on some of its citizens and, as at earlier periods of tension (and later), the foreign Chinese were often a target for Indonesian hostility. Nor was it always possible, in the heat of the moment, to distinguish between foreign Chinese and Indonesian citizens of Chinese descent. Nevertheless such hostility, while hardly to be condoned, is at least understandable in terms of the earlier privileged position of the Chinese, and the record many of them held as exploiters, supporters of the Dutch, and anti-nationalists in a period of rising national sentiment.

Although, by the end of the 1950s, Indonesian-Chinese relations had reached their lowest point in many years, in the period following this, as Indonesian policies at home and abroad increasingly isolated her not only from the Western powers but also from the more moderate Afro-Asian countries, these two isolates began to draw closer together. President Sukarno spoke of a Peking-Djakarta axis, and envisaged a new world body in which Indonesia and China would be foundation members. Yet, by 1966, Sukarno, President for Life, Supreme Commander of the Armed Forces, and Great Leader of the Revolution, was fighting a losing battle to retain any vestige of his former power.

30TH SEPTEMBER 1965 (GESTAPU) COUP AND ITS AFTERMATH. 1965-68

On 1 October 1965, just after 2 a.m., three large trucks, carrying almost a hundred armed soldiers of the palace guard regiment, appeared outside the house of General Nasution and began continuous shooting. In other parts of the city, six of the Indonesian Army's top generals were captured and taken to Halim Air Force Base outside the city, where they were mutilated and murdered. Although General Nasution escaped, his five-year-old daughter was fatally wounded. At 7:15 a.m., Lieut.-Col. Untung of the palace guard regiment declared on Radio Djakarta that a plot by a Generals' Council to overthrow the President had been thwarted and the President himself was safe.

Of the top Army leaders, General Nasution and General Suharto escaped the would-be assassins. Within a few hours of the beginning of the coup, General Suharto, head of the Army's strategic reserve, was able to mobilize army forces to take counter-action. President Sukarno himself seems to have sympathized with the actions of Untung's group, although he refused to give his public endorsement. By the evening of 1 October, it was clear that the coup had failed, though not at all clear who had been involved in it or what its effects would be.

Although some foreign observers have argued that the coup was primarily an internal army affair, led by younger officers against the older leadership, the official Indonesian view is that it was an attempt by leaders of the Communist Party (PKI) to take over control. It climaxed a period of growing hostility between the Communists on the one hand and the Army leadership on the other, both of whom were struggling to establish their position as heirs to President Sukarno. It has been argued that the President's ill-health during the preceding weeks precipitated this struggle for leadership. Whether the Communist leaders were responsible, or whether, as at Madiun in 1948, they were drawn into a situation not of their own making, may not be clear for many years to come. The result of the coup and its rapid suppression led to a discrediting of the Communist leaders, and within many villages where Communist and Moslem groups confronted each other, growing tension led ultimately to clashes in which a great number of Indonesians were killed. The official and unofficial estimates range from about 87,000 to about 800,000. The truth perhaps lies somewhere in between.

The period after the coup saw the gradual rise of General Suharto who, five months later, was given power by the President to 'take such action as he deemed necessary' to restore law and order. A year later, in March 1967, he was named Acting President, and Sukarno was stripped of his powers but retained an ambiguous claim to the title of President and the fiction that Suharto was acting on his behalf. Another year elapsed before Suharto was appointed President by the (Provisional) People's Consultative Assembly, which, with General Nasution as its Chairman, was no longer overshadowed by the former President but could reclaim its position as highest authority. In its hands lay the power to elect the President who, according to the Constitution, acted on its behalf. As Suharto gradually consolidated his position, the former President Sukarno gradually lost his pre-eminence, becoming more circumscribed in his activities. It was a slow-motion transfer of authority, aimed at preserving dignity all round, and at preventing any further bloodshed after the first short, sharp outbursts of violence. Those three years were ones of continuing tension as, to many Indonesians, the country seemed on the brink of civil war. Continuous pressure came from student groups, impatient with the cautious manoeuvrings of their elders. There was also a sober and realistic appraisal of the actual state of the Indonesian economy, a subject for which President Sukarno had shown such distaste that it had not received much public acknowledgment in past years, although its impact was being increasingly felt throughout the community. This realistic assessment was the first essential step toward the slow, unspectacular, painful process of restoring economic order after the cumulative effects of economic chaos and decline during the past thirty years.

The Army gained in strength despite the loss of so many of its top leaders, for in many ways Suharto's regime is an Army regime.

One of the most striking aspects of the period after the abortive coup was the rising influence of the students and intellectuals, organized into various Action Fronts. The Action Front of Indonesian Students (KAMI) was particularly active during the early part of 1966 as was the Action Front of Indonesian High School Students (KAPPI). Suharto, who has contrasted himself with Sukarno by saying, 'I am no expert in public speaking', took advice from those intellectuals at the University level whose opinion was most urgently needed—the economists. Although the students' political success was partly due to support from key groups in the Army, their movement was always a force in its own right, not merely a front for the Army. When Sukarno was attempting to reassert his power, the student groups served as the spearhead of the struggle, the Generation of '66 rising against the Generation of '45, and the students clashed with the Army on a number of occasions when student leaders protested against the Army's slow pace and its mildness in dealing with Sukarno.

The effects of the attempted coup on foreign policy have also been most dramatic. During April 1966 the Foreign Minister, Adam Malik, one of the group involved in the kidnapping of Sukarno and Hatta almost twenty-one years earlier, began to negotiate the settlement of the Malaysia dispute and the recognition of Singapore. When in May the President was forced to sign the document terminating confrontation, he said, 'I am keeping silent in one thousand tongues', but added that 'God willing at some time in the future I am going to open my mouth'. He did so on 17 August 1966, urging a return to history; but the appeal fell on deaf ears, or rather, the strong support which existed for the President in central and east Java was contained by the Army and the threat of civil war averted.

In September 1966, Indonesia resumed her United Nations membership. By March 1968, in a joint communiqué issued by the Dutch ministerial delegation and the Indonesian authorities, but inconceivable ten years earlier, the Netherlands announced its willingness to increase assistance to Indonesia in 1968 through grants and loans. This was one small part of the wide 'Aid Indonesia' programme supported by other Western nations concerned for Indonesia's stability.

Paralleling this rise in mutual co-operation between the West,

Japan and Indonesia was a decline in relations between Indonesia and China, whose relationship with the Indonesian Communist Party implicated it in the repercussions following the abortive coup.

For the majority of Indonesians the rhythm of their life is governed by the cultivation of wet ricefields, the constant round of hoeing, ploughing, regulating the flow of water, planting out the seedlings, weeding the ricefields, reaping, threshing and drying the rice; or in the swidden cultivation which still predominates in the less populated islands. An aeroplane of the Garuda Indonesian Airways may pass overhead, or a car or lumbering bus provide transport between the villages, but the bulk of internal traffic is still carried by ox cart, horse cart, or by *pikulan,* two baskets slung on either end of a carrying pole. Although inter-island shipping is now mechanized, offshore fishing is not. Fishing boats still dot the seas around the islands, returning at night 'like bees to the hive'.

In the cities, even in Djakarta the capital, Western-style buildings rub shoulders with huts of woven bamboo. Beggar and millionaire still jostle in the crowded streets. Pedestrians, *betjaks* and bicycles compete with army trucks, jeeps, taxis and modern cars in what seems a frenzied confusion. While nowadays the local inhabitants by far outnumber the foreigners, it is still possible to meet in Djakarta people from all corners of the globe.

We can trace too the continuing strands in Indonesian history. The co-operation and conflict between the trading empire and the land-based kingdom are still influential in more recent times. The conflicts between *adat*, religion, and the new influences of the Western world continue to find expression in the songs people sing, the customs they follow, and the values they cherish. The need for strong government, and the difficulty of achieving it in the face of the divisions which separate different groups within society, both continue. Underlying this diversity is the unity which has at its root the basic similarities between the different ethnic groups. It has been fostered by the common struggle which has united Indonesians for the past sixty years, and which has its roots in an even longer history of local conflict against foreign domination. It has been strengthened by the spread of the national language not only, as in the past, along the trade routes, but now through the new and expanding school system where it is the language of instruction from third grade onward, and the medium for teaching pride in country, including the

national history and national songs which the colonial government forbade as treasonable. While not all of President Sukarno's
concepts and slogans have been accepted by the New Order,
those which sprang from the underlying common cultural
elements within the nation and which he helped to make
articulate, are still cherished. Intermarriage between different
ethnic groups is also slowly having its effect, because marriage in
Indonesia links family with family on a much wider scale than
in Western countries where family ties are weaker and family
units smaller. Indonesians in the civil service may be appointed
to ethnic areas other than their own, and so make friends outside
their own ethnic group. Indonesia still faces tremendous economic
problems—too many people, too little foreign exchange, too little
land, too few jobs, too few factories, roads and ships—but under
the New Order she has begun to assess these realistically and is
slowly beginning the tremendous task of overcoming them.

In a television programme made early in 1968, the Australian
commentator interviewed a Sundanese peasant, one year older
than former President Sukarno, yet still working in the ricefields
of west Java. His face was lined and weatherbeaten; he spoke not
Indonesian but the local language, Sundanese, with his interpreter,
and said that he did not know whether Suharto was better than
Sukarno. He was not, he said, very clear what had been happening and why Suharto had replaced Sukarno. He seemed to
symbolize the continuing life of the land, underlying the activities
of the rulers, but not closely related to these activities. As in the
days of Madjapahit, little attention is focussed on peasant life
and most people are more interested in the activities of the
rulers; but, as a contrast between the old Indonesia and the
new, we could not find a more appropriate example than the
fact that, when the newly appointed President Suharto, son of a
peasant in Godean (near Jogjakarta), set out on his first Presidential visit overseas, he named as his Acting President Sultan
Hamengkubuono IX, descended from the rulers of the *kraton* of
Mataram, whose authority came, not from his princely descent,
but from the President appointed by the (Provisional) People's
Consultative Assembly established by the constitution of the
Republic of Indonesia.

Concerning a Time Line

A time line is a very useful device for sorting out when certain events happened in relation to other events, and a number of time lines were worked out in the course of writing this book. Some of them were quite gay, with several different colours to distinguish events in different places or different sequences on the same time line. Ideally it is best to have either a large enough sheet of paper or a small enough time scale to be able to represent the whole period with which one is dealing as a whole without having to turn pages, and this presents certain problems because, as you may have noticed, the time span shortens as we approach the present. Chapter 3, for example, moves from about 40,000 B.C. to about A.D. 1500, while Chapter 9 covers only ten years.

Before trying to work out the most helpful way of presenting a time line it was necessary to ask, 'Just what is the purpose of a time line?' Its main function seems to be to help relate together things which happen at much the same time but which, in order to present a history of the relationship of events, instead of a mere chronicle, cannot all be dealt with at once in the narrative. Its main value was gained not from having it in its final form but from the sorting process which went into making it in the first place. In other words *having* a time line is not nearly so valuable as *making* a time line. For that reason there is no time line included in this book but there is, I hope, sufficient information for you to make your own. If not, there are quite detailed timelines in the following books:

Cady, J. F. *Southeast Asia: Its Historical Development.* McGraw-Hill, 1964; pp. 606-615.
Hall, D. G. E. *A History of South-East Asia.* Macmillan, 1964; pp. 880-886.
(These are actually dynastic lists of rulers rather than time lines.)
Vlekke, B. H. M. *Nusantara: A History of Indonesia.* Van Hoeve, 1959; pp. 442-455.
　　(This is called a Chronological Epitome.)

277

Remember that, the earlier you go, the greater the margin of uncertainty, so that, at the time of Solo Man, a few thousand years either way is about as close as we can come to a date, while by August 1945 it may be important to know not only the day but even the hour when certain events occurred in relation to others.

Glossary

(including notes on pronunciation)

Although an effort has been made to introduce foreign words along with an English equivalent, they may occasionally have slipped in later unexplained. The glossary, along with foreign words, contains various place names and personal names which appear in different forms as used by different writers. They are listed according to the spelling used in this book but, in cases where the initial letter varies, they have been listed under both letters.

Indonesian and Malay both sound the same when spoken but are written with slight variations, Indonesian following Dutch, and Malay English, spelling. The most confusing difference between the two is the Indonesian 'j' (Malay 'y') and Indonesian 'dj' (Malay 'j').

To simplify the pronunciation for English readers, the 'j' has been replaced in most cases with a 'y' as in Malay, although the 'dj' has been retained. Other consonants are pronounced much as they would be in English. The diphthong 'sj' sounds like our 'sh' and 'tj' like our 'ch', and both of these spellings have also been retained.

Indonesian (and Malayan) vowels are pronounced as follows:

a — as in father (only rather shorter).

e — as in grey.

i — as in machine.

o — as in or (only shorter).

u — as in put In proper names this is sometimes spelt as 'oe' although in this book the spelling has been modernized and appears as 'u'.

There is very little stress on the separate syllables, although there is a slight one on the next-to-last syllable. For example, 'Su-kar-no' has a slight emphasis on the 'kar' and 'ba-tik' on the 'ba'. Once you have mastered these simple rules you need have no further problem with Indonesian pronunciation as, unlike English, it is consistently spelt phonetically.

279

Do not let the variations of spelling concern you unduly. They are inevitable when names and words are being transliterated from one script to another. Arabic script, for example, has no distinct letters to represent the different vowels. 'Moslem' and 'Muslim' are both acceptable spellings for the same word. Chinese and Japanese writing is spelt in different ways in English in an attempt to give an approximation of the pronunciation. The same applies to names derived from Sanskrit. The important thing is to know which are the same names with different spelling, and which are different names with similar spelling. You would be wise, as has already been suggested, to make your own Dictionary of Indonesian Biography and Geography, noting down the names of people as you meet them, and at the same time checking any variation of spelling as between different writers. (If you use a notebook with alphabetical tags you may find your list easier to use when you want to refer back to it.) In particular you need to notice different initial letters, as this can affect the ease with which you can find information in the index of the book. For example, 'Srividjaya' can also be spelt 'Çriwidjaya'; 'Amangkurat' is sometimes written as 'Mangkurat'; or 'Hayam Wuruk' as 'Ajam Wuruk'.

abangan	— the term is used by C. Geertz to refer to nominal Moslems among the village people, although, strictly speaking, it would also include the group which he classes as 'priyayi' who are mostly nominal Moslems also. It comes from the Javanese word 'abang' meaning 'red', distinguishing these people from the orthodox Moslems (*santri*) or white people, from the white robes worn for Moslem prayer.
adat	— customary law, which varies from one ethnic group to another.
Amangkurat	— ruler (s) of Java.
Ambon	— also Amboina/Amboyna. Island in the Maluku group.
Atjeh	— also Achin/Dachem. District in north Sumatra.
batik	— a process for decorating cloth by using wax to prevent some areas from absorbing dye.
bendahara	— treasurer, controller of the exchequer.
Bengkulu	— also Bengkulen/Bencoolen. District in south-western Sumatra.
benzoin	— a kind of aromatic resin used for incense and perfumes.
betjak	— bicycle rickshaw used for transport in Djakarta and other large and not too hilly cities.

Borneo	— see Kalimantan.
Borobudur	— Also Barabudur. Ninth century Buddhist monument in central Java.
Celebes	— see Sulawesi.
Cheribon	— see Tjeribon.
Conefo	— Conference of the New Emerging Forces.
Çriwijaya	— see Srividjaya.
dalang	— the puppet master who recites the stories and manipulates the puppets at *wayang* shows, which usually run from about 9 p.m. to 6 a.m. the following day.
damar	— a kind of resin.
Darul Islam	— the Domain of Islam, an Islamic rebel movement attempting to establish an Islamic state in Indonesia.
de facto	— in fact, whether by right (*de jure*) or not.
Digul	— Boven Digul or Upper Digul in West Irian on the upper reaches of the Digul River was used by the Dutch to intern political prisoners.
Diponegoro	— also Dipanegara. Nineteenth century Javanese prince.
Djambi	— also Jambi. City in south-east Sumatra.
Djapara	— also Japara. Port on north coast of Java.
djihat	— also jihad. Holy War in defence of Islam against the infidel.
gamelan	— Javanese and Balinese traditional orchestra.
Goa	— town in India, headquarters of the Portuguese Empire.
gotong royong	— mutual self-help as practised traditionally in the villages.
Gowa	— kingdom of south Sulawesi.
hadji	— title which indicates that its holder has completed the pilgrimage (the hadj) to Mecca.
halus	— refined, cultured, sensitive, delicate, gentle. The kind of behaviour which the Javanese seeks to emulate. (See *kasar*.)
Hayam Wuruk	— also Ajam Wuruk. Ruler of Madjapahit.
Hizbullah	— Moslem military auxiliary force established by the Japanese.
hongi	— raids to destroy any rival spice trading or growing in east Indonesia.
ikat	— 'to bind'. A method of dying cloth by tying off the sections to remain undyed. (See Wagner.)
Jakatra	— the old name for the modern city of Djakarta.
Jambi	— see Djambi.
Japara	— see Djapara.
jihad	— see djihat.

Jogjakarta	— *kraton* city in central Java, sometimes abbreviated 'Jogja'.
kafir	— infidel, one who does not believe in Islam.
kain batik	— a length of *batik* cloth worn as a long skirt with a jacket or *kebaja*. The traditional dress of Javanese women. *Kain* means cloth.
kampong	— also *kampung*. A village group within a city environment, often with the main disadvantages of both and the advantages of neither.
kasar	— coarse, ill-bred, rude; the opposite of *halus* and so the embodiment of all that a Javanese seeks *not* to be.
keramat	— holy, miraculous, supernatural power (Islamic). (Compare *kesaktian, semangat*.)
kesaktian	— influenced or animated by supernatural power, supernaturally gifted (Hindu-Buddhist). (Compare *keramat, semangat*.)
kiyayi	— Javanese, pre-Islamic word for a teacher of religion or one well-versed in religion, but now used as a title by local Moslem religious leaders in Java.
KNIL	— Royal Netherlands Indies Army.
KNIP	— Central Indonesian National Committee.
kraton	— the royal palace, residence of the ruler and centre of the early Javanese kingdoms.
kris	— ceremonial, sacred, wavy-edged dagger.
ladang	— unirrigated arable fields; rice grown without irrigation.
lontar	— palm leaf manuscript.
Makasar	— Macassar/Mengkasar. City in southern Sulawesi.
Malacca	— also Malakar. City on the Malay Peninsula.
Maluku	— also Moluccas. A group of islands in eastern Indonesia.
Mangkurat	— see Amangkurat.
Manipol-USDEK	— Political Manifesto of President Sukarno introducing guided democracy and guided economy.
Maphilindo	— acronym from Malaya-Philippines-Indonesia. Proposed regional grouping of these three countries.
marhaen	— the 'little people' of Indonesia, owning some of the means of production and some small portion of land and so not a landless proletariat, but still very poor.
Masjumi	— the Modernist Moslem party. Under the Japanese, a Moslem council attempting to unite Islamic groups in support of the Japanese.
milob	— an English acronym derived from *mil*itary *ob*server.
MPR (S)	— (Provisional) People's Consultative Council.

Nasakom	— acronym from Nationalism-Religion-Communism denoting a cabinet with all parties represented.
Nefo	— New Emerging Forces.
Nekolim	— *Neo*-colonialism, *Col*onialism and *Im*perialism.
NICA	— Netherlands Indies Civil Administration.
ningrat	— in a proper name denotes membership of the Javanese or Sundanese nobility. e.g. Suria*ningrat*; Kuria*ningrat*.
NU	— Nahdatul Ulama. Moslem Theologians' Party, sometimes called Moslem Scholars' Party.
Oldefo	— Old Established Forces.
panggeran	— governor or prince; title of member of ruling family in Java.
panglima	— commander.
Pantja Sila	— the Five Principles of the Indonesian state philosophy.
pasar	— market, usually open air, and from the same root as 'bazaar'.
pemuda	— young person.
peranakan	— Although this is used by some writers to distinguish between Chinese born in Indonesia and more recent arrivals born outside Indonesia, it means, literally, a person of mixed racial descent (see *totok*).
pesantren	— Moslem religious boarding school.
Peta	— Japanese-established Indonesian armed units in Java.
petji	— small black velvet cap, originally a sign of Islam but now worn as the national headdress by Indonesian men.
PKI	— Indonesian Communist Party.
PNI	— Indonesian Nationalist Party.
Priangan	— also Prianger. District in west Java.
priyayi	— member of the Javanese gentry, often in the higher civil service.
PSI	— Indonesian Socialist Party.
pusaka	— heirlooms or symbols of state, the possession of which determines the right to govern.
Putera	— also Poetera. All-inclusive nationalist organization set up by the Japanese in Java and Madura.
Raden, Raden Adjeng, Raden Aju	— aristocratic titles for Javanese men, single women and married women respectively.
Ramadan	— the Islamic month of fasting.
Ratu Adil	— the Just Ruler of Javanese mythology.
romusha	— Indonesian conscripted labour during the Japanese occupation.
Sabilillah	— village Islamic military units formed under the Japanese.

saikerai	— the ceremonial bow toward the Japanese Emperor, a part of Japanese Shinto worship.
salam, selamat	— greeting, wishing peace and protection.
sambal	— hot, sharp appetizer made of ground chillies and other spices, and used to give additional flavour to meals.
santri	— Javanese term for orthodox Moslems, used by C. Geertz to distinguish a particular group within Javanese society.
sawah	— irrigated ricefields.
semangat	— the inner soul or vital spirit; special spiritual force possessed by the individual destined to lead (Animist). (Compare *keramat, kesaktian.*)
shahbandar	— harbour master.
shaman	— priest possessed of magical powers and able to use these.
Srividjaya	— also Çriwidjaja, Sriwidjaya, Shih-li-fo'shi Che-li-fo-che. Maritime kingdom probably centred on south Sumatra.
stupa	— bell-shaped dome often containing a figure of the Buddha.
Sufi	— form of Islamic mysticism widely found in Indonesia.
sunan, susuhunan	— Javanese royal title.
Sunda Kelapa	— along with Jakatra, one of the early names of modern Djakarta.
Surakarta	— also Solo. *Kraton* city of central Java.
swidden farming	— slash-and-burn agriculture in tropical forest land.
Taman Siswa	— lit. Garden of Pupils. Nationally oriented school system established during the 1920s.
Tanah Merah	— see Digul.
teungku	— Atjehnese royal title.
tjandi	— sepulchral monument.
tjanting	— a small tool used in 'writing' *batik* on cloth with hot wax.
Tjeribon	— also Cheribon. Town in north central Java.
totok	— full-blood as distinct from person of mixed descent, used of foreigners resident in Indonesia. More recently it has come to be used of new arrivals born overseas as against those born in the country, or even of those people, Chinese in particular, whose loyalty is primarily Chinese as against those whose loyalty and citizenship is Indonesian. (Compare *peranakan.*)
trepang	— bêche-de-mer; a sea slug prized by the Chinese as a delicacy.
Trikora	— President Sukarno's triple command to regain West Irian.

trimurti	— the trinity of Hindu gods.
tuanku	— religious title in Minangkabau. Lit. 'my lord'.
Tumasik	— Singapore's earlier name.
tumenggung	— high Javanese official.
ummat	— the community (of Islam).
V.O.C.	— Dutch East India Company (Vereenigde Oostindische Compagnie).
waringen	— banyan tree, a large tree like a fig, but with aerial roots which, on touching the ground, produce new trees.
wayang	— shadow puppets.
wayang golek	— doll puppets, the three-dimensional carved wooden puppets popular in west Java.
wayang kulit	— another name for shadow puppets. Lit. skin/hide puppets, from the buffalo hide of which they are made.
wayang purwo	— old or original puppets, hence the shadow puppets which the audience sees only as shadows thrown on a white screen.
wayang wong	— performances in which the puppets are replaced by live actors whose acting and dancing is formalized in imitation of the puppets.
windhu	— Javanese period of time; a span of eight years.
Zakat	— tax or tithe given as alms to the poor by Moslems at the end of the Ramadan month of fasting.

[A very detailed glossary appears in
   Wagner, F. A. *Indonesia: The Art of an Island Group.*
   Methuen, 1962.]

Bibliography

In addition to the books listed in the introductory reading list on pages 16–17, the following should be available in most school libraries. Highest priority should go to those asterisked.

General References

*FitzGerald, C. P. *A Concise History of East Asia*. New York: Praeger, 1966.
*Geertz, C. *The Religion of Java*. Glencoe, Ill.: The Free Press, 1964.
*Hall, Daniel G. *Atlas of South-East Asia*. New York: Macmillan, 1964.
Hall, Daniel G. *A History of South-East Asia*, 2 vols., 3d ed. New York: St. Martin's, 1968.
Harrison, Brian. *South-East Asia*, 2d ed. New York: St. Martin's, 1963.
*Legge, John D. *Indonesia*. Englewood Cliffs, N.J.: Prentice-Hall, 1964.
Mintz, Jeanne. *Indonesia: A Profile*. Princeton, N.J.: Van Nostrand, 1964.
Tinker, Hugh. *South Asia: A Short History*. New York: Praeger, 1966.
*Vlekke, Bernard Hubertus Maria. *Nusantara: A History of Indonesia*. The Hague: Van Hoeve, 1959. (This history concludes in 1942.)

Primary and Secondary Sources Suitable for Use by Students

Benda, Harry J., and Larkin, J. A. *The World of Southeast Asia*. New York: Harper & Row, 1967.
Benda, Harry J., and Larkin, J. A., eds. *The World of Southeast Asia: Selected Historical Readings*, 2 vols. New York: Harper & Row, 1967.
Caldwell, Malcolm. *Indonesia*. London: Oxford University Press, 1968.

Castles, L., and Feith, H. *Indonesian Political Thinking: Selected Readings, 1945–1965.* Ithaca, N.Y.: Cornell University Press, 1966.

Douwes, Dekker E. ("Multatuli"). *Max Havelaar.* Translated from the Dutch by Roy Edwards. London: Heinemann, 1967.

Hanna, Willard A. *Bung Karno's Indonesia,* rev. ed. New York: American Universities Field Staff, 1961.

*Kartini, Raden A. *Letters of a Javanese Princess.* New York: Norton, 1964.

*Lach, Donald F., and Flaumenhaft, C. *Asia on the Eve of Europe's Expansion.* Englewood Cliffs, N.J.: Prentice-Hall, 1965. (A selection of extracts from contemporary materials.)

Mintz, Jeanne. *Mohammed, Marx, and Marhaen: The Roots of Indonesian Socialism.* New York: Praeger, 1965.

Palmier, Leslie H. *Indonesia and the Dutch.* New York: Oxford University Press, 1962.

Parrinder, Edward G. *A Book of World Religions,* 2 vols. Chester Springs, Pa.: Dufour, 1967.

Parry, J. H. *Europe and a Wider World, 1415–1715.* New York: Hillary House, Hutchinson University Library, 1962.

Purcell, Victor. *The Chinese in South East Asia,* 2d ed. New York: Oxford University Press, 1965.

Sukarno. *Toward Freedom and the Dignity of Man: A Collection of Five Speeches.* Djakarta: Department of Foreign Affairs, Republic of Indonesia, 1961.

Tarling, Nicholas. *A Concise History of Southeast Asia.* New York: Praeger, 1966.

Vlekke, Bernard Hubertus Maria. *The Story of the Dutch East Indies.* Cambridge, Mass.: Harvard University Press, 1945.

*Wagner, Frits A. I. *The Art of an Island Group.* New York: McGraw-Hill, 1959.

Wallace, Alfred Russel. *The Malay Archipelago, the Land of the Orang Utan and the Bird of Paradise: A Narrative of Travel with Studies of Man and Nature.* 1886. Reprint, Magnolia, Mass.: Peter Smith, n.d.

References for Teachers (and the More Adventurous Student)

The following books are listed mainly for the benefit of teachers, and many may be too difficult for all except the most enthusiastic students. Teachers are also referred to "Suggested Readings" in Legge, J. D., *Indonesia,* for valuable comments on the material available in English.

Allen, George Cyril, and Donnithorne, Audrey Gladys. *Western Enterprise in Indonesia and Malaya: A Study in Economic Development.* Mystic, Conn.: Verry, 1957.

*Alisjahbana, S. Takdier. *Indonesia: Social and Cultural Revolution.* New York: Oxford University Press, 1966.

Benda, H. J. *The Crescent and the Rising Sun.* The Hague: Van Hoeve, 1958.

Brackman, Arnold C. *Southeast Asia's Second Front: The Power Struggle in the Malay Archipelago.* New York: Praeger, 1966.

Callard, Keith B., *et al.* *Major Governments of Asia,* 2d ed. Edited by George M. Kahin. Ithaca, N.Y.: Cornell University Press, 1963.

Day, Clive. *The Dutch in Java.* New York: Oxford University Press, 1966.

Feith, Herbert. *The Decline of Constitutional Democracy in Indonesia,* 2 vols. Ithaca, N.Y.: Cornell University Press, 1962.

Furnivall, John Sydenham. *Netherlands Indies: A Study of Plural Economy.* New York: Cambridge University Press, 1967.

Geertz, Clifford. *Agricultural Involution: The Processes of Ecological Change in Indonesia.* Berkeley: University of California Press, 1963.

Geertz, Clifford. *Peddlers and Princes: Social Development and Economic Change in Two Indonesian Towns.* Chicago: University of Chicago Press, 1963.

Holt, Claire. *Art in Indonesia: Continuities and Change,* 2 vols. Ithaca, N.Y.: Cornell University Press, 1967.

*Kahin, George McTurnan. *Nationalism and Revolution in Indonesia,* 2 vols. Ithaca, N.Y.: Cornell University Press, 1952.

Koentjaraningrat, ed. *Villages in Indonesia,* 2 vols. Ithaca, N.Y.: Cornell University Press, 1967.

*McVey, Ruth T., ed. *Indonesia: Its People, Its Society, Its Culture,* 2d rev. ed. New York: Taplinger, Human Relations Area Files Press, 1968.

Meilink-Roelofsz, M. A. P. *Asian Trade and European Influence in the Indonesian Archipelago, 1500–1630.* The Hague: Martinus Nijhoff, 1962.

Palmier, Leslie H. *Indonesia,* 2 vols. New York: Walker & Company, Nations and Peoples Library, 1966.

Schrieke, B. *Indonesian Sociological Studies,* 2 vols. The Hague: Van Hoeve, 1955–57.

Soedjatmoko, ed. *An Introduction to Indonesian Historiography,* 2 vols. Ithaca, N.Y.: Cornell University Press, 1965.

*Van Niel, R.   The Emergence of the Modern Indonesian Elite.
The Hague: Van Hoeve, 1960.
*Wertheim, William Frederik. Indonesian Society in Transition:
A Study of Social Change. The Hague: Van Hoeve, 1956.
*Winstedt, R. Malaya and Its History. New York: Hillary
House, Hutchinson University Library, 1966.
*Wolf, Charles, Jr.   The Indonesian Story: The Birth, Growth
and Structure of the Indonesian Republic. New York: John
Day, 1948.
*Woodman, Dorothy. The Republic of Indonesia. London: Cres-
set, 1955. (Rather uneven, but in places very good.)

Valuable material can also be found in Cornell University's
Modern Indonesia Project, Interim Report Series, and in the
magazine Indonesia, published by Cornell University's Department of Far Eastern Studies.

Index

Italic figures indicate map references. Indonesian names may be listed under the first or second name according to custom.